Young Lawrence

A Portrait of the Legend as a Young Man

ANTHONY SATTIN

JOHN MURRAY

First published in Great Britain in 2014 by John Murray (Publishers)
An Hachette UK Company

1

© Anthony Sattin 2014

The right of Anthony Sattin to be identified as the Author of the Work has
been asserted by him in accordance with the Copyright, Designs
and Patents Act 1988.

Maps drawn by Rodney Paull

A CIP catalogue record for this title is
available from the British Library

ISBN 978-1-84854-912-8
EBOOK ISBN 978-1-84854-913-5

Typeset in Bembo MT Pro by Palimpsest Book Production Limited,
Falkirk, Stirlingshire

Printed and bound by Clays Ltd, St Ives plc

John Murray policy is to use papers that are natural, renewable
and recyclable products and made from wood grown in sustainable
forests. The logging and manufacturing processes are expected to conform to
the environmental regulations of the country of origin.

John Murray (Publishers)
338 Euston Road
London NW1 3BH

www.johnmurray.co.uk

Young Lawrence

Also by Anthony Sattin

Lifting the Veil: Two Centuries of Travellers, Traders and
Tourists in Egypt

Shooting the Breeze: A Novel

The Pharaoh's Shadow: Travels in Ancient and Modern Egypt

The Gates of Africa: Death, Discovery and the Search for Timbuktu

A Winter on the Nile: Florence Nightingale, Gustave Flaubert
and the Temptations of Egypt

Edited by Anthony Sattin

An Englishwoman in India: The Memoirs of Harriet Tytler

Florence Nightingale, Letters from Egypt: A Journey on the Nile

A House Somewhere: Tales of Life Abroad

For Johnny and Felix, setting out . . .

Contents

CONTENTS

PART III: The Young Spy

Maps

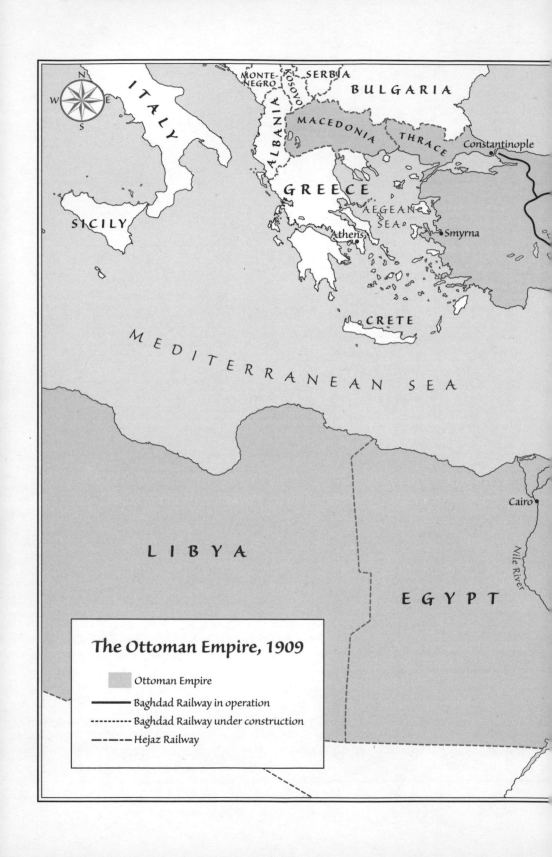

The Ottoman Empire, 1909

A Note on Spelling and Transliteration

The transliteration of Arabic words and the spelling of place names in the region covered by this story is problematic because there is no one system and no international norm. A city such as Aleppo, for instance, is also known as Halep, Halab and Alep, while Damascus is also known as Damas and as-Sham. Another layer of complication has been added by time: some spellings – and names – have changed over the century since Lawrence and his colleagues wrote them down. Constantinople is now called Istanbul. Beyrout, or occasionally Beyrouth, is now Beirut. The word for castle, qala, appears as kala in Lawrence's writing, so I have used it – Kalaat, not Qalaat al Kahf. Yet another layer of complication is added by the different usages of Arabs, Turks and others. I have adopted whatever has seemed most reader-friendly. I have not changed any of the archaic spellings if they are still obvious to us today, or if they refer to places most of us have never heard of. Similarly, with the prefixes al- and el-, I have favoured common usage over consistency. My intention, throughout, has been to let the words flow.

All men dream: but not equally. Those who dream by night in the dusty recesses of their minds wake in the day to find that it was vanity: but the dreamers of the day are dangerous men, for they may act their dream with open eyes, to make it possible. This I did.

T. E. Lawrence, *Seven Pillars of Wisdom*

I love all waste
And solitary places; where we taste
The pleasure of believing what we see
Is boundless, as we wish our souls to be.

Percy Bysshe Shelley, *Julian and Maddalo*

If I could talk it like Dahoum, you would never be tired of listening to me.

T. E. Lawrence in a letter to George Bernard Shaw, 1927

Prologue

The First Spark

The stories of his adventures and the hardships he endured on that trip would make the most thrilling reading; they would sound like the Arabian Nights.

Fareedeh el Akle[1]

Oxford, August 1914

A YOUNG MAN CROUCHES beside a fireplace and strikes a match. He is in the sitting room of a bungalow at the end of a garden, separated from the main house by a lawn, roses, perhaps also holly-hocks. The solid redbrick house, his family home, sits on a road just north of the centre of Oxford and could stand as a monument to Englishness. Identical to other Victorian houses in the area, it is almost anonymous. The bungalow, which has been purpose-built for the second of the family's five sons, has a small bedroom, elec-tricity, running water and, something of a novelty, a direct telephone line to the main house. The walls are hung with fine green cotton to encourage calm and there is a fireplace for warmth. But it is August, the summer has been good and the weather bright, so there is no need for heating and yet the young man holds the match to papers piled in the grate.

The man is T. E. Lawrence – Thomas on his birth certificate, Edward to outsiders, Ned to his family, T.E. to some of his friends, El Aurens to his Arab companions. He has just celebrated his twenty-sixth birthday and war has been declared. The bungalow is his retreat, commissioned while he was studying history at the nearby university and when he needed some personal space. For the past four years,

I

however, he has been an infrequent visitor, passing through in the summer, on one occasion causing a stir when he arrived with two Arab friends. For most of those years, he has been travelling and living in an area marked on his map – and he has become an expert on this region – as 'Northern Arabia', an area that includes the countries we know as Turkey, Syria, Lebanon, Israel, Palestine, Jordan and Egypt. Northern Arabia, divided into the Ottoman *vilayets* or provinces of Syria, Palestine, Mesopotamia and Egypt, is the setting for the story that is to unfold.

The fire takes, and pages curl in the grate, become blackened, flame-licked, and give up acrid smoke. He is burning the only copy of a book he has written about his experiences in the East.

Exactly five years later, in August 1919, the Royal Opera House in London was packed, twice a day, with people wanting to hear about the great war hero 'Lawrence of Arabia'. Not long after, when the man himself had changed his name and profession and was trying to disappear (but also, it must be said, popping into the theatre to see himself on the screen), he mentioned this 'youthful indiscretion book' to a friend who had also served in Arabia. 'It recounted adventures in seven type-cities of the East,' he explained, 'Cairo, Baghdad, Damascus, etc.'[2] Another time he dropped Baghdad from the list, which made sense because he had never been there, and referred instead to Cairo, Constantinople, Smyrna, Aleppo, Jerusalem, Urfa and Damascus, with all of which he was very familiar. 'It was a queer book,' he said, 'upon whose difficulties I look back with a not ungrateful wryness.'[3] A queer book about his years of adventure about finding happiness, about love.

The only reason he gave for destroying the manuscript was that it was immature. But that doesn't quite ring true. He had written other works – a description of Crusader castles in Syria, for instance, and the diary of a journey he made across the Euphrates River in the summer of 1911. Both of these unpublished manuscripts were immature, both had caused him difficulties, and both were in the bungalow at the end of the garden. So why burn the book of his adventures? A clue lies in the admission of 'indiscretion' and in the outbreak of war.

His brother Frank had already been commissioned into the army and had gone to fight. Another brother, Will, was on his way back from India, intending to enlist. Lawrence knew that soon – weeks perhaps – he would leave the bungalow, say goodbye to his parents and travel south to London and from there to war. In August 1914, at the very beginning of the conflict, no one had any idea of the slaughter that lay ahead in the Somme, at Ypres, in the Dardanelles and in many other places whose names we might otherwise not know, and which would claim the lives of both Frank and Will the following year. In August 1914, many people expected World War I to be over by Christmas: it was inconceivable that it would last four years, claim eight and a half million lives and bring an end to four empires.

Lawrence had already offered his services to the war effort. He had lived in and travelled around the Middle East for the previous five years and he knew that this would be a conflict unlike any other. He knew, because he had watched it take shape, growing from a small fight in Libya to major battles in the Balkans to a war that would destroy his life. He was certain that he had a role to play in this conflict. In fact, he had already dreamed of the glorious challenge: he would start a new crusade by raising a wave of fighters out of Arabia and rolling them before the breath of an idea, to crash against the walls of Damascus. In so doing, he believed, they would free the Arab lands from Ottoman control. He had already laid his plans. He knew the terrain, the combatants and the tactics that would win the prize of freedom for the people he loved. Now he was watching nations lining up to fight, waiting for the Turks to join the war.

It seems natural, under these circumstances, at some point, if only during the black hours of night, hours he knew well, that he would consider his own mortality, because he might not return from this war. He was certainly aware of that possibility when his brother Frank went to join the 3rd Gloucestershire Regiment. 'I didn't go to say goodbye to Frank, because he would rather that I didn't, & I knew there was little chance of my seeing him again; in which case we were better without a parting.'[4]

If Lawrence was aware that there was little chance of his returning from the war, then burning his 'immature' manuscript with its 'indiscretions' must have been part of the tidying of his affairs. Which raises the question of what the book might have contained that he would not have wanted to leave behind, that he did not want his parents, or the world, to know about.

Like the words of great poets, Lawrence's name is carried on the wind. It reached me at an early age and, one way or another, it has hung about me ever since. As a child, I saw David Lean's film *Lawrence of Arabia*, with Peter O'Toole's intelligent if not wholly accurate portrait of the man – he did, at least, capture the wayward nature, the staring into space, the smiles, the love of pranks and obscure comments, that mix of shyness and irrepressible liveliness in the man. The film is based on the extraordinary book Lawrence wrote in the 1920s, which describes in vivid detail and with passion his war experiences and which he called *Seven Pillars of Wisdom*. On the brown cover of the first public edition of 1935 are a pair of crossed swords and the words 'the sword also means clean-ness + death', so troubling to my impressionable young mind.

Half a century after its first publication, engaged in the Middle East myself, I remember reading the book. Since then, on many occasions in and near the desert in Jordan and Egypt, I have been encouraged (by Bedouin, camel hawkers and others) to 'be' Lawrence, by which was meant that I should mount a camel, tie a *keffiyeh* on my head and ride into the sands, although I, like the young Lawrence, prefer to walk. But in spite of all this exposure, at no point was I swept away by the man or his myth. I took the view that the importance both of the Arab revolt of 1916–18 and of Lawrence's role in it had been overplayed, that the revolt was little more than a sideshow in the war and that Lawrence, while he may have done considerably more than was expected of a junior liaison officer, had neither created nor led the uprising. But time changes many things.

In the 1990s, I travelled through the Syrian mountains where, I was told, I would find the remains of extraordinary Crusader-era castles. Looking for books to read before I started out, I came across Lawrence's *Crusader Castles*, the final incarnation of his under-graduate thesis. As I followed the trail, from Aleppo to Sahyun, from Markab to Masyaf, from Crac des Chevaliers to Safita, I realised I was also following the man. Lawrence was twenty years old when he started on that journey in the summer of 1909. I was older when I made mine. I had had more difficulty getting into Syria, which was then ruled by Hafez al-Assad, because something I had written about the country had upset someone in the Syrian government so that for several years my visa applications were turned down. When I was finally allowed to visit, the Syrian travel agent who organised my trip took me to meet the man from the ministry and smoothed my way. He also warned me to look out for myself while travelling in the remote hills. Similar words were said to Lawrence before he set out.

All of those warnings melted away when I reached the old Assassin stronghold at Kalaat el-Kahf, a remote rocky outcrop where the remains of the castle had mostly disappeared beneath greenery. The day was sunny and warm, my thoughts as clear as the air – as my memory is now of that moment when I began to wonder about this young Englishman who had been there before me. I knew why *I* was there: I had been living in Cairo for a couple of years and wanted to see and understand more of the region and its people. But what would drive an exceptionally bright Oxford undergraduate to leave the comfort and safety of home to see the remains of Crusader castles in the Middle East in 1909? Why would he choose to walk at a time of great political and social unrest in the Turk-controlled provinces, and in midsummer, when the experts at home had advised against it? This moment is more important for me to fix, and to hold in my memory, than the first time I came across the Lawrence legend. Much has been written and argued about the part he played in the Arab contribution towards the defeat of the Turks in World War I. But nothing I read then, or have read since, told the story I wanted to read: how the second son of a quiet, comfortably off, apparently unexceptional Oxford family came to play a role – any role – in the Arab uprising, how an archaeologist became a spy, how an introvert became an outspoken leader, how and why 'Ned Lawrence of Oxford' became 'Lawrence of Arabia'.

At the first village beyond Kalaat el-Kahf, a middle-aged man stopped me and, as people like him have been doing for longer than we can know, he invited a traveller into his house. Over a glass of tea, with his children staring from the safety of the doorway, he gently led me through a series of questions that established who I was, where I had come from, where I was going and why. I in turn asked about his land and what he grew on it, the size of the harvest and of his family, the state of the countryside and, eventually, the pinch of the government. Curiosity satisfied on both sides, I continued on my way with his blessing, his younger sons herding me out as though I were some stray goat, until their father called them off and the breeze carried his blessings to me.

Lawrence went through this ritual every day that he travelled in the region and each time it happened, he was more charmed, more fascinated. So much so that when his parents tried to lure him home – this was after he had been away for a couple of years – he explained, in almost exactly the words I used to relay the same message to my parents, that 'I don't think anyone who has tasted the East as I have would give it up.'[5]

I don't think anyone who glimpsed this side of young Lawrence would give up on him either, at least not before getting to the heart of the puzzle of why he stayed in the Middle East for most of the five years leading up to the war that was to change his world. But then Lawrence's life is punctuated by mysteries, as his friend Sir Ronald Storrs, one of the pall-bearers at his funeral, mused long after his death, when he described Lawrence's motive for getting involved in the Arab revolt as 'a tragic mystery that can never be revealed'.[6] The Lawrence who fought in the war and, even more so, the Lawrence who looked for peace in the 1920s and 1930s, is a deepening mystery, a character who becomes ever more complex and opaque and, as the years pass, who poses greater challenges as the truth is hidden behind ever more convoluted ambiguities. That older Lawrence might never be fully understood, although some have come close to revealing him. But the young Lawrence of the years before World War I is both more approachable and easier to understand, seen through actions and comments that are not coloured by his coming greatness or reinterpreted in the light of his enduring legend. A closer look at the five years Lawrence spent travelling around and living in the Middle East before the war reveals a great deal about the motives for what followed. There is also, I believe, a fascination, a joy even, to be had in following a young man as he falls for another culture, for another people, and for one person in particular.

I did not know, as I followed his trail through the Crusader castles then, or on subsequent journeys, that I would become obsessed by the story of *Young Lawrence*. This book is the result of a long, slow process of gestation. But several years ago, when conflict spread from Tunisia to Egypt and then Syria, I remembered some of the people I had met, whose generous hospitality I had enjoyed. And I recalled what Lawrence had written about the artificial boundaries being created in the aftermath of World War I as a result of a deal between Britain and France, the Sykes–Picot agreement, which he strongly opposed. I remembered how he had said that youth could win but it could not hold its victories, that the old men came out and made their same old mistakes. I realised then how much the pre-war years resonate today. The geographical divisions of the Middle East that Lawrence knew in the years leading up to the great conflict made more sense – politically, socially, ethnically – than the configurations do today. This goes some way towards explaining why the states that were created after World War I are still under so much stress.

Geography and politics form a background, part of the bigger picture of this book. But I have been drawn into his story by a need to understand why he went, why he stayed and how he became Lawrence 'of Arabia'.

Most people's image of Lawrence starts with David Lean's film. The earliest moment of his life as shown in the film presents a blue-eyed, fair-haired, silver-tongued, twenty-eight-year-old man in uniform, surrounded by maps, at British army headquarters, Cairo. The year was 1916 and Lawrence was about to leave Egypt, for Arabia, seeking to understand why the Arab revolt was failing, 'to see and consider its great men . . . and [to look for] the leader with the necessary fire'.[7] From November 1916, when Lawrence was officially posted as a liaison officer to the Arab revolt, until October 1918, when he asked General Allenby, Commander of the Allied forces in the Middle East, to let him leave Damascus, he fought, schemed and dreamed to create the circumstances out of which independent Arab states might emerge. It was to be the crucible from which the legend of

Lawrence, the uncrowned king of Arabia would also emerge.

A hundred years after the outbreak of World War I, very few individuals who fought in it exist in our popular imagination. In 1918 Allenby was one of the most famous fighters to have survived the war, but now he is mostly forgotten. The show that opened in the Royal Opera House in 1919 and packed theatres around the world in the 1920s was originally titled *With Allenby in Palestine*, before being changed to *With Allenby in Palestine and Lawrence in Arabia* when it became clear that the crowds wanted to see Lawrence: more than four million people worldwide went to see the lecture and screening. Lord Kitchener, the British field marshal who reminded Britons that their country needed them, is remembered, as are Rupert Brooke, Wilfred Owen, Siegfried Sassoon and the other war poets. But none has retained the standing, in the popular imagination, that Lawrence enjoys. In part this is to do with the nature of his exploits during the war, in part due to the way his story was exploited afterwards. Reporting his death on 20 May 1935, an editorial in *The Times* noted that his place in history was assured. 'Other British officers helped the Arabs of the Hejaz in the campaign that has changed the political face of the Near East, but none so effectively or so intelligently as this young archaeologist who had studied war in his school days and had had original ideas of its conduct.'[8] When the publication of *Seven Pillars of Wisdom*, his account of his wartime exploits, was announced weeks after his death, fifty thousand advance copies were sold, a record at the time. My grandfather was among the many people eagerly awaiting that publication. His copy sits on the shelf beside my desk.

Reviewing *Seven Pillars of Wisdom*, Winston Churchill thought it 'will be read as long as the English language is spoken'. So far, that has proved to be the case. But in the stream of books, articles, lectures and discussions about the nature and value of Lawrence's wartime exploits and what we now call his legacy, his post-war reputation, popularity and significance have waxed and waned. He has been hailed as a hero and denounced as another imperialist out to exploit the less fortunate, both championed and derided as a homosexual, and dismissed as a self-publicist, a fantasist, a fake.

In the controversy, we have lost sight of the man. But in his pre-war story, in the tale told in the manuscript he burned in Oxford in 1914, we can see the man without the distortions of legend. *Young Lawrence* sets out to reconstitute from his own letters and from the papers and stories of those who knew him at the time some of what was lost in the grate of the bungalow at Polstead Road. It is intended as a prequel to the better-known exploits of Lawrence of Arabia as told in the post-war *Seven Pillars*. Only by knowing the story of how this extraordinary young archaeologist, so awkward at home, found himself – his role and his passion – among the Arabs, Kurds and Turks of Ottoman Syria, can one understand how he achieved what he did during the war. Only when one understands the depth of feeling he had for the villagers who had brought him happiness, and for one of them in particular, can one understand why he wanted to help to raise the Arab armies against the Turks and why, when it was done, he had no choice but to change his name and to hide from the legend that had been wrapped around him.

PART I

The Young Scholar

Imagination should be put into the most precious caskets, &
that is why one can only live in the future or the past, in
Utopia, or the wood beyond the World.

T. E. Lawrence to his mother, August 1910,
The Home Letters of T. E. Lawrence and his Brothers, p. 110

I

Landing

Learn to dream when thou dost wake,
Learn to wake when thou dost sleep.
Learn to water joy with tears,
Learn from fears to vanquish fears.
　　　　Francis Thompson, 'The Mistress of Vision'[1]

Beirut, Tuesday 6 July 1909

THE PORT SAID steamer dropped anchor off Beirut at around
six o'clock in the morning. The roadstead was as busy as ever.
Ten ships were expected during the day, and a cluster of skiffs and
rowing boats rocked on the crystal water, ready to bring off passengers and cargo. From the deck, a young Englishman was staring out
at the merchant-favoured city spread before him and up the slopes
behind the quay to the clutter of white and grey stone houses with
pointed, red-tiled roofs. The hum of human activity – prayer and
industry – rose like a mist above the roofline as the sun climbed
over the shoulders of Jebel Sannine and the Lebanon Mountains and
the city began its day. At this early hour, the light was soft, the air
still cool and damp. Later, writing his first letter home from the
Middle East, he described it as being 'most delightfully warm, and
the bay of Beyrout [sic] lovely'.[2]

The man from Thomas Cook came to clear his bags through
customs, although there was not much to be inspected: a change of
clothes, something to read, a notebook to record observations, a
German-made revolver and a camera with lenses, in a large leather
bag. If any eyebrows were raised among the port officials, it was not

because of what he was carrying but at his lack of luggage. He was travelling with considerably less than most British visitors, but then he was not like them.

The extent of his difference would become apparent later. If he stood out among the passengers, agents and porters being rowed the short distance from steamer to quayside that morning, it was perhaps for his youth, his bespoke suit with its many pockets, for his low, soft voice with its 'donnish precision of speech'[3] and, above all, for the coiled potential that many people remembered hanging about him. He was a month off his twenty-first birthday, travelling alone, a reserved, confident, Oxford history undergraduate. At five feet five inches, he was shorter than many of his family and friends in England. But in Beirut, where people were shorter, he stood out more for his thick head of fair hair, combed from a parting far to the right and, above all, for the icy blue of his eyes. One of his Oxford tutors commented on the 'depth and seriousness of purpose in that steady and unyielding gaze with which with head slightly bowed, he looked up into the eyes of those who spoke to him'.[4] No one spoke to him now, but the gaze was the same, fixing this place he would come to know so well.

He had consulted his Baedeker guide to Palestine and Syria and although Cook's office was in the Grand Hôtel d'Orient, the city's finest, right there on the waterfront, he preferred the sound and the lower rates of the nearby Hôtel Victoria. He was expecting to stay in the region for a couple of months, to do some touring and sightseeing, and like many visitors he spent that first day in preparation. He had been thinking about his route for several months and he knew very well what he wished to see. He had come to walk around the surviving Crusader castles, up to Urfa beside the Euphrates River in the north and then down to the southern outposts in the desert beyond Jerusalem. He had also made some advance introductions and now walked out of the old town and past the Turkish barracks to the British Consulate, where he was expected. Because he was intending to visit some of the more remote districts of Palestine and Syria, he had already applied for a permit to travel from the imperial government in Constantinople. At the Consulate, he now heard that his papers, known as *iradés*, had been posted from the capital and 'should arrive shortly, but the Turkish P.O. is irregular'.⁵ From the Consulate, he walked a mile or so through 'streets full of camels, donkeys, and mules, and of millions and billions of dogs'⁶ to the American College.

Lawrence had an introduction to the American College* and held court in the teachers' Common Room that afternoon. He was by habit shy, even introverted, but if he felt on safe ground, and especially if there was a trick or a joke to be played, as there was now, he was happy to rise to the occasion. His brother had recently taught him some lines from the ancient Greek poet Theocritus, and Lawrence now dropped these into conversation at the College, the city's premier institution for higher education, with the desired effect. He mused afterwards that 'a reputation as a classical scholar is easily gained'.⁷ Equally easy was the arrangement he had made with some of the young Americans who taught at the College and who were about to break for the summer. 'The tutors', he wrote home that first evening, 'have been taking walking tours in their summer holidays for years, exactly as I propose to do. On Thurs I start with a party of them (s) [south] down the coast: we may keep together for a week or more. The country is quiet.'⁸

The country is quiet . . .

Elsewhere in this first letter he wrote that 'I am setting out to enjoy myself, as everybody, from the Consul downwards, tells me that travelling is as ordinary as in Europe.' The Consul had also asked him to keep in touch, to be sure this young man with his bespoke suit, hobnail boots and fair hair was safe. Because in spite of Lawrence's comment that travelling in the area was as ordinary as in Europe, the truth was more troubling. A year earlier, there had been a revolution in Constantinople. The Committee of Union and Progress, better known as the Young Turks (although the key players were far from young), had not removed Sultan Abdul Hamid II from his divan, but they had forced him to hand over power. The empire was to be ruled by constitution, by parliamentary law, not by the Sultan's decree. This might seem nothing more than a comma in the long and twisted story of Ottoman decline, but the effects were

* Now the American University in Beirut.

significant and they rolled, wave after wave, out of the capital and across the empire, reaching even its most remote provinces. Perhaps especially to the remoter corners of the provinces. One of the many consequences was that the imperial government's grip was weakened; the centre struggled to hold the outer edges. This situation was made worse in April 1909, less than ten weeks before Lawrence landed in Beirut, when the old Sultan attempted a counter-coup. Abdul Hamid had reigned for more than thirty-two years, but when his counter-coup failed, he was sent into exile in Salonica and replaced on the throne by his more compliant half-brother, Mehmet V. The new Sultan had spent at least half of his sixty-four years in the Topkapi Palace harem, many of those in solitary confinement. He emerged now into the bright light of the Bosphorus with a greater interest in Persian poetry than in divan politics. This suited the Young Turk leaders. Absolute power over an empire that still stretched across three continents, from Bosnia to the tip of the Arabian peninsula, from Basra on the Persian Gulf to the Tunisian border, now lay in the hands of a group who had little experience of ruling. Their policies exacerbated divisions among the many religious and ethnic groups ruled by the quiescent Sultan.

So while the country may have been quiet, as Lawrence wrote home, it was not entirely safe for travellers, as a letter to *The Times*, reprinted in the Constantinople-based *Levant Herald & Eastern Express*, made clear: 'The peaceful cultivator or merchant and the Arab sheikh cannot exist side by side; the settled population must drive the Beduin from out their borders . . . With the lack of roads and the insecure state of the few that exist, the best intentioned Vali [Governor] of Aleppo, Damascus, or Baghdad will find his hand too short to reach the limits of his vilayet [province].'[9] The correspondent's concern was validated six days later when the same paper reported that Miss Gertrude Bell, 'a traveller and authoress, had been robbed of her horses and baggage by Kurds'.[10] Bell, the intrepid forty-year-old British writer and archaeologist, had been travelling in the empire's furthest provinces looking at Syriac orthodox churches around Tur Abdin, close to the Tigris River. She was on her way back towards the Mediterranean coast when her entourage pitched tents at a village by the name of Kotch. They assumed, as they were back in Syria, that they need post no sentries. 'We had grown careless with months of safe journeying in dangerous places,' the redoubtable woman later remembered, 'and the thieves had found us an easy prey.'[11] Her notebooks were among the stolen baggage, 'the result of four months' work'. What was not reported in the local press was that several days after the theft all her belongings were returned apart from some cash, and this was later refunded by the Ottoman government. 'It may well be questioned', she concluded, 'whether any other govt would have recognized a like liability.'[12]

And yet in spite of Miss Bell's parting comment, and of Lawrence's reassurances to his family, it was clear that travel in some parts of the region was not as safe as it had once been. So why would a young man risk his possessions and perhaps his life? What, in this remote place, could possibly be so important to him? What was this passion driving him eastwards?

2

Origins

Indeed you shall have it very plain, my friend. My mother says
I am his son: for myself I do not know. Has any son of man
yet been sure of his begetting?

          Homer, *The Odyssey*, Book I, translated by Lawrence[1]

Who could have supposed that this childhood punish-
ment . . . would determine my tastes and desires, my passions,
my very self for the rest of my life?

          Jean-Jacques Rousseau, *Confessions*[2]

1903–8

LATER, AFTER THE adventures, the war, the shame and pain, the
years of hiding and then his death in a motorbike accident at
the age of forty-six, his family and friends would remember his early
fascination with the medieval world, his love for the monuments of
crusading knights and his work with glass and pottery dug from
under the streets of Oxford.

He had been making brass rubbings since he was a small boy.
Something about the romance and chivalry of men who went to
fight in the Middle East some eight hundred years earlier, the
Crusader knights whose brass tomb-images he was copying, appealed
to him from an early age. There was also the freedom he was given
to pursue this hobby. He started by touring churches in and around
Oxford, but when he was older he cycled around England in search
of famous brass, and the walls of his bedroom – this was when he
was still sleeping in the house, before the bungalow was built – were

hung with treasures found on these outings, a parade of life-size figures of knights in armour and priests in elaborate vestments. Pride of place was given to rubbings of the two oldest knightly brasses in England, Sir Roger de Trumpington and Sir John d'Abernon. It was typical of Lawrence that his interest should become obsessive. His principal collaborator, his childhood friend Cyril Beeson, known by his school nickname of 'Scroggs', remembered that 'it was no collector's hobby. There were experiments in the technique of rubbing with different grades of heelball [a mix of lamp-black and wax] and paper, assisted by friendly advice from shoemakers and paper-hangers whose shops supplied our raw materials.'[3] Another schoolfriend described the outings as 'a ransacking'. Nothing stood in Lawrence's way, so if brasses were hidden behind some pews, 'Lawrence, already ruthless, made short work of the obstruction, and I still hear the splintering woodwork and his short laugh, almost sinister to my timorous ears.'[4] A third friend, Charles ffoulkes,* remembered an occasion when they forgot their heelball: 'There was a serious discussion as to the possibility of removing the brass, taking it home for rubbing, and replacing it.'[5]

Research led Lawrence and his friends into Oxford's libraries and then to London, to the armouries at the Wallace Collection and the Tower of London. They were just fifteen years old and yet their passion led them to study techniques for making armour and chain-mail, trace the development of heraldry and copy arms on to sheets of paper. The terminology was also mastered; 'a herald's jargon was permanently acquired', Beeson noted, and 'eventually enriched the vocabulary of the *Seven Pillars*'.[6]

Oxford was a happy place to live for someone with a passion for the past as it was home to numerous societies devoted to antiquities and antiquaries. There was also the Ashmolean Museum, the city's treasure house, whose collections were started in the seventeenth century. Lawrence became a regular visitor and a teenage volunteer, while the museum's senior staff played an important role in his life. In the summer of his eighteenth birthday, 1906, he also became a

---

* ffoulkes later became Curator of the Imperial War Museum, London and an expert in armour. Lawrence bought him a chainmail vest from the last blacksmith capable of such work in Damascus.

donor. There was a large amount of demolition work in Oxford's city centre that summer – in the Cornmarket, the Leopold Arms and Civet Cat pubs were pulled down, while other buildings were cleared along the High Street and at Hertford, St John's and Jesus colleges. Many people saw these works as a nuisance, but Lawrence recognised an opportunity and made friends with some of the workmen who told him they had been finding pieces of old pottery and glass, but had been throwing them away. Lawrence persuaded them to keep them. Beeson went with Lawrence on these visits and remembered that 'to ensure that the specimens were carefully dug out and preserved, the workmen were bribed with a few pence a piece. We made our rounds almost daily and were often rewarded by the recovery of a fragment of a greybeard or bottle months after the first portions were turned up.'[7]

It seems extraordinary in a place of learning such as Oxford that a pair of teenagers should be salvaging antiques from city-centre excavations. And it wasn't just confined to that summer – they bought pieces from several sites over two or three years. 'It yielded a fine series of vessels of pottery, glazed ware, blown and moulded bottles, pipes, coins and tokens, etc., mostly fifteenth- to seventeenth-century work.'[8]

Shards and fragments were carried to Polstead Road, where Lawrence began the process of reassembly. Restoration – of broken objects, ancient cities and fractured nations – became his lifelong mission. His mother, who watched over all his activities, described how 'he put the fragments together with plasticine, and built up many fine pots and jugs, etc., of things broken and thrown away hundreds of years before.'[9] As with everything he devoted himself to, there was something profoundly romantic about it – a schoolboy recovering fragments from a construction site and restoring them to something like their original condition. There was also a seriousness of purpose, and ambition, because he and Beeson then took the best pieces to the Ashmolean. The curators were delighted to receive the gifts: the Keeper's *Report* noted 'considerable disturbance of the ground for foundations of new buildings in the city' and also that 'owing to the generosity of Mr. E. Lawrence and also C. F. C. Beeson, who have by incessant watchfulness secured everything of antiquarian value which has been found, the most interesting finds have been added to the local antiquities in the Museum'.[10] Before long, he was helping to rearrange the museum's medieval collection.

Brass rubbing and friendship with Beeson also led south to France, in an indirect sort of way. His father had long encouraged him to cycle and to photograph, both hobbies the older man was able to share with his sons. His mother, in spite of wanting to control his every action, was happy to allow her second son to roam the counties in search of brasses to rub and Roman sites to excavate. At the end of July 1906, Lawrence prepared his bike and a very small bag for a journey to France. He had cycled there the previous summer with his father and remembered it as 'a dream of delight'.[11] This time he spent August cycling from medieval churches to castles. He was based in Dinard, Beeson was there for two weeks and they stayed with family acquaintances, and yet he achieved something he had long craved: a sense of independence. A mark of his independence can be seen in the long letters filled with closely observed detail of things seen and people met, but giving very little about the state of their author. He addressed this, probably in reply to a prompt from his inquisitive mother. 'You want more details of myself,' he wrote on 14 August, 'I really have none to give.'[12] A week later he explained to his father that there was no personal information in any of these letters because 'the buildings I describe will last longer than we will, so it is only fitting that they should have the greater space.'[13] A week later still, again to his mother, he stressed that 'there will be no private or family messages in [this letter], although there has not been anything of the sort in any letters of mine up to the present.'[14]

Most young people crave independence at some stage of their development. Many are excited by the prospect; some want it but are terrified at the thought of loosening family bonds. Lawrence's urge for independence, his desire to stand alone, was acute because it was driven by a very private thought: he believed he was illegitimate.

The truth of his birth was not confirmed until after World War I, by which time he was over thirty and his father was dead. Then he learned that he was indeed illegitimate, the son of unmarried parents. His father was Sir Thomas Robert Tighe Chapman, an Anglo-Irish baronet with an estate and a large manor house in County Westmeath, some fifty miles north-west of Dublin in Ireland. He had a wife and four daughters. Into the house came a young Scottish woman, Sarah Lawrence. She was an excellent governess and the girls adored her. Unfortunately so too did Sir Thomas Chapman.

Sir Thomas seems not to have been a complicated man. Brought up in Ireland, educated at the famous English private school, Eton, and then sent to Cirencester's Royal Agricultural College to learn about running his estate, he enjoyed many of the privileges his status and wealth allowed him, and had a passion for hunting and drinking. Perhaps he liked to drink too much, but then so did many people around him and it would not have been a problem had he not married a dour woman with a very public passion for God. With hindsight, they appear to have been an unusually bad match. She seemed also unable to bear him a son.

Chapman was careless in his passion for the governess. When she became pregnant in the summer of 1885, he arranged for her to move to Dublin. When she bore him a son, he gave the boy his name, Chapman, and christened him Montagu Robert, later known as Bob. With his mistress and son in Dublin and his wife and four daughters on his estate, Chapman's life became complicated and then, somewhat inevitably, began to unravel. When he and Sarah were spotted in Dublin, his wife confronted him and issued an ultimatum. The choice would have been a hard one, for whatever he felt about his wife Chapman had been happy with his life, his land and his daughters, aged between six and twelve. But he was in love and he chose Sarah and their son. There was no possibility of a divorce, so Chapman could never marry Sarah Lawrence. Instead, he gave up his estate, fortune and family name and moved with her and the baby to Wales, to the sleepy town of Tremadoc, where they were not known and where they set up home as Mr and Mrs Thomas Lawrence. When their second son was born in 1888, he was christened with his father's first name and his parents' assumed name, Thomas Edward Lawrence.

The social stigma attached to living in sin was especially poignant in Victorian Britain; having children out of wedlock was considered an even greater sin. (Sarah Lawrence would have known all about that as she was herself illegitimate: her real family name was Junner.) Lawrence and his brothers were bastards and the knowledge of this, the fear of being exposed, kept their father away from places where he was known. It also haunted him to his death and at some point, for it is undated, he wrote a confession even though he expected no absolution. It was addressed to his sons, but with the instruction that it should not be opened until after his death or until their mother wished. In it he explained how he had left his wife and how she turned down his repeated requests for a divorce – 'How often I wish there had been! You can imagine or try to imagine, how your Mother and I have suffered all these years, not knowing what day we might be recognised by some one and our sad history published far and wide. You can think with what delight we saw each of you growing up to manhood, for men are valued for themselves and not for their family history, except of course under particular circumstances.' The pain in this letter, written after years of shouldering a crushing sense of sin, reaches a crescendo: 'I can say nothing more, except that there never was a truer saying than "the ways of transgressors are hard". Take warning from the terrible anxieties and sad thoughts endured by both your Mother and me for now over thirty years!'[15] This, then, was the unspoken truth present throughout their childhood, the guilty secret that poisoned each day and that kept them moving, always scared of being exposed. From Wales they moved to western Scotland where their third son, Will, was born. Frank, the fourth, was born four years later on the island of Jersey, although by then they were living in seclusion outside Dinard on the Brittany coast. They moved to the edge of the New Forest in Hampshire, southern England, the following year and in 1896, when eight-year-old Ned and his elder brother were in need of a good school, they settled in Oxford and found the large, redbrick house on Polstead Road. Arnold, the youngest of the five brothers, was born at home in Oxford in 1900.

There was never a suggestion that the five Lawrence boys had an unhappy or even an unsettled life. They moved more often in their first few years than most families moved in a lifetime, but they were close knit and well loved. When their father gave up his name, he also signed away his right to the revenues from his estates, but in return he received an annual income that allowed him and his new family to live comfortably. Because he had neither the need nor any great urge to work, Thomas Lawrence spent more time with his children than was usual for a father at that time and it was from him that Ned acquired a passion for shooting, for photography and for long-distance cycling. His relationship with his mother was more complicated.

Lawrence began picking up clues about his illegitimacy from an early age, perhaps because he overheard a conversation between his father and a lawyer: there is no suggestion that he shared his suspicions with his four brothers. Ned certainly understood that there was an ulterior motive behind his father's infrequent visits to Ireland. He claimed that he understood the situation by the time he was ten, although it seems he misunderstood it. Charles Bell, Assistant Keeper at the Ashmolean Museum, claimed that he heard before the war that Lawrence had confided that he was illegitimate. The story Bell recorded, which we must assume is what Ned believed, was that Sarah Lawrence was indeed the boys' mother, but that Mr Lawrence was not the father, that he had adopted them when he and their mother had married. This is a 'milder' version of the truth, but even this was enough to hang a weight on Lawrence's shoulders. He believed that if the truth about his birth were known, he would not be accepted in society and might find it difficult to teach or carry out postgraduate work at Oxford. Even if he had not understood this himself, he would have gleaned something of it from an early age by watching his parents' behaviour. Their hiding away in Wales, the New Forest and France could be easily explained if one understood that they were driven by a fear of being exposed. Their reluctance to be seen at anything but church gatherings made sense for the same reason. One of their neighbours at Polstead Road spoke later of how the family was considered a little strange. And yet none of the other boys nor any of the people they knew guessed their secret, only their precocious second son.

He would have to play along with the charade for everyone's sake, but he found the hypocrisy at home sickening. He seemed to blame his father less than his mother and as a result had a happier, if less intense relationship with a man he described as being on 'the large scale, tolerant, experienced, grand, rash, humoursome, skilled to speak, and naturally lord-like'.[16] Most of his letters were addressed to his mother, who was also the one who wrote to him, as she had looked out for him when he was at home. The supposed 'truth' of his birth made her intrusiveness unacceptable and they fought. In a letter to Charlotte Shaw, wife of George Bernard Shaw and one of the confidantes of his later life, he expressed the terror he had felt of his mother finding out what he thought or wanted or believed, because she would use it to dominate him. He saw his mother as a woman who had sacrificed herself to her family, but at the same time as someone who was dominant in her marriage, who held his father 'as her trophy of power'.[17] Because of this complex woman and the equally complicated situation in which he grew up, he had a horror of families. He also seems to have found the idea of a sexual relationship with a woman repellant, although there was one, Janet Laurie, who claimed he had proposed to her in 1910. Laurie had known the Lawrence brothers since childhood and was a welcome visitor to Polstead Road. Several of the young men seem to have been in love with her. Mrs Lawrence had hoped that Bob would marry her, but after dinner one evening it was Ned who took her aside and popped the question, only for her to decline. He never mentioned his passion for her again, and nor did he propose to anyone else.

Much can be made of the strain his illegitimacy and his struggle with his mother placed on his relations with his parents: this, I assume, is why they built the bungalow for him at Polstead Road, to get him out of the main house, to defuse the tension between mother and son. But consider also how the parents' situation would have affected some of the more obvious things in his life. What stories were told when it came to explaining the family's background? How were differences in his parents' education, expectation and manners explained? What of the lack of mementoes of former lives? How did they explain the years Thomas Chapman lived in Ireland with his wife? There were presumably no photographs or portraits of ancestors, nothing that might give away the truth of his bloodline (which could be traced back to Sir Walter Raleigh) or of Sarah Lawrence's illegitimacy. Instead, in Ned's bedroom, there were brass rubbings of noble men who went crusading in the belief they would make the world a better place and in the hope of salvation. This lack of grounding in a family history made it all the easier for the teenager to imagine himself a nowhere man. His life was to be fashioned out of opportunity, luck and very specific dreams.

Lawrence left Oxford High School at the end of July 1907. He was nearly nineteen and had won an exhibition to read modern history at Jesus College, Oxford.* Looking back on his schooling after the war, he wrote that he had been educated 'very little, very reluctantly, very badly' at Oxford High, which sounded damning, but was better than his views of how he was educated at Jesus College, which was 'not at all'.[18] To one of his early biographers he described his school years as 'an irrelevant time-wasting nuisance, which I hated and contemned'.[19] The nuisance, frustration and hatred was about to be replaced by the 'heaven' of undergraduate life.

He was an erratic student. Although clearly extremely bright, there was a flaw in his character: if something interested him, he would excel, but if not, he would do no more than pass. L. C. Jane, Lawrence's private tutor at Oxford, noted his pupil's enthusiasm for less obvious reading. 'I should not call him a scholar by temperament,' Jane wrote, 'and the main characteristic of his work was always that it was unusual without the effort to be unusual.'[20] Ernest Barker, one of his medieval history tutors, went further and doubted that 'Lawrence ever was, or wished to be, an "historical scholar" in the ordinary sense of the word. He was not interested in historical fact for its own sake. He took the Oxford History School because it came in his way, and because it was a hurdle to be jumped on the road that led to action.'[21] The road first led back to France.

He had chosen to write a thesis on medieval military history and strategy as part of his final year's work and, to help with his research, in July 1908, at the end of his first year at university, he prepared

---

* Jesus College had a bias towards Welsh students, and Lawrence had been born in Wales.

for the longest bike ride of his life. Between the middle of July and early September, he rode some 2,400 miles across France. If he had done nothing more than cycle, at an average of more than fifty miles a day, every day, for six or seven weeks, even on the finest bike one could buy at the time (which he had), this feat of endurance would have tested most people. But cycling was not the purpose of the journey: it was simply a way to move between the buildings he wanted to study. He gave detailed descriptions of these buildings in long letters home, made plans of castles, took photographs of the significant ones and everywhere he went expressed an opinion. The eleventh-century Norman basilica at Vézelay, for instance, was 'superb', but for its sculpture – not, as most people claimed, for its proportions. The twelfth-century cloister of St Trophinus at Arles was 'unimaginably fine' and the black basalt cathedral at Agde 'has a front seat in my thesis' (in the end, it did not), while the fortified town of Carcassonne was 'the most interesting and most valuable object-lesson in military architecture . . . and it happens also to be wonderfully picturesque'. There was much more, but he was always withholding the important thought, the imaginative one that would have brought these places to life, that would have repeopled them. Then he reached Chartres.

He had assumed the Gothic cathedral of Notre-Dame at Chartres would be a disappointment in the way that great monuments can be, and also that it would be over-restored as others he had visited had been. So he popped out of his hotel to 'do' it before breakfast, and he was still there in the evening. 'It is . . . the noblest building that I have ever seen, or expect to see.' His long description peaks with the statement that 'it must be one of the noblest works of man, as it is the first of the middle ages'. He then reaches an epiphany:

> All day I was running from one door to another, finding in each something I thought finer than the one I had just left, and then returning to find that the finest was that in front of me . . . it is overwhelming, and when night came I was absolutely exhausted, drenched to the skin (it had poured all day) and yet with a feeling I had never had before in the same degree – as though I had found a path (a hard one) as far as the gates of Heaven, and had caught a glimpse of the inside, the gate being ajar.[22]

Sarah Lawrence, to whom this letter was addressed, would have been delighted and rewarded by her son's description, for both she and Thomas Lawrence were devout and active Christians. They had encouraged their sons in their belief and practice, leading them to attendance at St Aldate's Church and at the Bible study lessons conducted by the church's rector, Canon Alfred Christopher. Sarah Lawrence would have been cheered by the more personal nature of this and other letters Ned was sending home from France because there was plenty of detail about how he felt, what he ate, how far he was pushing himself, and he was always pushing himself and taking pleasure in depriving himself, as if in preparation for an even greater challenge. 'I'm riding very strongly,' he told her after a week in the saddle,

> & feel very fit, on my diet of bread, milk, & fruit . . . I begin on 2 pints of milk & bread, & supplement with fruit to taste till evening, where more solid stuff is consumed: one eats a lot when riding for a week on end at any pace. My day begins early ('tis fearfully hot at mid-day) there is usually a chateau to work at from 12–2, and then a hotel at 7 or 8. I have no time for sightseeing: indeed sometimes I wonder if my thesis is to be written this Nov. or next, I find myself composing pages and phrases as I ride.[23]

His excitement was palpable and it rose the further he rode along beautiful country lanes with their ox-carts, and up to high roads where he was chased by wild dogs. At the beginning of August, he reached Provence and the Mediterranean. It was a cloudy day and he was standing at the top of a valley near Les Baux-de-Provence, above Arles, still some miles from the sea. A green valley and sunburned fields stretched out beneath him. Beyond there was a great grey sliver of horizon. He stood for a while to take in the enormity of the view across the landscape and, as he did so, the sun came out and 'a sort of silver shiver passed over the grey: then I understood, & instinctively burst out with a cry of *thalassa thalassa* that echoed down the valley, & startled an eagle from the opposite hill'.[24] The young man from the north was quoting the famous cry of Xenophon and his ten thousand Greek soldiers when, in 400 BC, they caught sight of the Black Sea on their way home from Mesopotamia. Lawrence had just caught his first glimpse of the Mediterranean. In his excitement, he had shouted so loudly that two French tourists came running to see whether someone was being murdered. They were not. This was a beginning, not an end.

He cycled down through Arles to Aigues-Mortes, where the town thrilled him with its intact medievalism, 'a lovely place . . . with hardly a house outside its old walls, still absolutely unbroken, & hardly at all restored or in need of it. From it St. Louis started for his crusades, & it has seen innumerable events since. Today it is deserted by the world, & is decaying fast.'

He had now arrived at one of those rare moments when the way forward in life becomes clear. He went to bathe in the Mediterranean just outside the town. 'The great sea,' he wrote that night, 'the greatest in the world: you can imagine my feelings: the day was lovely, warm, a light wind, & sunny: the sea had not our long rolling breakers, but short dancing ripples.'[25]

Then he quoted lines from the poet Shelley. 'I love all waste and solitary places; where we taste the pleasure of believing what we see is boundless, as we wish our souls to be.'[26] It could stand as a motto for the next phase of his life. He longed to be unbound and thought of what might lie beyond Oxford for him. What would there be after he had loosened the ties that held him to his family, his medieval obsessions, his sleep watched over by crusading knights? Much later, in *Seven Pillars of Wisdom*, he remembered that he 'had dreamed, at the City School in Oxford, of hustling into form, while I lived, this new Asia which time was inexorably bringing upon us. Mecca was to lead to Damascus; Damascus to Anatolia, and afterwards to Bagdad; and then there was Yemen.' Some of that youthful urge drove him as he looked on to the flat sea near Aigues-Mortes. 'I felt that at last I had reached the way to the South, and all the glorious East; Greece, Carthage, Egypt, Tyre, Syria, Italy, Spain, Sicily, Crete . . . they were all there, and all within reach of me . . . I fancy I now know better than Keats what Cortes felt like, silent upon a peak in Darien. Oh I must get down here, – farther out – again! Really this getting to the sea has almost overturned my mental balance: I would accept a passage for Greece tomorrow.'[27]

3

Father Confessor

Though it is over six and a half centuries since the last Crusaders embarked for Cyprus, the architectural imprint of the Crusades lies heavy on the Syrian littoral.

Robin Fedden, *Syria*[1]

1908–9

Back in Oxford, in the bungalow at Polstead Road, he arranged his plans, notes and photographs and then, his yearning to go east as bright as coals in the grate of the new fireplace, he went to the Ashmolean Museum to share his summer discoveries.

Charles Bell, the museum's Assistant Keeper, had accepted Lawrence's offerings of glass and pottery, and recognised his unusual abilities. A friendship had developed. When it was decided that the museum should be reorganised, Lawrence volunteered to help arrange the medieval pottery. 'We were talking one day about what his next step should be,' Bell wrote later, discussing how Lawrence might develop his thesis on medieval military history and strategy, when the older aesthete suggested, 'Why don't you go to the Holy Land and try to settle once and for all the long contested question as to whether the pointed arch and vault were copied or developed from Eastern sources by the Crusaders, or whether it was they who taught their use to the Arabs?'[2]

The suggestion appealed for it would satisfy his desire to go east and his enduring passion for the medieval world. The Crusades, a series of invasions and wars waged by Europeans in the Middle East in the name of religion – officially to guarantee access to the Holy

30

Land for Christian pilgrims, but more often for political and financial gain – were not such a loaded topic in the early 1900s. Interest in them stirred with the rise of Arab nationalism and continued through the twentieth century.* There were nine main crusades between 1095, when Pope Urban II called on European leaders to free the Holy Land, and 1272 when the last Christian strongholds in the region were lost. Lawrence had no strongly held view of the politics of the Crusades, at this point, but their influence was present in every part of his life, from the medievalism on which Oxford was built, to the knightly stories he so enjoyed reading, to the brass rubbings that had hung over his bed. Of greatest interest to him were the traces the Crusaders had left behind, tombs, tales and castles.

Bell's suggestion that Lawrence write a thesis on the origins of the pointed arch provoked the young man's curiosity about the medieval world. But Lawrence decided to take a broader view of the topic and to question whether the skill to build a castle – not just a pointy arch – had come from the East. The accepted view, championed at that time by Charles Oman, Professor of History at Oxford, was that the Europeans 'marched East with hardly any understanding of fortifications and learned from the Byzantines how to build the magnificent castles they have left in the Levant'. According to Oman, much of what Lawrence had admired in France had its origins elsewhere. But neither Oman nor any of the other scholars who had written about this period had travelled in Syria and Palestine to see the buildings, relying instead on historical documents for evidence to support their theories. Bell sensed that Lawrence's attention to detail and love of the unorthodox would allow him to challenge the accepted view, just as he might delight in a journey that would allow him to visit the magnificent buildings the Crusaders had constructed in an attempt to control the land they deemed sacred.

The idea quickly took hold and before long Lawrence was in the university's Bodleian Library reading Charles Doughty's *Travels in Arabia Deserta*, which Lawrence's generation considered the definitive

---

* Interest was stirred again in 2001, a week after 9/11, when President George W. Bush said that 'This crusade, this war on terrorism is going to take a while.' The late US journalist Alexander Cockburn picked up the reference a year later when he called President Bush and his supporters the Tenth Crusaders.

work on travelling among Arabs. Lawrence's plan was probably not entirely fixed in his mind, nor agreed with family or college, until early the following year, and the catalyst was a new arrival at the Ashmolean.

The Ashmolean Museum had been growing rapidly, acquiring some 2,000 objects a year from Europe and the Eastern Mediterranean. In the 1890s, it was gifted the Fortnum collection of classical and Renaissance bronzes and ceramics, along with £10,000 to construct a new, larger museum building. The new structure retained Charles Cockerell's mid-nineteenth-century neo-classical façade, with its columns copied from the Temple of Apollo at Bassae. In 1908, it was decided to move Oxford University's fine art collection to the museum, putting Dutch masters and Constables beside medieval ceramics and ancient sculptures. The enlarged museum also had a new Keeper (Director), David (D. G.) Hogarth.

Hogarth was forty-six years old when he took over running the museum. He was a graduate of Magdalen College, Oxford and, like Arthur Evans, his predecessor at the Ashmolean, already had a reputation for mixing scholarship with an ability to work in troubled places. The round-faced, balding archaeologist had spent much of the past twenty years in the Levant, from Greece through Syria, Palestine and Egypt. He had a fascination with Alexander the Great, had excavated in Egypt, Crete and Greece, had served as the Director of the British School in Athens and, briefly, as a correspondent for *The Times*. He was also the author of five books, one of which, *The Penetration of Arabia*, indulged his fascination with travelling among the Arabs, even though he had not done so himself. As he explained in the preface to that book, his 'sole qualification for writing the story of Arabian exploration rests in the study of the literature of the Arabian travel.'[3] The course of his life must have seemed obvious, a happy mix of travel, excavation and writing, a life on the move, carefree and curious. But Hogarth had married in 1894 and his son was now seven years old, in need of a settled life. The museum post seemed to suit him perfectly, as both he and the museum straddled academic and more populist worlds. More important for this story, Hogarth was to become the most significant influence on Lawrence's adult life. In *Seven Pillars*, Lawrence calls him 'our father confessor and adviser . . . our referee, and our untiring historian, who gave us his great knowledge and careful wisdom even in the smallest things'.[4] At this earlier stage of the story, he was more of a father than a confessor.

In his introduction to *Accidents of an Antiquary's Life*, Hogarth noted that 'your true Antiquary is born, not made. Sometimes an infirmity or awkwardness of body, which has disposed a boy to shun the pursuits of his fellows, may help to detach the man for the study of forgotten far off things.'[5] He was certainly not writing about himself, for he goes on to admit that, even though he had the required illnesses as a child, he was no born antiquary. But as he wrote these lines in Oxford in 1909, it is tempting to think that he had in mind his new young acquaintance. If not, it is a remarkable coincidence because Lawrence fitted the description perfectly, right down to the infirmity: five years earlier, when he had just turned sixteen, he had broken his leg in a fight at school.

The incident, like much else in his youth and childhood, has been embroidered into legend, but the fight – during the eleven o'clock break – and the injury were real enough. The fight is sometimes presented as one in which he was trying to protect a vulnerable friend from an older bully, which would certainly be true to type. Whatever the cause, the damage was extensive, although Lawrence either did not think so, or put up with it, and continued with lessons. The pain must have been apparent at lunch because his brothers wheeled him home on a bicycle and his mother called the doctor. The leg, broken just above the ankle, was set in a splint. 'He was out of school for a term,' his mother reported, 'it took a long time to get right.' And she added, 'He never grew much after that.'[6] It is true that he stopped growing then – and was the same height as Charlie Chaplin and Marilyn Monroe – but his lack of height was more likely due to his mother's genes than to the broken leg.

The injury exacerbated Lawrence's reluctance to join in. His eldest brother Bob remembered he was 'good at gymnastics, and took part in games in the playground',[7] but Ned admitted that 'I've never, since I was able to think, played any game through to the end. At school they used to stick me into football or cricket teams, and always I would trickle away from the field before the match ended.'[8] The obvious reason for this might have been physical, but Lawrence

33

later thought there were other, more complex issues behind his avoidance of team sports – 'because they were organised, because they had rules, because they had results'.[9]

Whatever the complicated combination of factors that helped to shape Lawrence's character, when Bell introduced him to Hogarth in January 1909 it must have been obvious to the new Keeper that he was naturally disposed towards 'the study of forgotten far off things'. Perhaps there was something in Lawrence's manner and his passion for the Crusader world that made the older man pay more attention to him than he might otherwise have done to a visiting undergraduate. The writer Robert Graves, who came to know Lawrence in the 1920s when writing his biography, described his face as having a 'kindly, almost maternal' upper half and a 'severe, almost cruel'[10] lower part. He liked to stand with his arms folded across his chest and his head tilted to one side. 'He can sit or stand for hours at a stretch without moving a muscle. He talks in short sentences, deliberately and quietly without accenting his words strongly. He grins a lot and laughs seldom.'[11] Perhaps the two things that struck Hogarth most forcefully – two things which continued to impress him as their friendship grew – were the intensity of those cool blue eyes and the matching intensity of concentration once the young man had decided on a course of action. Lawrence had decided on a journey through Syria to study Crusader architecture.

When he revealed his plan for the coming summer, Hogarth was concerned.

'This is the wrong season to visit Syria: it is too hot there now.'

'I'm going,' Lawrence replied.

'Well, have you got the money? You'll want a guide and servants to carry your tent and baggage.'

'I'm going to walk,' the student explained.

'Europeans don't walk in Syria,' the Keeper corrected him, with the authority of someone who had spent several months the previous spring travelling around the Euphrates River region. It was true: no European was seen walking there and for several good reasons, one being that 'it isn't safe or pleasant'.

'Well, I do,' said Lawrence, speaking as someone who had cycled a couple of thousand miles through France the previous summer and who was as confident about his physical abilities as he was about overcoming the intellectual challenge of his thesis.[12] Almost twenty years later, just after Hogarth had died, Lawrence wrote that he 'was a wonderful man . . . first of all human, and then charitable, and then alive. I owed him everything I had, since I was 17, which is the age at which I suddenly found myself.'[13] Lawrence was now twenty and had just found some of the humanity, the charity, the life in Hogarth. Out of respect, he listened when the older man suggested he write to ask advice from Charles Doughty, the expert on Arabia.

Doughty replied on 3 February 1909, writing from his house overlooking the English Channel at Eastbourne.

Dear Sir,

I have not been further North in Syria than lat. 34 [the level of Baalbek in Lebanon, north of Damascus and south of Homs]. In July and August the heat is severe by day & night, even at the altitude of Damascus (over 2000ft.). It is a land of squalor, where an European can find little refreshment. Long daily marches on foot a prudent man who knows the Country would I think consider out of the question. The populations only know their own wretched life, & look upon any European wandering in their Country with at best a veiled ill will.

The distances to be traversed are very great. You will have nothing to draw upon but the slight margin of strength which you bring with you from Europe. Insufficient food, rest & sleep would soon begin to tell.

A distinguished general told me at the time of the English expedition against the Arabs that no soldier under 23 years old, who went through the Campaign, had not been in hospital.

I should dissuade a friend from such a voyage, which is too likely to be most wearisome, hazardous to health & even disappointing.

A mule or horse, with its owner should, at least in my opinion, be hired to accompany you.

Some Arabic is of course necessary.

If you should want to ask any further questions I shall be happy to reply so far as I can do so.

Yours sincerely,

Charles Doughty[14]

Lawrence's response, written five days later, shows him to be undeterred, but also aware that the walk would be more challenging than a bike ride round France:

'My little pleasure trip appears to be more interesting than I had bargained for. I have fortunately a few months to think about it in.'[15]

4

On Foot and Alone

Pass not beneath! Men say there blows in stony deserts still a rose
But with no scarlet to her leaf – and from whose heart no
  perfume flows.
Wilt thou bloom red where she buds pale, thy sister rose? Wilt
  thou not fail
When noonday flashes like a flail?
James Elroy Flecker, 'The Gates of Damascus'[1]

July 1909

THE DAY STARTED cool and damp on the coast, but the sun warmed as he walked on the south road out of Beirut and his excitement rose with the temperature. He was twenty years old, bright, perhaps even brilliant, resourceful, physically extremely tough, with the summer and the Middle East before him, money in his pocket, a pistol in his bag. Why would he not be happy?

He was wearing a lightweight suit he had had made before he left home – with extra pockets to carry his papers and other essential items – and a fine woollen shirt, also bespoke, fastened (for some reason best known to himself) by tiny glove buttons. He carried a small bag and great expectations. Great reserve too, although he was excited by the freedom that lay ahead. He had dreamed of this moment of departure, and had planned for it for the past six months. In his bag were his camera, a spare shirt, sunhat and water bottle. He was travelling light but heavy with intent: he wanted to enjoy himself, he hoped to have an adventure, and he needed to find material to prove that 'the Crusading architects were for many years

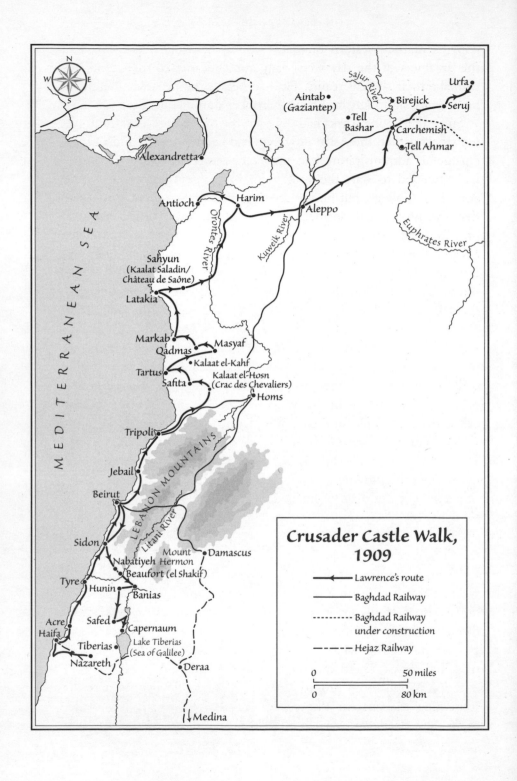

Crusader Castle Walk,
1909

→ Lawrence's route

— Baghdad Railway

---- Baghdad Railway
under construction

—·—·— Hejaz Railway

0 ——————— 50 miles
0 ——————— 80 km

MEDITERRANEAN SEA

Urfa
Birejick
Seruj
Sajur River
Aintab
(Gaziantep)
Tell
Bashar
Carchemish
Tell Ahmar
Euphrates River
Alexandretta

Antioch
Harim
Aleppo
Kuweik River
Orontes River

Sahyun
(Kaalat Saladin/
Château de Saône)
Latakia

Markab
Qadmas
Masyaf
Kalaat el-Kahf
Tartus
Safita
Kalaat el-Hosn
(Crac des Chevaliers)
Homs

Tripoli

LEBANON MOUNTAINS

Jebail

Beirut

Litani River

Sidon
Nabatiyeh
Beaufort (el Shakif)
Mount
Hermon
Damascus

Tyre
Hunin
Banias

Acre
Safed
Haifa
Capernaum
Tiberias
Lake Tiberias
(Sea of Galilee)
Nazareth
Deraa

↓ Medina

N
W E
S

copyists of the Western builders'.² Later, he would recognise that
the dreamers of the day were dangerous because of their tendency
to make their dreams reality. He had begun the process of fulfilling
his dreams, although he knew there were problems ahead.

Since the Young Turks had deposed the Sultan in Constantinople,
ten weeks earlier, the Asian provinces had been unsettled and a recent
change of administrators had made the situation worse. Lawrence
had intended to start the walk with some young tutors from the
American College, but he wrote home that one of them was ill and
that the group had decided to delay their tour. The illness was
probably a fabrication and the tutors were more likely to have delayed
because the roads were unsafe. Whatever the reason, Lawrence was
too impatient to wait. So, with the pine, cedar and mulberry-covered
mountains to his left, the summer-blue Mediterranean on his right,
Baedeker's *Handbook to Palestine and Syria* as his guide, he walked
along the carriage road towards the ancient city of Sidon.

It is easy to imagine his excitement. It had taken three weeks to
reach Beirut – there was a long slow cruise to Port Said, days wasted
waiting for a ship up the Palestine coast, more days in Beirut, and
now . . . *now* he was on his way. To Doughty in February, he had
called this a little pleasure trip. But on the ancient coast road, along
which Alexander the Great and other great warriors had marched
before him, with the July sun on his head and dried-out *maquis*
lining the route, giving an unfamiliar accent to the dust beneath his
boots, he felt the thrill of independent action and a chill of anxiety.
Doughty had been blunt in his warnings about the heat, the squalor,
the lack of refreshment, the hard marches over great distances and
the ill will of the people. What would be his fate?

There is no hint of anxiety in his letters home, just the joy of
walking thirty miles in a day along a road rich in history, but curiously devoid of any great sights. At Nebi Younes, the only place he
thought of any significance that day, tradition suggests Jonah was
cast ashore by the whale but Lawrence found nothing more than
trees and rocks. There was more to see in Sidon.

Sidon is built on a promontory and has a good natural harbour,
something the ancient Phoenicians recognised when they settled
there. His Baedeker warned that 'the present town contains few

attractions',³ but Lawrence found interest. 'Its streets are so narrow,' he told his mother, '& all built over above with houses: some were so narrow that 2 men could only with difficulty pass, and in others I had to bend even my head to pass.'⁴ And while he agreed with Baedeker about the quality of attractions – 'there are two castles, one standing on a mound of purple shells: neither very interesting'⁵ – he was amazed that the guidebook writer had missed the antiquities. Sidon, he wrote, was 'a perfect treasure ground'. He was immediately offered a small intact statue of Venus emerging from the sea, which he thought was second-century BC and, at £60, was well beyond his budget. 'There are other nice pieces of carving, and terracottas, much glass, & dozens of seal-stones (many fired).'

The coast road was well laid and well used, safe, and easy to walk. What lay beyond was more challenging, a week's trek into the 'waterless' Lebanon Mountains and then down into Galilee through a town called Nabatiyeh. Nabatiyeh was *en fête* when he arrived.

> I had the usual things to look at, the people in the shops chaffering over infinitesimal sums, sweetmeat sellers, the icedrink man who sells syrups, crying out 'Take care of thy teeth' or 'Refresh thy heart', 'This for a metallick' (1½d.), or the man with plain water in a goat skin with brass spout, then the fruitsellers, 'if an old woman eats my cress she is young tomorrow'; and funniest of all men with women's ornaments crying 'appease your mother in law', and then as you are looking on at this, comes a hoarse gasp of *dahrak* (your back) and a porter crashes into you with a fresh killed sheep on his back, or a load of charcoal, or perhaps a camel loafs through the crowd with its bell round its neck giving notice.⁶

His family might have wondered how his Arabic had suddenly become fluent enough for him to catch the humour of street sellers, but then he admitted that at Nabatiyeh he 'got a guide or chaperon or whatever you like to call it (male!) to go to Banias whose people have the finest castle, and the worst reputation in S. Lebanon'.⁷ The tone is brief, terse, and suggests that he was not entirely happy at having to resort to a chaperon. It also suggests that he finally realised that he needed one.

He was now walking along one of the main routes south from Damascus to Palestine, a track that for centuries had been watched over by the brooding towers of medieval castles. Here, more than along the coast, he found the setting for some of his childhood dreams, a place where courtly knights in chainmail and armour had displayed their heroism.

Whatever notes he made as he travelled through the country that summer have not survived, so we must rely on the long, infrequent letters he wrote home, and the text of his university thesis, for clues to how he travelled and what he saw. His letters are revealing – 'intentionally personal' he called them – in contrast to the ones from France the previous year, more revealing and with more complaints. 'The roads in Palestine are awful,' he wrote, 'either they are basalt, or limestone, in huge blocks, often a couple of feet high, & with smaller ones strewn about at random. As the whole country is made up of these stones it is a little difficult sometimes to distinguish the road. When one has found it one proceeds gaily by jumping from one stone to another, & as they are all angular, & some of them tottering, progress is painful. Occasionally however I found a road made of little stones no bigger than my fist or even of dust, & then I made good way.'[8] Road surfaces were not the only challenge, for he was also walking through hills. 'The roads are never at rest, indeed climbs & descents of 1500–2000 feet into valleys (usually dry) & up the most scorching hillsides are regular things.' And, being high summer, most of the countryside was burned out and brown: 'an olive tree is a delight to the eyes'.[9] But if he had any regrets about not heeding Doughty's warnings, he kept them to himself.

From Nabatiyeh, the track wound through a series of valleys, the hills became more fertile, his spirits rose and the countryside inspired him – he wrote of the sweetness 'of the varied bells of a caravan of half a hundred camels in a valley'[10] – as did the welcome of villagers.

When I go into a native house the owner salutes me, & I return it and then he says something to one of his women, and they bring out a thick quilt, which, when doubled, is laid on the rush mat over the floor as a chair: on that I squat down, & then the host asks me four or five times how my health is, and each time I tell him it is good. Then comes sometimes coffee, and after that a variety of questions, as to whether my tripod is a revolver, & what I am, and

41

where I come from, & where I'm going, & why I'm on foot, & am I alone, and every other thing conceivable: and when I set up my tripod (sometimes, as a great treat) there are cries of astonishment and 'Mashalla's', 'By the life of the Prophet,' 'Heavens,' 'Give God the glory' etc. etc. Such a curiosity has never been seen and all the village is summoned to look at it. Then I am asked about my wife & children, how many I have etc. I really feel a little shamed of my youth out here. The Syrian of 16 is full grown, with moustache & beard, married, with children, & has perhaps spent two or three years in New York, getting together enough capital to start him in business at home. They mostly put my age at 15, and are amazed at my travelling on foot & alone. Riding is the only honourable way of going, & everyone is dreadfully afraid of thieves.[11]

The villagers even went armed into the fields.

The people are pleasant: very childish & simple of course, & startlingly innocent, but so far quite honest. Very many men in all the mountain villages have visited America, & they love to display their English before their fellow-villagers . . . They usually wear baggy trousers, & short coats, or shirts, with a sash round their waist, but further from the coast they approximate mostly to the Bedouin dress: for headgear, sometimes the fez, sometimes the keffiyieh, the black coiled rope of the desert Arab. They all carry revolvers, some of them guns [rifles], & you see them ploughing the fields, or eating at home in a belt of 150 cartridges: enough for a campaign.

By now it must have been obvious to his family that there were several reasons for Lawrence's decision to hire a guide in Nabatiyeh. The least likely was that he was uncertain of the route to the castle at Banias, in what is now Israel, and then to Safed. More likely, he was concerned about security – if villagers were going armed to the fields, he, as a fair-haired, blue-eyed foreigner, young, short, travelling alone and on foot, might have felt too easy a target, although he too was carrying a revolver.

Doughty had warned him that 'Some Arabic is of course necessary,'[12] and part of his preparations for the journey had been to take lessons. He had approached the Orientalist David Margoliouth, Professor of Arabic at Oxford, who had introduced him to a Syrian Protestant clergyman by the name of Nasar Odeh. But Lawrence's mother remembered that 'Ned was with him only a short time and knew very little when he started for Syria,' although 'he studied hard on the way out'.[13] His Arabic was still poor when he arrived in Beirut, but the guide from Nabatiyeh will have helped, giving the Arabic words for crops in the fields they passed, for the basalt and other stones they were walking over, for a man, a rifle, a cartridge belt, for the camel he was leading, for thirst, water, cold milk, Crusader, castle . . .

Beaufort – 'Kalaa't el S'ch'k'if',[14] he called it (more properly el Shakif) – was 'a splendid castle'. The Arabic name means the Castle of the High Rock, which is appropriate as it sits on a peak from where it dominates the Litani River and the mountain pass from Sidon to Damascus. Crusaders built the castle in the twelfth century, but it had suffered much over the years, and in his thesis Lawrence mentions only the keep, 'of small size, and much damaged'.[15] The chapel, however, was in better shape and through one of its windows he tossed a stone that bounced twice off rocks as it fell 1,600 feet (some 500 metres) to the river below. What most impressed him was the view over the coast, and some twenty miles along the Litani. 'Across the low foothills & plain of the Jordan springs to the East we could see [Mount] Hermon, still with snow in its valleys, and the mountains of Bashan and to the north half the Lebanon. Southward hills near Safed and Nazareth rather blocked the view. Still even so it was fine and very refreshing to catch a breeze, & find a spring of water on the top.'

It took him an hour following goat paths to walk down into the gorge. On the way, his guide began to sing. He claimed to have one of the best voices in the district, but Lawrence, unimpressed, complained that 'he yelled all the time like a Syren [sic] (of the modern sort)'.[16] At midday, with the sun shining directly into the gully, he tried swimming in the river, 'with a raging current and full of rocks. No swimming was possible; one just hung on a rock and waved about in its eddy like a fish's tail. Still it served to wash the dust off. The banks of course were all oleander.'[17] There was more climbing – a thousand feet up – and then they were at Banias.

As it sat on the Damascus 'road', Banias, one of the sources of the Jordan River, was fortified, but Lawrence was more interested in another fortress an hour's climb above the town. Kalaat es-Subeibeh, known as Nimrod's Castle, was one of the strongest of the Crusader strongholds but it had long been abandoned, and when Lawrence reached it the following morning he found the inner courts choked with decades of brushwood and creeper. A different sort of visitor might have accepted that there was no way in, but Lawrence cleared a passage by setting fire to the overgrowth. 'The owner was a little surprised but did not expostulate,' he recorded, 'as it was inaccessible to anything but a mountaineer or a spider. He had never got to it (entrance on the 1st floor of course, & the walls elsewhere still intact). It must have made a jolly bonfire from a distance, for there was a space of 30 yards square of old thorn trees.'[18] By the evening the owner was calm, the ashes cool, and Lawrence was able to inspect the castle.

For once he was happy to defer to Baedeker: the castle was 'one of the best-preserved and largest in Syria'[19] and, perched on a rock some six or seven hundred feet high, also offered some of the finest views in the region. The rest of the guidebook's description – that 'the greater part of the castle was erected by the Franks [Europeans], who held possession of it from 1139 to 1164' – he dismissed as 'drivel'.

Before leaving England, Lawrence had contacted Harry Pirie-Gordon, an Oxford graduate who had been part of the British School at Athens and another contact made through Hogarth at the Ashmolean.* Pirie-Gordon had visited some of these castles the previous year, going with some friends, and his mother, on a tour organised by Thomas Cook. They had met in London 'at the end of May 1909 (I think) while I was lunching at the Holborn Restaurant', Pirie-Gordon later remembered.

> He had followed me from where I was staying, as he was, he later explained, in a hurry, and wanted to talk to me about Syria and Palestine . . . We had finished lunch, but he sat with us over coffee and asked questions about the country and the castles . . . Lawrence

---

* Pirie-Gordon, Lawrence and Hogarth all worked at the Arab Bureau in Cairo during World War I.

told me nothing of his plans . . . and he must have been bored with much of the information imparted to him, as it concerned travel in comfort on horseback with a caravan . . . For nearly two hours we talked about the castles of the Crusaders, and how they might best be reached, and from where they might best be seen.[20]

Lawrence was travelling with Pirie-Gordon's map and his ground plan of the castle at Banias. In his thesis, he described Banias as 'probably the first castle the Hospitallers* put up in Syria'.[21] The feature that impressed him the most was platforms built over towers, from which stones could be dropped on people below. Known as *machicoulis*, they were unique in Syria. 'And yet this [Hospitaller] architect must have had frequent opportunity of building such machicoulis, since only by use could their distinctly decorative quality have been developed. Similar ones do not appear on any other Crusading castle in the country: and when the Arabs adopted machicoulis they were not of this shape.' Lawrence decided, therefore, that this sort of elaboration was imported from Europe and yet, as he knew, 'the common view is that machicoulis were invented in Syria'.[22] He had spent less than a fortnight in the region, but was already beginning to overturn accepted theories concerning the development of military architecture. He tipped the owner of the castle when he left at the end of the day, and walked down through olive groves to the village.

Lawrence had been warned about his own safety in Banias, but it was his guide who had trouble. When he returned from Kalaat es-Subeibeh, he found 'the villagers very anxious to murder my man, as he was a Christian'. Lawrence knew 'they would not have ventured to touch him as long as he was with me for fear of the consequences', but they did not stay the night to test his conviction. In the morning, 'one of the hottest days of all',[23] he left his guide at Hunin, where the castle was unremarkable except for the fleas. 'The Arabs say that the king of the fleas lives in Tiberias, but I can guarantee that he has summer residences elsewhere as well.'

The next day he reached Safed, a town with a mostly Jewish population, famous for its mystical philosophers. It had been a

* The Knights of St John of Jerusalem.

difficult day's walk, perhaps because it was hot, but maybe also because he was now without a guide and might have lost his way. By the time he reached Safed, his thoughts were more physical than spiritual.

> In the day's march I went up & down the height of Mt. Blanc – and Palestine is all like that: a collection of small irritating hills crushed together pell-mell, and the roads go up & down all the time, or wind in & about the rock of the valleys, & never reach anywhere at all. Nobody ever built a house except on a hill-top or half-way up, the path is only a piece of land from which the smaller stones have been pushed; all day one steps from one sharp rock to another which is not only tiring to the feet but to the brain also for one has to be continually on the alert, to find the best place for the next step, & to guard against slips . . . The alternative is a field path which is much better; these paths are very easily made & have an odd trick of dying away in the middle of a square mile of thistles from one to three feet high of a blue grey colour & very hard. To walk through them for any length of time is rather painful.[24]

Safed was worth the pain, for it was unlike anywhere else he had visited. High up in the lush Galilee hills, it was well watered and cool. It was also a city of twenty thousand people, over half of them Jews. Among them was Dr Anderson, the town's physician, who lived with his English wife and their four children. 'He gave me the most admirable reception,' he reported. 'I stayed 4 nights & thoroughly refreshed myself.' Lawrence was even more impressed by Dr Anderson's work than with his hospitality: the doctor saw more than two hundred outpatients a day, as well as those under his care in hospital, and still found time, one evening, to take his young visitor to the town's ruined castle.

From Safed, Lawrence walked south through Bible lands, to Capernaum, Jesus' base during his ministry in Galilee, and then along the Jordan valley to Lake Tiberias. The road south was more comfortable than many he had known, but he was still provoked by the walk, thinking that 'it is such a comfort to *know* that the country was not like this in the time of Our Lord. The Renaissance Painters were right, who drew him and his disciples feasting in a pillared hall, or sunning themselves on marble staircases: everywhere one finds remains of splendid Roman roads and houses and public build-ings, and Galilee was the most Romanized province of Palestine.'[25] In the place of pillared halls and marble steps, he found twenty miles of thistles. Along the lake shore, he passed 'dirty, dilapidated'[26] tents whose Bedu owners called to him while their dogs snapped at his heels.

Tiberias was as far south as he would go and he now walked across Galilee to the Mediterranean coast, on to the great Crusader port of Acre – 'so quaint & unspoiled a town'[27] – to Tyre and Sidon, and from there back up the coast road to Beirut. 'Now all the corn is out so that all day one walks over varying greys, and browns, & whites, & reds, never a touch of green, except small thorny oaks or at times a fig tree where there is water under the surface: one does so rejoice in a spring.'[28] He had averaged 'only' about twenty miles a day, every day – 'and the people here think that good'.[29] His mother will have worried about his health, covering such distances in the heat. What she didn't know was that by the time he reached Beirut he had had what his brother Bob called 'a bad attack of fever', probably malaria, and needed to rest for some days before continuing north.

He had been more forthcoming about his diet than his health. From Safed, he had written to say that he was enjoying bread, fruit and milk (he had given up eating meat before he left England). Laid up in bed in his hotel room near the Beirut waterfront, he now gave a detailed description of his diet.

> Native bread is of two kinds, one, with small loaves, about 6–10 inches across, circular, & of double thickness of material: it is lumpy outside, but not thinner than cardboard of some stoutness, & when fresh very good. Everybody likes to eat it hot, & when I get to a house in its district & ask for a loaf (proffering a half-penny) the woman goes out at once with her tray, made of straw closely woven, so as to be quite stiff, about 2 feet in diameter, slightly concave, on which are loaves already mixed up but not cooked, & in about 6 minutes she is back with the whole thing ready, sprinkled with grains of sesame & cummin [sic], is it? I forget. At any rate Bread No. 1 is good, when not dry . . . Bread No. 2 is more doubtful. It is light grey in colour, deepening to brown, very large, sometimes

up to 3 feet across, & of course circular. It is very thin, quite as thin as ordinary brown paper, tough, & pliable, almost leathery when fresh, but when dry becomes brittle like a cheese biscuit or oatcake (it really does rather resemble oatcake, though not one third as thick). To bake it they plaster it against the side of the oven, so that on the surface it is lightly dusted with clay. To eat leben, or burghul (boiled wheat) with it (the regular thing) one tears off a small part of one's loaf, & doubles it up on a spoon or poke-bonnet shape:– this then makes a splendid dipper. Leben is when fresh rather thick and lumpy: when old it gets like cheese (cream-cheese that is) and has a distinctly acid taste. In colour it is pure white, with a sourish smell . . .[30]

The rest of his diet was equally 'local', something he admitted was lunacy. Hogarth, after all, had told him he would need porters to carry supplies of the tinned and dried food he was more used to eating.

If I have slept the night in a native house then [breakfast] will be 'Haleeb' ordered overnight. The people do not usually take this, since it is fresh milk, (boiled, or heated rather, they fight shy of it cold), with quantities of sugar in it. They prefer their milk soured as a rule: though some take haleeb. With this will be eaten a sheet of bread No. 2 (the more common variety). If I feel thirsty after it they bring me a bowl of prickly pears, & cut them open for me till I am satis-fied. Prickly pears are the cheapest, most plentiful fruit, very refreshing, above all in the cool of the morning, &, with all the rind cut away, the prickles are never happened on. Then at midday I eat another sheet of bread . . . next a spring, if there is one: if not it is consumed on the march, moistened with an occasional drop from my water-bottle. Sometimes, but only in exceptional country I can get figs, or even grapes or water melons: when I can there is a great feasting: nothing is more refreshing than to march for an hour up a dusty road, eating the melon in one's arms: it is as pleasant as loitering in a country lane in England.[31]

By the time he was back in Beirut, he had been out of England for more than six weeks and was clearly both sick and homesick. Two days after telling his mother about his diet, he wrote a short, practical note to his father to say that he had been averaging twenty-two miles a day – thirty-six miles one day – and that his money and his clothing were holding out, which 'speaks well for boots'.[32] He admitted to having had a 'touch of malaria (not noticeable)', but was now sufficiently recovered to prepare for the second part of his journey. Thinking back to the walk he had just completed, he wrote that 'Palestine was a decent country then [at the time of the Romans], and could so easily be made so again.' He was quite clear how this transformation could be achieved: 'The sooner the Jews farm it the better: their colonies are bright spots in a desert.'[33]

He had been making long walks over demanding terrain on a simple diet, through lawless villages and in the hottest month. Perhaps, as Doughty had predicted, the journey had worn him down. Whatever the circumstances in which this comment emerged, it is striking that the man whose name has since become synonymous with the struggle for Arab independence should approve so strongly of Jewish settlements on Arab land. But in those less charged political circumstances before World War I, the logic of his conclusion must have seemed as irrefutable as the observations on which it was based. Jewish-owned farms and settlements in Galilee were thriving – and spreading, on land sold by Arabs to Jewish European migrants.

5

A Glorious Country for Wandering In

He is crazed with the spell of far Arabia,
They have stolen his wits away.

Walter de la Mare, 'Arabia'[1]

August–September 1909

LAWRENCE HAD HOPED to leave Beirut for the north on 3 August 1909, but was still there three days later, held back by exhaustion and fever, and still waiting for his travel permit.

Before leaving Oxford, he had asked the Principal of his college, Sir John Rhys, for help with obtaining an official permit from the Turkish authorities. Rhys had referred him to the university's Chancellor, Lord Curzon. Curzon's name still commanded respect – he had served as Governor-General of India until 1905 – and it was expected that the Turkish authorities would issue an *iradé* that would give Lawrence some protection, should he run into trouble with provincial officials. When he had first passed through Beirut, the documents were still in the post. They had now arrived at the British Consulate and he was amused to see that he was described as a 'Professor of University & Artist'.[2]

He was more likely to need these papers on the next part of his walk. As well as picking up news that the French pilot Louis Blériot had just become the first person to fly across the English Channel, Lawrence had also heard about instability in the provinces where he was hoping to walk. 'Don't be nervous about me,' he wrote disingenuously to his father, 'I can't see any cause for unease,' while warning that there might be no more letters for a while 'if country beyond is disturbed'.[3]

The first stage was an easy day's walk: from Beirut, he crossed the Dog River to Jebail. There were at least two good reasons for him to stop in Jebail.* Baedeker described it as 'an unimportant little town',[4] but also noted that it had been an important port during the Crusades and mentioned a Crusader castle and two churches, one of which was 'fine'. Another reason to stay in Jebail was that then, as now, it was a very pleasant place in the summer. Fruit trees ran down the slopes above town, promising shade and abundance, while the area above the gold-sand beach was scattered with ancient ruins and more modern square stone houses. One of these houses belonged to Miss Holmes, an American missionary to whom he had an introduction. Here, we catch a rare glimpse of young Lawrence, for Fareedeh el Akle, daughter of a local family and a teacher at the American Mission School, remembered 'a weary young traveller' knocking at the school gate during the 'hot summer of 1909'. 'The maid who opened the door, seeing the dusty, tired-looking traveller with the bundle tied to his back, thought him one of the German tramps that were going about the town at that time.'[5] If he was a tramp, he was a forceful one for he 'did not wait to be asked in; he followed the maid. At the top of the stairs he met the Principal, and after a few words had been exchanged between the two of them he was immediately welcomed.'

Baedeker makes no mention of the American Mission, but the school and its twenty-seven-year-old Beirut-born teacher Miss Fareedeh were to play an important part in Lawrence's life in the Levant before the war. At this stage of his journey and of his immersion into the Arab world – and also at this stage of his recovery from malaria – he was comforted by the welcome, the calm, the English conversation and the food. 'Miss Holmes, the American missionary . . . was most exceedingly kind in feeding me up,' he wrote to his parents, '& as she has plenty of books & a

* Also known as Byblos.

marble-paved hall, with water ad lib. and trees (real green ones) in her garden I was happy.'⁶ The word *happy* occurs so rarely in Lawrence's writing, as in his life, that its appearance here should be noted.

It wasn't just the welcome at Jebail that made him happy. He thought the American Presbyterian Mission was 'doing much the most wonderful work in all of Palestine, & has the most brilliant men at the head of it'.⁷ The American College in Beirut, which he had visited on his arrival in the country, and whose President, Dr Howard Bliss, he had met, was the mission's centrepiece. 'Here the chief study is Medicine, & Pharmacy: but Law, Agriculture, Dentistry, and teaching are now commencing. Nearly every educated Syrian in Beyrout has been through some part of this college, & all through the country one finds the leading men in the village its graduates.'⁸

There were several consequences to this spreading Western influence, some of which he had already noticed on his walk. Along the Lebanese coast, as in Palestine, many people he met had lived in the United States, usually just long enough to earn some money to return home and start a business. Because of this, someone – some people – in each village usually spoke English. Another, more far-reaching consequence was the exposure of these émigrés to some of the ideals of American society: democracy, the right to freedom of expression and of religious belief. None of these freedoms had been present in the region during the centuries of Turkish rule. 'These men', Lawrence wrote from the coast, referring to the American College graduates, 'are all eager for reforms in Syria, & dissatisfied with the government.'⁹*

Many graduates returning from the US believed that Arabs should be ruled by Arabs, but there was still no united nationalist movement in 1909, 1914 or, as Lawrence was to discover, after 1918. The term 'Arab' was too diverse to allow that. Palestinian Christians and Syrian Alaouites, Wahabis from the Hejaz and tradition-bound Sunnis

---

* This urge was not new. As far back as the 1820s, the Albanian-born leader of Egypt, Muhammad Ali Pasha, had sent a group of promising students to study in Paris in the hope that when they returned they would help modernise their country.

from the Nile valley might have shared a language but in many other ways found little common ground. With such a diverse group, it was inevitable that not every Arab dreaming of freedom agreed with the call for independence. Many were happy with the idea of Arab autonomy or self-rule within the Turkish empire. Others believed that Arab nationalism could only go hand in hand with a resurgent and highly politicised Islam, with the re-establishment of the caliphate.

The last paragraph of the final version of *Seven Pillars of Wisdom* suggests that Lawrence was already aware of the movement, and that he had no time for nationalists who would settle for continuing Turkish rule, or for the division of Arabs along religious or tribal lines. He claimed he had dreamed, while still at school, of helping to shape a new Asia, and part of that was going to be created by Arab nationalists. Perhaps it was with the memory of that dream that he wrote home to say that 'the secretary of the government of the Lebanon (a high Turk) said to me – "the recent reform of the constitution in Constantinople (i.e. the revolution) is entirely due to the American mission." They have so educated the country (without touching on politics) that public opinion rejoiced in reform.'[10] He left the comfort of Miss Holmes's mission in Jebail in August 1909 aware that a process of political transformation was under way, but equally aware that it had a long way to go before achieving its goals.

He moved more slowly now, because of the malaria and the unsettled state of the country. Tripoli was a larger and more important town than Jebail, with a British vice-consul and a choice of hotels, although he chose to stay with American missionaries again, claiming that 'they take care of me in the most fatherly (or motherly) way:– they have all so far been as good as they can be'.[11] There was much for him to see. 'The aspect of many streets is quite medieval,' Baedeker notes, suggesting that it would be 'best surveyed from the castle-hill'.[12] But the castle, or castles, because Lawrence mentions two or three, were uninteresting hybrids, unlikely to delay a young scholar of Crusader architecture. He had equally little to say about himself: 'I am very well, & very hot, my clothes are all well, & my stockings still unholed, & my boots look as if they have hardly been worn.'[13]

Tripoli turned out to be a good place to collect information about the road ahead. 'It will take me at least 3 weeks to go to Aleppo,' he warned his father in the middle of August, knowing that he would need to extend his stay, 'and from there to Edessa another week. Then to return will take 10 days, to Damascus. Altogether it will take till the end of September.'[14] And even then he would not be finished: from Damascus he was hoping to take the Hejaz Railway to Kerak (now in Jordan), one of the greatest of all Crusader castles, built to defend the southern approaches to the Kingdom of Jerusalem. 'Dr. Bliss [President of the American College in Beirut] told me that it was the most interesting castle in Syria and Shobek (Monreale) is only two days further.' Going that far south would mean that he would not get back to Oxford before 20 October, long after his university term had started. And then there was Jerusalem . . .

> This will give you an idea of how it is: my wishes are of course evident: this is a glorious country for wandering in, for hospitality is something more than a name: setting aside the American & English missionaries . . . there are the common people each one ready to receive at night, & allow me to share in their meals: and without a thought of payment for a traveller on foot. It is so pleasant, for they have a very attractive kind of native dignity.[15]

He would have to wait for an answer. If the post was on time, he might hear when he reached Aleppo; if not, it would have to wait till Damascus. He knew he would be able to walk up through the hill country between Homs and Aleppo, and then on to the Euphrates River and Urfa, returning to Beirut via Damascus. He had enough time and money for that, so long as his mother would forgive him not bringing home a silver tea pot – 'but seriously', he warned his father, 'they don't make tea out here if they can help it: and I don't think she would much fancy the Damascus silver work: it is mostly filigree, & I think a little finnicking: also it would be hard to clean.'[16]

The following day, 16 August, he celebrated his twenty-first birthday by walking out of Tripoli, his bag on his back and one of the region's great castles ahead. Above Tripoli, the road divided, one branch continuing up the coast to Tartus and Latakia. The other, which Lawrence followed, curved along the north end of the Lebanon

Mountains and into a lowland plain, the Homs Gap. This was one of the region's most fertile areas but, more important, it was also the easiest passage between the desert, Damascus and the Mediterranean Sea. Easy travelling for caravans and armies – even the ancient Egyptians had marched this way during their war with the Hittites – and easy enough to protect, if you built a castle on one of the foothills leading into the mountains, which is what the Crusaders had done.

The night after his birthday, he was the guest of a high-born Arab called Abdul Kerim, 'a young man very lively, or rather wild, living in a house like a fortress on top of a mountain: only approachable on one side, & then a difficult staircase'.[17] Abdul Kerim turned out to be as exciting as the location, a man with a passion for guns who had recently bought himself a Mauser – presumably of the sort issued to Turkish soldiers. He 'blazed at everything with it. His bullets must have caused terror to every villager within a mile around.'[18] Lawrence doesn't mention whether he produced his own Mauser from his bag.

From Abdul Kerim's house – and perhaps watched through the sights of the young nobleman's rifle – he walked up to Kalaat el-Hosn, the Crusader castle of Crac des Chevaliers, about which Baedeker was even less instructive than usual. Perhaps the writer was lost for words. Providing a sentence on the history – built by the Hospitallers in the 1180s and lost to Sultan Beibars in 1271 – and another on its strategic position, the author noted that 'a village and the residence of a Kaimmakam [Governor] are now established within the building'.[19] Gertrude Bell, the British traveller whose robbery beyond the Euphrates had been recently reported, described riding there four years earlier:

through such delicious country that every step of it was delightful . . . The great castle on top of the hill was before us for five or six hours. The sun shone on it and the black clouds hung round it as we rode up and up through flowers and grass and across running streams. But it was a long way and the animals grew very tired. At sunset we came to the dark tower. I rode through a splendid Arab gateway into a vaulted corridor which covered a broad winding stair. It was almost pitch dark, lighted only by a few loop-holes; the horses stumbled and clanked over the stone steps – they were shallow and wide, but very much broken – and we turned corner after corner and passed gateway after gateway until at length we came into the court in the centre of the keep. I felt as if I were somebody in the Faery Queen, and almost expected to see written upon the last arch, 'Be not too bold.'*[20]

Lawrence thought the Crac was 'the finest castle in the world: certainly the most picturesque I have seen – quite marvellous'.[21] It is interesting to see how restrained his description is compared to the more mature style of *Seven Pillars of Wisdom*. In his thesis, he describes the Crac as 'a finished example of the style of the Order [of Hospitallers], and perhaps the best preserved and most wholly admirable castle in the world, [which] forms a fitting commentary on any account of Crusader buildings in Syria'.[22] Admitting that its defences were not of the same standard as the castles at Coucy in France or Caerphilly in Wales, he still found it more impressive because it was neither a ruin nor a showpiece. And it was still in use: 'a few years back it withstood a siege on the part of a neighbouring district with complete success, and were Beibars [the thirteenth-century Mamluk ruler of Egypt who succeeded where Saladin failed when he took Crac from the Crusaders] to reappear he would think it as formidable as of old'.[23]†

The most impressive part of the castle was the *donjon*, reached by a final flight of stairs from the courtyard Gertrude Bell had mentioned, and containing an upper terrace and three towers. 'They overtop by many feet any other tower in the fortress, and are magnificently built of huge blocks of stone. The governor of the province now inhabits

---

* This phrase ends a stanza of Edmund Spenser's *The Faerie Queene* (Book III, Canto XI), which starts with a very different injunction:

> And as she look'd about, she did behold,
> How over that same Door was likewise writ,
> *Be bold, Be bold*, and every where *Be bold*;
> That much she mus'd, yet could not construe it
> By any riddling Skill, or common Wit.
> At last she spy'd, at that Room's upper end,
> Another iron Door, on which was writ,
> *Be not too bold* . . .

† Combatants in the Syrian civil war had similar thoughts in 2013, when Crac was once again used as a stronghold, this time by fighters opposing a Damascus regime. Government jets subsequently bombed the castle, with the *donjon* taking a direct hit.

them, and his harem and his divan, and his own private rooms rather obscure the arrangement of the Eastern half of the platform.'[24] In a letter home, he described the Kaimmakam, with whom he stayed for three days, as 'a most-civilised-French-speaking-disciple-of-the-Herbert-Spencer-Free-Masonic-Mohammedan-Young Turk'.[25]

Safita was the next in a string of castles built within sight of each other. It had a Norman-style keep and its original battlements were intact: 'the like is not in Europe: such a find'.[26] Of more concern to his parents would have been his mention of an escort, which the Kaimmakam had insisted upon for his protection. A couple of days later it was Lawrence who was doing the protecting. Stopping to sleep the night on a threshing floor, on a bed of dry straw, and dozing to the sound of villagers threshing their wheat, he was woken at 2 a.m. by one of the villagers who asked him to keep watch. 'I was a [sic] Inglezi & had a pistol.' But who was he protecting the wheat from? He found the answer the following day, having walked to the coast at Tartus, where he discovered that the villagers were worried that their landlord might see how much wheat they had grown and demand a greater share; he would not come if Lawrence were standing guard. 'Isn't that charming? These dear people wanted to hide the extent of their harvest.'[27]

From the coast he climbed back into the mountains, travelling through territory that had been held by neither Crusaders nor Arabs, but by the Assassins. The Hashashin, as they were more properly known, were a sect of Persian origin who acquired a formidable reputation during the Crusades as political killers. Being Shi'ite Muslims, they saw both Christians and Sunni Arabs as potential enemies, and potential allies. At one point in the twelfth century, they operated out of a string of castles in the Syrian highlands, led by Rashid al-Din Sinan, popularly known as 'the old man of the mountains'. Lawrence visited two of Sinan's castles: Masyaf, 'the capital city', and Qadmas, which had been Sinan's main base. The young traveller would certainly have known something about their tactics, but he was about to learn more.

The sect never had sufficient supporters to engage their opponents in open battle. So they became adept at avoiding setpiece conflicts and chose, instead, a more fluid and dangerous combination of expedient alliances and political assassinations. Lawrence knew of the story of Saladin's march into the mountains of the Assassins in the summer of 1176, when the Kurdish-born leader laid siege to the 'chief' Assassin castle of Masyaf. He had a vastly superior army and should, by his own invariably correct calculations, have been successful. And yet he retreated out of the hills without his victory. What led to this about-turn? Saladin already knew about the reputation of his adversaries and, concerned for his safety, had had his tent surrounded by guards and also by a ring of chalk and ashes, which would show the footsteps of anyone daring to cross. In spite of these precautions, the great warrior woke in the night to find a note pinned to a poisoned dagger, inviting him to withdraw or die. He had superior numbers and huge battle experience, but Saladin recognised that he had been outplayed and immediately retreated down the mountain.

Lawrence has been credited with inventing guerrilla warfare as it is known today, but this is exaggerated. In *Seven Pillars of Wisdom* he explained the idea with his usual clarity, and beauty. 'Suppose we were (as we might be) an influence, an idea, a thing intangible, invulnerable, without front or back drifting about like gas? Armies were like plants, immobile, firm-rooted, nourished through long stems to the head. We might be a vapour, blowing where we listed.'[28] This was how the Assassins had conducted themselves: Lawrence merely replaced remote mountains with remote desert. When he read about their tactics, and heard stories of their exploits while sleeping in the 'chateau' of the Assassin's leader – as I did years ago while visiting one of the Assassin strongholds in the Syrian mountains – the young man who, from an early age had dreamed of crusading knights, who walked through the landscape they had known and who imagined, as he was imagining, how those wars were fought, realised that the Assassins were precisely that 'influence, an idea, a thing intangible', an invisible force so great that even the mighty Saladin, scourge of the Crusader armies and master of the Middle East, was forced to back down rather than risk being killed. Here was a lesson from history that Lawrence, the eager student, could not have failed to learn.

But there was a limit to what he could take in. At Oxford, during the months of preparation for this journey, which were also months of seminars and lectures and essays, he had taken classes in Arabic and drawing. His drawing instructor was an artist and architectural illustrator. by the name of Edmund (E. H.) New. New was a fan of the Arts and Crafts, black-and-white, pen-and-ink style of illustration, and shared Lawrence's admiration for the work of William Morris. New's architectural precision suited the young man's needs, for he had discovered during his bike ride across France that there were features of some castles that he could not capture with his camera. Up in the Syrian mountains he now used the techniques New had taught him to produce several detailed drawings of Crac des Chevaliers, which he would use alongside photographs to illustrate his thesis. But he never thought his work did justice to the buildings he was seeing. 'I wish I was a real artist,'[29] he complained in the face of a particularly spectacular building.

He was thinking of these illustrations several days later when he wrote from Latakia, the northern port, that his thesis was now 'assured'. He was also becoming aware that this journey through a landscape, history and culture was affecting him in a way he had not anticipated. He had lived off stale bread for much of his time in Crac and Safita, but Latakia had 'native' restaurants and a particular dark tobacco, cured over pine or oak fires. 'No smoking yet, though here every man woman and child does: Latakia tobacco, which Father knows all grows here: the peasants dry & smoke their own, all in cigarettes.'[30] By this point, after two months on the road, he realised – and relished the fact – that he was becoming Orientalised and he warned that he would 'have such difficulty in becoming English again, here I am Arab in habits & slip into talking from English to French & Arabic unnoticing'.[31]

It was a typical piece of Lawrentian self-mythologising and it was misleading for, while he might have shed some of his English reserve along those broken roads, he was Arab neither in his bespoke suit, fine-spun woollen shirt and hobnailed walking boots nor in his habits, even if he had, finally, grown to like the local staple dish of leben. So however comfortable he felt sleeping on a roof or eating with his hands out of a communal dish, the people he met were in no doubt that he was a foreigner, as had become apparent up in the

Assassin stronghold when 'an ass with an old gun', a muzzle-loader, 'put in a shot at about 200 yards'.[32]

There are several accounts of this attack, including one from Fareedeh el Akle in Jebail, who described the assailant as 'a huge cruel-looking'[33] Turk. Lawrence, who only told his parents about the attack some weeks after the event – and, still wary of causing alarm, assured them that 'there is no chance of a repetition of the joke: which is why I tell you: it is not very sensational I fear' – said he fired back with his Mauser and grazed the man's horse, which then bolted half a mile or so. 'He stopped at about 800 yards away to contemplate the scenery, & wonder how on earth a person with nothing but a pistol could shoot so far: & when I put up my sights as high as they would go & plumped a bullet somewhere over his nut he made off like a steeple-chaser.'[34]

'I'm rather glad that my perseverance in carrying the Mauser has been rewarded,' Lawrence himself added with typical understatement, 'it is rather a load but practically unknown out here.'[35]

After the incident, he complained to the local Governor, who sent askari (policemen) to look for the attacker, without success. The assumption was that the man had spotted a foreigner and hoped to scare him into handing over some money. Doughty had warned Lawrence about this sort of opportunism when he had written of a 'veiled ill will' towards Europeans, while Baedeker, more specific, warned that 'most Orientals regard the European traveller as a Croesus, and sometimes as a madman – so unintelligible to them are the objects and pleasures of travelling. They therefore demand bakshish almost as a right from those who seem so much better supplied with this world's goods.'[36] The attack was not unexpected: why else was he carrying the Mauser? And if that was the case, then the hospitality he had enjoyed for most of the past two months was all the more remarkable, explained in part by the fact that he was travelling on foot and alone, instead of riding through as part of a Cook's caravan with guide and porters. Except that now he was not alone.

The Governor to whom Lawrence had complained insisted that he continue through the hills to Aleppo with an armed escort, something he was obliged to agree to. What he did not agree to was to ride himself. 'It is rather charming to contemplate a pedestrian guarded carefully by a troop of light horse,' he wrote jokingly, adding, 'of course everybody thinks I am mad to walk, & the escort offered me a mount on the average once a half-hour: they couldn't understand my prejudice against anything with four legs.'[37]

Less amusing was the road itself. The distances were bad enough – he covered 120 miles in five summer days, sometimes walking thirteen hours in the heat – but the terrain made it harder as he went 'stumbling, & staggering over the ghastly roads'. But there were consolations because the landscape was beautiful – 'almost English in parts' – and there was the castle of Sahyun. Known also as Kalaat Saladin and the Château de Saône, Sahyun was a revelation. Unlike Crac des Chevaliers, which dominates the Homs Gap and can be seen for hours before it is reached, Sahyun is tucked into the hills between Latakia on the coast and the broad, lush Orontes valley. This was no obvious statement of power and yet, as he wrote home, Lawrence thought it was 'perhaps the finest castle I have seen in Syria'.[38]

The first view, across rolling hills, was impressive, looking down on to more of a fortified town than a conventional castle, filling a ridge and protected by sheer drops into deep ravines. There was romance in the setting and strategic power in the location, which is why it was used as a stronghold long before Alexander the Great marched his army up the nearby coast road. But Lawrence was most impressed by the details of the place, by 'a splendid keep, of Semi-Norman style, perfect in all respects: towers galore: chapels, a bath (Arabian) & a Mosque: gates not original'. As he drew closer, he realised that the castle was defended by a rock-cut moat, which he measured as being '50 feet across in one part, 90 feet in another, varying from 60–130 feet deep: there is a setting for you'.[39] Still in the moat, looking for a path up to the castle, he came to 'the most sensational thing in castle-building I have seen'.[40] In the middle of the clearing, between the two hills, rose a single, slender finger of rock, left over when the moat was cut. It pointed some ninety-two feet into the air (Lawrence miscalculated it at 110 feet) and had been left to support a drawbridge that would have joined the 'island' castle to the rest of the hills. Having found a way up to the castle, he also found what he called hundreds of other points of interest and stayed two days as a guest of the local Governor.

In his thesis, he slightly qualified his original judgment about Sahyun, calling it 'probably the finest example of military architecture in Syria',[41] but admitting to difficulties examining the site. It 'is of such colossal size, and so deeply set in inhospitable hills that a complete examination of it is a matter of some exertion and discomfort', made worse by the fact that he was suffering from a bad bout of malaria (something he had omitted to tell his parents).

He made sketches of the moat and the many towers guarding the south-east wall, but the keep impressed him most. It was the biggest keep in Syria. 'In form it is roughly a square about 90 feet each way: the height is 76 feet, and the thickness of the walls on the first floor some 22 feet.'[42] In a footnote, he explained the imprecision of his calculation: 'there is a lusty colony of snakes on the ground floor, preventing exact measurement; above all since it is in total darkness'. The upper floor had *garderobes* and withdrawing rooms, 'like any keep in Normandy', and 'most admirable latrines, with as usual a strong draught through them'.[43]

He walked into Aleppo, accompanied by his mounted escort, on 6 September and made straight for Baron's Hotel. Visitors to the city, before it was sucked into its latest civil war, tended to focus on antiquity, enthusing about Aleppo's ancient citadel with its Crusader-era battlements dominating the maze of medieval souks, the mosques and madrassas, houses and hammams. Visitors in the months before Lawrence arrived in 1909 were more concerned with security: a German journalist had reported in June that year that there was great anxiety in the city, that Armenians and Sicilians in particular were leaving in significant numbers and that martial law would be imposed 'as soon as reliable troops come from Constantinople'.[44]

Lawrence makes no mention of the disturbances, presumably not wanting to worry his parents. Nor did he write about the monuments of Aleppo because, as the Crusaders never managed to take Aleppo, they were not relevant to his thesis. After all the castles and antiquities and landscape he had seen over the past couple of months, what struck him most was the European feel of the city, where the streets were paved and even had pavements. For once, he agreed with Baedeker, when the guidebook explained that 'a characteristic feature is the numerous passages with pointed arches. The houses, which are mostly one-storeyed, are built of solid stone, and their courts are usually handsome in a simple style.'[45]

The city was already home to at least 200,000 people, a mix of Muslims, Christians and Jews, of Syrians, Kurds, Greeks and Armenians. Yet, in spite of the extent of the city, the Kuweik River, on which they all depended, was still lined with orchards of walnut, quince, pistachio and olive trees, and its water was still clear enough to drink. The Governor of Aleppo ruled as far as the Euphrates River, where Lawrence was hoping to go.

For now he was happy to settle beneath the high ceilings and wheeling fans of Baron's Hotel. Baron's, like the American School in Jebail, would become an important refuge for Lawrence in the coming years.* When Lawrence arrived in September 1909, it sat on the edge of a new suburb, Safiyeh, a place that was still sufficiently rural for duck and other game to be bagged, occasionally, from the hotel terrace. Lawrence was more interested in what lay inside the hotel: hot water and a bath – he had been unable to wash for the past ten days – a hot meal in the restaurant and news from home. There was no reply from his father to his request for more time and money to reach the castles beyond the Dead Sea, so he wrote to his mother. 'I have wired Beyrout in case you mistook my directions: I hope nothing has happened.'

Lawrence now prepared for what was going to be a very different journey, across the rolling hills and the Euphrates valley to the castle at Urfa.† The seventy-mile journey there, and then down to

---

* A bill for accommodation and, unexpectedly (seeing that he rarely drank alcohol), a bottle of champagne, in Lawrence's name and dated June 1914, was still hanging in reception when I first visited in the 1980s. The elderly, elegant patron, Krikor Mazloumian – 'everyone calls me Koko' – was still there when I first visited in the 1980s, his head full of stories about Lawrence, Agatha Christie and other famous guests, stories that flowed like sherry, or Armenian brandy, on a Sunday lunchtime in front of his sitting-room fire.

† As Edessa, Urfa had been an early Christian enclave in a predominantly Muslim region. It made an easy target for Baldwin of Boulogne, who separated from the main army of the First Crusade and set himself up as Count of Edessa in 1098. Edessa was the first Crusader state to be created and also the first to fall, captured by the ruler of Aleppo in 1150.

Damascus, should have been easy and interesting – there was no shortage of sights to see along the way. The terrain was less challenging, becoming increasingly flat as he neared the Euphrates. And because he needed to be in Damascus in a fortnight, perhaps also because he had been warned of lawlessness along the way, he had hired a carriage with two horses and two coachmen. It was expensive – at £7 it was one-tenth of the cost of his entire summer journey – but he had no choice because, with no word from his father, he assumed he had to be in Oxford for the start of the new term.

Hogarth of the Ashmolean had travelled that way the previous year in search of a suitable site to excavate, and of antiquities he could buy. When he had told Lawrence that Europeans did not walk, alone, in Syria, and certainly not in the summer, he was speaking as someone who had found conditions challenging, even on horseback, in company and in the early spring. But Hogarth had also found antiquities, and a site that few foreigners can have seen since the great armies of the Persians and Greeks marched through. He was particularly interested in finding inscriptions in the Hittite cuneiform script, sometimes called nail-writing. Travelling through that region in the early 1890s, the archaeologist had been offered a variety of Hittite seals in the souks of Aintab (Gaziantep), all of which were said to have come from a place called Tell Bashar, one of the high mounds that stick out of the flat Euphrates plain. 'I doubted their story,' Hogarth had written then, 'knowing how natives will combine to say that small antiquities come from the most notable ruin in their district, whatever its age.'[46]

But as a skilled hunter after antiquities, he was not going to leave Tell Bashar unvisited, especially as he knew that no antiquary had mentioned visiting there before. There was a good reason for this: 'the place was reported to us in Birejik and Aintab to be a spot where a stranger would not be well received. The nearest village was a home of outlaws.'[47] Hogarth and his companions had gone prepared, with a guide, guard and attendants.

The threat was real enough, for he noticed that even the camel drivers on the main caravan trail were carrying guns. At the village of Bashar, not far from the *tell*, even the welcoming sheikh who offered them coffee was nervous. When the subject of Hittite seals was raised, word went round and, an hour or so later, a crowd of villagers appeared. To Hogarth's disappointment, all that was offered were two defaced coins. There was more disappointment at the *tell*: Crusader towers had survived, but the larger, more ancient site had been ploughed under and all the surface stones removed. Hogarth returned, dejected, to his tents on the edge of the village to decide on his next move.

> It was after sunset when the first fruits of the harvest we sought appeared at our tent-door. They were two seals of steatite, gable-shaped and engraved, which had been strung on a woman's necklace in the company of modern charms to avert the 'eye'. No price was asked, but what we chose to give. We paid well, and had not time to finish supper before spoil of the Hittites – their cylinders, their beads, their seals, gable-shaped, conical, scarabaeoid – flowed in from all sides, and the source of the Aintab objects was beyond all doubt.[48]

So many villagers turned up to trade their charms and heirlooms that the sheikh came with minders to close the 'market'. The following morning the villagers returned with more heirlooms. 'Collecting was too easy a business here to be a sport at all; but the bag consoled us.' He noticed that almost every woman in the village was wearing some sort of ancient seal around their neck – to bring prosperity, ease the pains of childbirth, keep their men attentive. He ended by buying almost sixty Hittite seals and other objects. No wonder he hoped his brilliant young Oxford scholar might strike it lucky when he passed through the region.

The description of Lawrence's journey to Urfa is the least informative of all his writing that summer. He was driven in a carriage, ferried over the Euphrates near Tell Ahmar, the Red Hill, another of the area's important ancient sites, and continued over the low rolling countryside to Urfa. Then as now, the ancient town huddled around a pool that legend connected to the patriarch Abraham, and was overlooked by a sheer wall of rock topped with the remains of massive Crusader fortifications. Lawrence climbed up to inspect the ruins.

In his thesis, he described the ruined castle as 'Byzantine with Arab additions', drawing attention to the moat, which he had photographed. Like the moat at Sahyun, it had been cut out of the rock; at 500 feet long, 60 feet deep and 30 feet wide, it was 'too huge a work for the Latins ever to have undertaken in their insecure tenure of the place',[49] especially as he was certain the walls above the moat were Byzantine. But it was the pier, the little finger of rock left in the middle of the moat, that interested him most. It was necessary, he now realised, because the only trees in the area tall enough to span the thirty-foot moat were poplars. And poplarwood, extended over that distance, would have flexed too much to have been useful as a drawbridge. The remedy was to use a pier to steady the wood. More significant for his thesis was the fact that the only example he knew of this in Europe was many hundreds of years later.

On his way back to Aleppo, Lawrence found the *tell* that Hogarth hoped he would visit, and bought some Hittite seals. Then his luck ran out.

Afterwards, back at Baron's in Aleppo on 22 September, he wrote to his mother to say that his camera had been stolen. He wrote that the theft had happened in a place called Seruj, about halfway between Urfa and the Euphrates, when he had left one of the coachmen to look after his things. When he returned to the coach, both the sleeping man and the camera were missing. Elsewhere on that return journey, he told his mother, the carriage had overturned although no one had been hurt. This was all a lie to explain the fact that he had been injured. But it was no accident: he had been attacked and robbed, and his wounds seem to have been serious enough for him to have them dressed in hospital, while the incident was of sufficient interest for a report – of his murder – to have appeared in the Aleppo newspaper. 'The [Baron] hotel people received me like a ghost.'[50]

On 24 September, from Baron's, Lawrence wrote a different account to Sir John Rhys at Oxford in which he stated that he had had 'a most delightful tour', had seen thirty-seven of the fifty or so castles on his route, some of them previously unrecorded, and had bought about thirty Hittite seals, the best of which he would offer to the Ashmolean. 'My excuse for outstaying my leave must be that I have had the delay of four attacks of malaria when I had only reckoned on two.' There was also the fact 'that only last week I was robbed & rather smashed up'.[51] He ended with a postscript asking Sir John not to mention the robbery or injuries should he meet Lawrence's father. 'I want to be returned reasonably whole before [the news] comes out.'

Lawrence had already provided a more detailed description of the attack to E. T. Leeds, Hogarth's assistant at the Ashmolean, while explaining why he was bringing home so few Hittite seals. 'I meant to buy more,' he explained – and this was three days before he wrote to his mother – 'and found some rather jolly ones in a Turkish village one hour north of Tell Bashar [where Hogarth had bought so many]; – but a beggar followed me from Mayra and bagged all my money and valuables (not content with pounding me behind the ear with a stone and biting open the back of my hand). I re-covered most; but with such work that I was too sick of the district, and had (after due baksheeshing) too little cash to spare to search further.'[52] Later, back in England, Lawrence had given more details to Harry Pirie-Gordon, who had asked about the bloodstains on his map of the castles. 'He had been attacked by Kurds who had beaten him and left him for dead in indignation at finding that the "treasure" which he had been reported to be carrying consisted of no more than his clothes, shabby after his remarkable tramp through Syria in the heat of the summer, some Hittite cylinder seals, which he had bought in Aleppo, and a few beshliks. They had taken most of his clothes and all the money, but had left the seals and the map as being valueless.'[53] Presumably they also left the Mauser (he later sold it in Beirut), but took his camera.

Once we learn that he had been attacked, 'rather smashed up', robbed and hospitalised, the letter he wrote to his mother from Baron's on 22 September reads very differently. The opening is abrupt: 'After all I am coming home at once, for lack of money'.[54] He would be leaving his clothes and boots at Beirut because 'I would never get them past the sanitary inspection at P. Said,'[55] although if Pirie-Gordon remembered correctly Lawrence was just covering the fact that his suit and boots had been stolen in the attack. But more than the information – and he did tell his mother about the local paper publishing an 'absurd canard' about the death of Mr Edvard Lovance – his tone and attitude had changed. The weather was now 'horrid', with temperatures still in the 40s Centigrade (around 106 Fahrenheit), in the shade. At the same time, the rain had started early, '& one couldn't walk in the rain'. And even if he could, his feet were in a bad way. He had gone by carriage to Urfa and back and yet his boots were suddenly shredded and his feet 'all over cuts & chafes & blisters'. And although he had avoided getting food poisoning, which was the big challenge for foreign visitors, he knew he had reached the limits of what he could endure. 'I am tired, & . . . would like to stop.'

He would go to Damascus by train, and spend a few days there, but not the ten days he had originally planned, and then he would go to Beirut. Instead of taking the fast route via Marseille or Toulon, and up through France, he would sail all the way home. 'It will be pleasant to have 14 days with no sightseeing, nothing to do but eat.'[56] It would also allow time for the wounds to his head and hand to heal, and it would give him time to consider how local events had interfered with his plans, how reality had ended his dream of adventure. In the future, he would want things to be the other way round.

6

Pushing the Boundaries

He who has once seen palm-trees and the goat-hair tents is never the same as he had been.

T. E. Lawrence to his mother, 11 May 1912[1]

1909–10

'I WILL HAVE SUCH difficulty in becoming English again,' he had written from Latakia at the end of August 1909, 'here I am Arab in habits.' The thought was a fallacy. As his journey from Urfa to Aleppo had taught him, Arabs who possessed anything that anyone might want were not in the habit of travelling alone and on foot. Thinking about the incident while he recuperated, he must have realised that he had made himself a target, and the realisation would have hurt as much as the pain inflicted on his body. But he will also have known that he might have been attacked earlier (although there was the man who shot at him near Masyaf) and that he had been lucky not to have been permanently injured, or even killed.

If that was a lesson he had learned the hard way, others had come more easily. Travelling alone and on foot had been risky and had put him in danger, but it had also been useful and he was justified in his claim (to Sir John Rhys) that 'I have perhaps, living as an Arab with the Arabs, got a better insight into the daily life of the people than those who travel with caravan and dragomen.'[2] The question that was not so easily answered was what he would now do with this knowledge.

After World War I, in *Seven Pillars of Wisdom*, he wrote of the consequences of attempting to live and think and act as an Arab, describing it as a Yahoo life. 'The efforts for those years to live in the dress of an Arab, and to imitate their mental foundation, quitted me of my English self, and let me look at the West and its conventions with new eyes: they destroyed it all for me. At the same time I could not sincerely take on the Arab skin: it was an affectation only.'[3] That, of course, was for the future – he had been conspicuous in Syria for walking in his bespoke suit and backpack, and for travelling with camera and tripod. So he returned home to Oxford, in the middle of October 1909, not as an Arab but as an Englishman who had just acquired a unique and valuable insight into the people, the history and the landscape of the region with which his name would become inextricably linked.

Oxford was a sufficiently cosmopolitan place for Lawrence's summer escapade, and his malaria-withered features to be accepted without too much comment although one of the university's history tutors, Ernest Barker, remembered vividly Lawrence returning that October.

> I was lecturing in a lecture room at St. John's, on the original authorities for . . . the history of the first three crusades. At the end of the lecture a man came up to me whom I did not recognize – a man with a very fine face, which seemed thinned to the bone by privation. When he spoke to me in his low, quick voice, I found that it was Lawrence. He told me that . . . with a small sum in his pocket, he had gone to Palestine; and living simply, on the food of the countryside, he had made his way from one castle ruin to another. He had climbed the walls barefoot: he had had his troubles with Bedouin, and once (I think he told me) been assaulted and left unconscious: but he had seen for himself what he intended to write about, and he had brought back his own plans and photographs to illustrate what he wrote.[4]

Arab or not, he soon settled into life at college and at home, no doubt with new stories to fill the evenings, to replace the boyhood one his brother Bob remembered him telling 'of adventure, and successful defence of a tower against numerous foes'.[5] In the bungalow, once again the centre of his world, he set up the main trophy he had brought back for himself, not from Syria but from Italy. On his return, the ship had docked in Naples long enough for him to see the spectacular collection of ancient bronzes in the National Museum, and then to visit a bronze factory. Most of the work for sale was beyond his modest budget, but he was able to buy a faulty cast of Hypnos, the spirit or god of Sleep. He placed it in the bay window of his study and would stare at it for hours, a reminder of the journey, and bearing an uncanny resemblance to Janet Laurie.

He had eight months until his Finals and, to help with the work, he was tutored again by L. C. Jane. These were clearly not standard tutorials, for Jane recalled Lawrence arriving at his rooms between midnight and four in the morning. Other evenings, and nights, were spent reading in the bungalow, working up into finished pen-and-ink drawings some of the rough sketches he had made on the journey, and writing letters, including one to Charles Doughty.

In many ways, Doughty had given sound advice. Walking in the summer *was* a bad idea and did weaken even this strongest of young men. Villagers were tempted to see him as a source of revenue. The landscape did wear him down, the food was dull, the beds hard. But what the grand Arabophile had failed to appreciate was that Lawrence had relished these privations and challenges. So there is a triumphal tone in the undergraduate's letter, which begins with a reminder of 'my writing to you in the beginning of the year, to ask your opinion on a walking tour of Northern Syria. This has ended happily (I reached Urfa Edessa my goal) and the Crusading Fortresses I found are so intensely interesting that I hope to return to the East for some little time. It struck me that I ought to see you first . . .'6 He then flattered the old man, saying that, such was Doughty's fame, Lawrence had been mocked by an Arab in Palestine for not knowing him. If Lawrence made no mention of Doughty's discouragements, the reply that came by return of post reminded him: 'I am glad to hear from you that you have returned safe & sound & successful from your Summer expedition to Syria. You will have been able to judge from actual experience, how far I was right in advising you of the excessive heat in the plains & the long distances that must be traversed from point to point.'7

Lawrence went to Eastbourne to visit Doughty in December. Huddled around the fire on a winter's day on the English coast, and with the author of *Arabia Deserta*, the prospect of returning to Syria the following summer, as a graduate, would have seemed more seductive than ever. Lawrence did fervently hope to return. But he also had another, apparently contradictory plan, to set up a printing press in a windmill overlooking the sea with an Oxford friend, Leonard Green. The idea was to produce what Green called 'only rather "precious" books',[8] exquisitely hand-printed. The project was inspired by the work of William Morris, the British designer, artist and writer, whose Kelmscott Press had produced some of the most beautiful and admired volumes of recent years. Like Morris and Kelmscott, Lawrence hoped his press would hark back to a time before mass printing, producing books that would be beautiful to hold and, with their elaborate type, slow to read. He had already begun to buy type from Morris's Kelmscott Press. But there was a typically Lawrentian twist to the plan: the books would be bound in vellum stained purple by Tyrian dye, the same used exclusively by Roman emperors to mark their rank. To this end, he had brought back murex shells from the Syrian coast. And if the venture were successful, he would have to collect more: all roads were leading him back east.

But first he had to write his thesis and much depended on it, for he was hoping to earn a good enough degree to continue into postgraduate study. He was probably aware that there were tutors, as there would be examiners, who suspected him of posing, and doubted whether his work was good enough to be awarded a first-class degree. But 'The Influence of the Crusades on European Military Architecture – to the End of the XIIth Century' did exactly what Lawrence, and Bell at the Ashmolean, had hoped. It brought out the best in him by allowing – requiring – him to challenge the accepted view. In all things at Oxford and later in life, this was his preferred position, standing at an angle, in opposition to the majority. The Oxford tutor Ernest Barker had noticed how Lawrence 'liked the curious; he studied and did curious things. He had no taste for organized life and its conventions and institutions; it was his instinct to be against them, and he readily indulged his instinct.'[9] His thesis allowed him to indulge this instinct to the full.

'The classical view of the subject', he starts in the finished work, 'may be summed up in the statement that the "Western builders were for many years timid copyists of the crusading architects." The idea is that the Franks marched East with hardly any understanding of fortifications more elaborate than earthworks.'[10] On their way through Greece and Turkey and into Syria, early Crusaders found their inspiration in the surviving work of Byzantine architects. He cites the case of Château Gaillard, Richard I's castle in Normandy, which he had visited in 1908 on his French cycle tour and had described as having a marvellous plan, wonderful execution and perfect situation. 'Château Gaillard', he notes in his introduction, 'is supposed to have drawn the greater part of its excellences from the East; sometimes it has been said that Syrian workmen were employed to build it; at least that Richard was incapable of it before his experience in Palestine.'[11] Lawrence rejects this idea outright. 'The early [Crusader] castles erected in Syria', he insists, 'were of a purely western pattern.'[12]

The thesis fell into four sections: an examination of castles in Europe from the Romans to the eve of the Crusades; Byzantine military architecture; Crusader castles in the East; and, finally, what was built in Europe in the second half of the twelfth century. It was capped at a maximum of 12,000 words and had to be submitted by 19 March 1910. Lawrence worked on it solidly through the winter, matching his intellect to his experiences in Britain, France and the Middle East. As he sat at his desk surrounded by the groundplans and sketches he had made, by the many photographs he had taken and by postcards bought along the way, as he ordered his material and structured his argument – the pile of volumes by 'authorities' he was about to attack standing like a mountain to be climbed – the freedoms and adventures of his Syrian summer must have seemed even more attractive.

The work, finally typed for submission – and published only after his death – is a brilliant synthesis of wide reading and extensive on-the-ground research. All the instantly stated judgments made on his travels – that Crac des Chevaliers was 'perhaps the best preserved and most wholly admirable castle in the world',[13] that the castles at Edessa, Antioch and Birejick were 'a little disappointing', that Sahyun was 'probably the finest example of military architecture in Syria' – are here, and fully justified. But so too are finely argued details over design and construction of walls and battlements, the decline of the central keep, the problems of access over moats and earthworks. The thesis concludes with a complete rejection of the accepted theory, having shown, on the contrary, that 'Crusading architects were for many years copyists of the Western builders.'[14]

Lawrence knew he was pushing the boundaries by submitting so much supporting material and illustration, but that was in his nature. 'I fully expect Theses will be frowned upon,' he told his brother Will, 'partly my fault, in straining the statute far beyond what was ever intended. Simple pieces of secondary work were supposed.'

On 20 June, having sat eleven exams, including a translation paper and with a month to wait for his results, he went to Farnborough in Surrey to join the summer camp of the Oxford University Officers Training Corps. The corps had been created in the autumn of 1908 as part of the War Office's programme to prepare likely men for service: in Oxford, that summer of 1910, this included the Prince of Wales. Lawrence never wrote anything about the experience, but a report in *The Times* noted that over seven hundred people were in camp that summer, including one hundred cavalry. There are two photographs of Lawrence in uniform at the camp. One shows him sitting cross-legged on the ground with a bandolier over his shoulder, and unexceptional in a group of fourteen cadets. The other, taken in a rare moment of sunshine, shows him sitting on a tent rope, in uniform with puttees, but – as would become his habit and would so annoy his superiors – without hat or belt. His exceptional blue eyes were sunk in the shadow. It is difficult to imagine that this young man had either the physical or mental strength to make his way across Syria, nor that he was preparing to do even more extraordinary things in the region.

When the Oxford History School published its results, Lawrence was among ten students who graduated with first-class honours. And yet opinion of his work was still mixed. His private tutor, L. C. Jane, described his degree work as being so brilliant that the examiners held a dinner to celebrate it (though it should be noted that Jane was not one of them). Another examiner referred to the records and reported that 'his thesis was marked "most excellent", but it was not that which won him his first class, but the other papers which were all good and some very good'.[15] Ernest Barker also thought the thesis 'proved conclusively . . . that the old theory of the influence of the castles of Palestine on western military architecture must be abandoned'.[16] Which makes it all the more puzzling that he doubted that Lawrence 'ever was, or wished to be, an "historical scholar"' and that 'he took the Oxford History School because it came in his way, and because it was a hurdle to be jumped on the road that led to action'.[17] Even stranger, given that Lawrence was hoping for an academic research posting now that he had the top degree. But Barker was right in one thing: his road was leading inexorably towards action.

First it led him back to France where he went on a cycling holiday with his younger brother Frank. There were many differences between the two brothers. Frank was a sportsman and a team player with none of Lawrence's enthusiasm either for history or for books. In one letter home he complained that 'each time I have a bath he [Ned] goes and buys a book instead'. Nor did he feel passionate about castles. When they reached Richard I's masterpiece at Gaillard, which Lawrence had written about in his thesis, Frank noted that 'Ned went up to Château Gaillard this morning at 11.0, and he just came back now at 6.30. I have not been with him all the time.'[18] Clearly not, as Frank had judged the castle to be 'a very poor place'.[19] Ahead of them lay a string of castles and churches, which Ned approached with his camera, sketchbook and a fifty-foot measuring tape. When Frank finally went home, Lawrence continued cycling around northern France with his brother Will. Curiously, only one letter to his mother has survived from this summer. Perhaps it was the only one he wrote, but it is one of his more revealing letters, for it expresses his need to be apart, to escape – if only into his reveries – at the same time as it exposes his loneliness. And there is something else, perhaps already a touch of nostalgia for home, an awareness that, with his degree done, life would never be the same again:

> You know, I think, the joy of getting into a strange country in a
> book: at home when I have shut my door & the town is in bed –
> and I know there is nothing, not even the dawn – can disturb me
> in my curtains: only the slow crumbling of the coals in the fire: they
> get so red & throw such splendid glimmerings on the Hypnos & the

brass-work. And it is lovely too, after you have been wandering for hours in the forest with Percivale or Sagramors le desirous*, to open the door, & from over the Cherwell [River] to look at the sun glowering through the valley-mists. Why does one not like things if there are other people about? Why cannot one make one's books live except at night, after hours of straining? and you know they have to be your own books too, & you have to read them more than once. I think they take in something of your personality, & your environment also – you know a second hand book sometimes is so much more flesh & blood than a new one. – and it is almost terrible to think that your ideas, yourself in your books may be giving life to generations of readers after you are forgotten. It is that speciality which makes one need good books: books that will be worthy of what you are going to put into them. What would you think of a great sculptor who flung away his gifts on modelling clay or sand? Imagination should be put into the most precious caskets, & that is why one can only live in the future or the past, in Utopia, or the wood beyond the World. Father won't know all this – but if you can get the right book at the right time you taste joys – not only bodily, physical, but spiritual also, which pass one out above and beyond one's miserable self, as it were through a huge air, following the light of another man's thought. And you can never be quite the old self again.[20]

After he had his degree, he had to wait a little longer for the next step to become clear. He was still hoping there might be a way for him to return to Syria, for he had made reference to 'the Syrian camera I may want' in that same letter to his mother. And around that time, he asked his friend Vyvyan Richards to look out for a first edition of Doughty's *Travels in Arabia Deserta*, and a copy of Hogarth's *Wandering Scholar in the Levant*, which he rather generously called 'one of the best travel books ever written'.[21]

While Lawrence had been finishing his degree, Hogarth at the Ashmolean had been making plans and had been in long discussions with the British Museum about opening a dig in Syria. The museum's

---

* Lawrence had an enduring passion for knightly tales, particularly the adventures mentioned here and recorded in Sir Thomas Malory's *Morte d'Arthur*, one of the books he was to take to Arabia and reread during the Arab revolt.

Keeper of Babylonian and Assyrian Antiquities, the renowned and prolific Dr E. A. Wallis Budge, had travelled in the area in the year of Lawrence's birth, 1888, and had identified a place called Jerablus, a huge *tell* or mound on the banks of the Euphrates, as the most promising place to dig. Nothing happened for the next twenty years, until Budge heard that an American mission was also interested in excavating in the area. When Hogarth was sent to see whether things still looked as they had in the 1880s (that was the journey on which he had bought the Hittite seals), he reported that Jerablus 'contained more than other sites and represented a more important Hittite centre'.[22] The museum had approached the authorities in Constantinople in June 1908 for permission to dig, but the idea lapsed in the unrest that followed the Young Turk uprising against the Sultan. Hogarth must have been in touch with the museum in the spring of 1910, perhaps jogged by Lawrence's account of his travels the previous summer. In May, the museum heard that Constantinople had approved the request and that Hogarth would be granted a two-year permit. But when it was finally issued in September 1910, just as Lawrence returned from cycling in France, it came on the condition that digging would start within three months. Hogarth could not mount his excavation so quickly, so he went to Constantinople himself to rearrange the dates.

In the uncertainty, Lawrence had applied to Jesus College to do a postgraduate B.Litt. in 'Mediaeval Lead-Glazed Pottery from the 11th to the 16th Centuries', an area of research suggested by Charles Bell at the Ashmolean, the same person who had proposed the Syrian tour to him. Although he failed to be appointed to a fellowship, he was elected a scholar at Jesus, with a grant of £50 a year and an expectation that he would undertake research in European museums. While Lawrence was waiting for the university's central board to approve this appointment, Hogarth returned to Oxford with the dig dates rescheduled.

If he did not know about Hogarth's Jerablus plan before, Lawrence certainly heard about it now because he went to ask E. T. Leeds at the Ashmolean if he knew of any digs he might join. 'Why on earth didn't you speak sooner?'[23] Leeds asked, for he knew about Hogarth's intention to dig at Carchemish. 'Lawrence,' he later wrote, 'who had already travelled in Syria, was obviously a suitable assistant; but the excavation staff had already been decided, with R. Campbell Thompson as second in command. I lamented that Lawrence was seemingly too late, but when he offered to go for his bare expenses I sent him at once to Hogarth, knowing the admirable impression he had made the previous year. Hogarth's influence won the day against official stickiness.'[24]

On 1 November, the university approved Lawrence's grant and confirmed his post as scholar; he left for France the same day. But the following day he wrote from Rouen to say that 'Mr. Hogarth is going digging: and I am going out to Syria in a fortnight to make plain the valleys and level the mountain for his feet.'[25] He had found his way back east.

PART II

The Young Archaeologist

We dug hard for 6 months and I used to travel for the rest of the year. We were there for 4 years and it was the best life I ever lived . . .

T. E. Lawrence to B. H. Liddell Hart, 1931

7

Forgotten Far Off Things

> To do the best of anything (or to try to do it) is not a waste
> of opportunity.
>
> T. E. Lawrence to his brother Will, 31 January 1911[1]

Winter 1910

WHAT COULD BE more exhilarating for someone fresh out of
university and with a romantic imagination, than to be employed
by a great museum to travel to the Euphrates River and search for
a Bible-mentioned city? Especially one that had been the scene of a
major battle between combined Assyrian and Egyptian armies and the
forces of a young Babylonian king called Nebuchadnezzar II.

The journey out took longer than expected. Lawrence travelled
overland through France and from Marseille took passage on a
Messageries Maritimes ship bound for Naples, Athens, Smyrna and
Constantinople. The *Sagholien* was not the newest ship afloat and
had already seen thirty years' service, the past dozen spent running
across the Mediterranean. 'Run' is being generous because, as he
wrote home, 'The boat is slow, very slow (11 m.p.h.), but comfortable.' He was travelling in second class, but as December was not
the preferred season to visit the Middle East the boat was only a
third full and he had the four-berth cabin to himself. The food,
familiar from French hotels, involved a good, solid breakfast, a 'huge'
meal at 10.30 a.m. and dinner at 6.30 p.m. He passed three calm,
comfortable days afloat, enjoying the space, and the time to read,
the only slight irritation being that lights in the public areas were
switched off at 11 p.m., 'a very primitive custom'.[2]

Anticipating their approach to Athens, he was excited by the idea of seeing the Acropolis come into view, until he realised they were due to arrive at night, 'a horrible tragedy'.³ The *Sagholien*, however, was no respecter of schedules and they were late again, docking at Piraeus, the port of Athens, at dawn. 'As we entered the Piraeus the sun rose, & like magic turned the black bars to gold, a wonderfully vivid gold of pillar and architrave and pediment, against the shadowed slopes of Hymettus. That was the Acropolis from a distance:– a mixture of all the reds & yellows you can think of with white for the high-lights and brown-gold in the shadows.'⁴ A painterly description, but also a surprisingly under-achieved response from the author of *Seven Pillars of Wisdom*.

In a tram from the harbour, he rattled across green fields and thin, fast, winter streams, the air smelling of pines as he arrived in this puzzling city, which he found too bright to be European and yet too clean to be Asian. From the station, he walked to the Acropolis. As it was still early, the absence of porters, guides and other visitors allowed his imagination to roam.

> I walked through the doorway to the Parthenon, and on into the inner part of it, without really remembering where or who I was. A heaviness in the air made my eyes swim, & wrapped up my senses; I only knew that I, a stranger, was walking on the floor of the place I had most desired to see, the greatest temple of Athene, the palace of art, and that I was counting her columns, and finding what I already knew. The building was familiar, not cold as in the drawings, but complex, irregular, alive with curve and subtlety and perfectly preserved.⁵*

His response to the spirit of the place was more significant than his appreciation of its architectural importance. Walking uphill, he imagined he was seeing things that would have greeted an ancient Greek traveller. 'The further I went the stranger became a curious sense of unreality, almost of nightmare. Here was a town full of people speaking the same tongue & writing the same characters as

---

* His failure to mention the Parthenon marbles is interesting, for they had been hanging in the museum for which he was now working for almost one hundred years.

the old inhabitants of 3000 years before.'[6] On the way down from the Acropolis, the spell was broken: he still saw that link between past and present, but now recognised differences as well. And he realised that the power the stones exerted over his imagination made it impossible for him to write about the place; only Tolstoy, he felt, could have found sufficient distance to see it as it was, not, as Lawrence knew he was doing, as he wished it to be, a glorious ideal. He hoped to return the following year to stay longer, look harder and understand more. In the meantime, he summed up his response in this way: 'there is an intoxication, a power of possession in its ruins, & the memories that inhabit them, which entirely prevents anyone attempting to describe or estimate them'.[7]

Constantinople was easier to describe, partly because the *Sagholien*'s engines broke down 'finally' and he spent a week there, the ship tied up in the busy waters of the Golden Horn beneath the minarets of the grand imperial mosques. His first impressions were positive: 'I remember great parts of it from my reading of Gibbon and Porphyrogenitus and Cecauminus and the rest of the party.'[8] This is a typically playful Lawrence line, showing off his knowledge of Gibbon's *Decline and Fall of the Roman Empire* and of the works of the Byzantine Emperor Constantine VII and the writer Kekaumenos.

'Constantinople is most beautiful from every point of view, & besides is very clean . . . full of interest in the people & artistically.'[9] Clean, coming to the end of one of its regular cholera epidemics, and decked out for Bairam, the big feast commemorating Abraham's willingness to sacrifice his son Isaac. Lawrence was thrilled by 'Cannons firing all round, & all the people feasting in the streets',[10] although the risk of cholera meant eating on board, mostly in the company of three French-Canadian priests heading for Jerusalem.

His was a very particular take on Constantinople. Instead of seeing the sights, as he had in Athens, he spent each day walking along the old Byzantine walls. 'To reach the walls means a walk of four or five miles through the town each way, and as the walls are four miles long, to reach the various daily sections I have, at one time or another, passed across every part of the modern town.'[11] Where Athens was wrapped in the sleep of ages, Constantinople was all noise and movement, the call from hundreds of mosques, the stench of a million people, a chill wind blowing along the Bosphorus, the waterway that separates Europe from Asia. He found the ancient walls more impressive than the great Byzantine basilica of Hagia Sophia, admiring their design, wondering at their preservation, but above all relishing the stories that clung to them. The later monuments seemed less impressive and even the work of the great architect Sinan, the glory of the early Ottoman Empire, failed to move him. Educated on the austere and restrained beauty of early medieval churches and castles, he complained that whatever the Ottomans built, they ruined by over-elaboration and decoration. 'The early Arab work is as fine as the Mediaeval,' he concluded, 'but Turkish art in Constantinople is of a period of decadence.'[12] Then, perhaps realising how damning he had been, he added that 'these are of course only private opinions and a little hasty'.[13] On better acquaintance, he thought his eyes might find another way of looking at this new aesthetic.

He found street life more exciting:

> Everybody (except the women) lives & works & eats in the open, and the markets and shops are busy with movement and colour. To walk down the great fruit-market at sunset, when each man's basket of oranges or apples is lit by a candle fixed in among the fruit, and when they are all redoubling their efforts to rid themselves of their stock before the evening prayer is a regular orgy of activity: the fruit I avoid for cholera's sake, but besides them are sweetmeat sellers with splendidly-varied stalls, and bread-shops, and the vendors of coloured and perfumed drinks, and the red-leather shoe shops, and a whole street of copper-smiths, creating most glorious shapes of cauldrons & basins & ewers in a deafening clatter of hammer on metal.[14]

The excitement that is palpable in his letters was not always infectious: although he persuaded the French-Canadian priests to follow him to the bazaar, where he showed them some of the local attractions – how 'Kamreddin', a paste of boiled apricots, was made, for example, and how the ubiquitous fez was flattened – the clergymen could not see past the chaos. The young traveller complained that the priests talked only 'of the dirt & disorder of things, of the lack of shops and carriages and what they pleased to call conveniences (which are more trouble than they are worth). They seemed too narrow to get outside their own civilization, or state of living.'[15] In view of what he went on to achieve, of the way he moved far outside his own 'civilization', this is a far-reaching and significant judgment. Disappointed by their inability to see beyond the dust at their feet, or to enjoy the spectacle of the great imperial city at feast, he posed a question, as much to himself as to his parents back home in Oxford: 'Is civilization the power of appreciating the character and achievements of peoples in a different stage from ourselves?' The wording is important: 'different', not 'less advanced'. The answer, if he did not know it already, would be found further east, when he went to live among Arabs.

He had said that he was going to Syria to smooth the way for Hogarth's arrival, but his mentor had first been smoothing the way for him. Although Lawrence had already been approved for a scholarship to study medieval pottery at Jesus College, Hogarth knew that it would not cover his costs. He also knew that the British Museum would not agree to pay for two British assistants on his dig. So he had approached Magdalen College, where both he and Charles Bell were fellows and, on 14 December, heard that Lawrence had been awarded a senior demyship – a research fellowship – that would last for five years and came with an annual grant of £100. The best thing about it was that it would allow Lawrence to study Crusader architecture in the Levant. Things were to get even better when Hogarth pressed Frederic Kenyon, Director of the British Museum, to agree at least to cover Lawrence's living costs on the dig. It seems the matter of language difficulties at Carchemish was raised, and Lawrence's fluency in Arabic exaggerated, because towards the end of the month Kenyon wrote to the Lords Commissioner of the Treasury, who had ultimate control over the museum's budget, with the news that 'an offer has been received from Mr. T. E. Lawrence (an Arabic scholar, acquainted with the country, and an expert in the subject of pottery) to join the expedition at Jerablus and to take part in the excavations. Mr. Lawrence is willing to give his services (which will be of very material value) without salary, but I would ask your Lordships to sanction the payment of his actual living expenses while engaged on the excavations, and of his travelling expenses from Beyrout to Jerablus and back.'[16]

Lawrence now had the bursary from Oxford University, worth £100 a year, and a guarantee that the British Museum would cover his expenses in the Middle East, which could be for at least six months a year. To put this in perspective, the average salary for a man in Britain at that time was £70 a year (women averaged considerably less, at around £30 a year). Yet while he might be relatively well off compared to many at home, he came from a wealthy and privileged family, his father had never had to work, and his Syria walking tour the previous year had cost more than £70.

It might have been a season of uncertainty and insecurity, of adventure and romance, but at least this time he was expected at Miss Holmes's American School and he made himself at home.

'I am on a divan,' he wrote to Leonard Green, one of his Oxford friends, although he was in fact on an American bentwood chair, 'inhaling haschich . . . and dreaming of odalisques.'[17] The inhalation was not hashish but the stink of animal skins being cured in the nearby tannery, and mention of odalisques would have made his friend smile at the improbability of his having changed his celibate habits: the flesh had been conjured out of a glimpse of the upper housemaids at work.

Fareedeh el Akle, then twenty-eight years old, remembered Lawrence arriving on Christmas Eve, when the nights are cold and damp, but the days can be bright and uplifting. His natural sense of reserve and an instinct to stand aside, which he called his 'Scotch' caution, gradually eased. As soon as the Christmas festivities were over, he began Arabic lessons with the 'wonderful' Miss Fareedeh and French lessons with her colleague, Emily Rieder. Rieder, New York-born, British naturalised, divorced from her French husband, was the more literary of the two women and enthused about French authors Lawrence had never read. At first, he had greater rapport with Miss Fareedeh, who gave him lessons in conversation and – along with one of Miss Holmes's pupils, a young man called Omar – in reading Arabic.

Hogarth had clearly exaggerated Lawrence's fluency in Arabic when persuading the British Museum to employ him, for however brilliant the young man's mind – and there is no doubt that he was brilliant – it was beyond even his ability to pick up the language in the few months he had walked through Syria and Palestine. In the eight weeks he spent at Jebail, he worked hard to improve. 'Notwithstanding the difficulty of the language,' Miss Fareedeh remembered, 'he made rapid progress; he was able to read, write and speak very simple Arabic in this short time.'[18] But for someone who, as a schoolboy, had ridden across counties to produce a rubbing of the best brasses in England, 'very simple' would not be enough. 'To do the best of anything (or to try to do it) is not a waste of opportunity,'[19] he wrote while still in Jebail. So as well as taking lessons, he bought 'an Arabic prayer book of 1145 A.D. small, but very well written'.[20] He chose it because he thought the handwriting was perfect, much better than modern script, and it is easy to imagine him at his table, the old pages beside him, copying the sweep and curl of consonants, the dots and dashes of vowels into his exercise book.

Miss Fareedeh remembered him being 'so full of humour that the hard Arabic lessons became the most enjoyable time for both student and teacher'.[21] Clearly this was no exaggeration because Lawrence wrote home after a few weeks to say how helpful she and Omar were being, and that he would have to find a way to thank them.

Weeks passed in hard work and sunshine, in excitement and fascination, in becoming used to the sea air, the mulberry-covered slopes, the sound of the muezzin. He was up for the dawn – around 6 a.m. – and usually still there past midnight. Early and late it was cold, but the days were 'roasting hot, with a glaring sun, & clouds of flies & mosquitoes. We can pick ripe oranges in the gardens, and roses and violets in Miss Holmes' patch (facing N.): everything is green and flourishing, for there have been two or three showers since I landed. Still the heat, & the perfect calm, and the exquisite twilight effects are nearly equal to summer's. I need a sun-helmet, really.'[22]

The light, and the long days and nights of reading, took their toll and he suffered eyestrain. Forced to ease off studying, he spent more time with antique dealers, who were as keen to make the most of the wealthy young man's presence as he was to indulge his passion for purchases. Beside the twelfth-century prayer book, other antiques and antiquities that caught his eye included 'some 5 good flint saws: much prehistoric pottery'.[23] He bought a selection of *bishliks, nahasis* and other coins for his youngest brother Arnold.

But more than shopping, he took time during these days to consider what he would do after this season of uncertainty and insecurity, of adventure and romance, after the excavations at Jerablus. The thought was provoked by the possibility that the work, or his part in it, might last for only one season. Not that he was short of options. He had research to do, and he was confident that his grant would continue for some years to come. He also had ideas for two books he would like to write. One he described as a monumental work on the Crusades, presumably building on the Crusader element of his thesis and drawing on experience gained the previous year. The other was a book about his experiences in the Middle East. It was called *Seven Pillars of Wisdom*, the only copy of which he was to burn in Oxford in August 1914.

He was also still pursuing the idea of setting up a boutique printing press, now in connection with another Oxford friend, Vyvyan Richards. Richards, two years ahead of him at Jesus College, remembered their first meeting: 'it was reported that there was a queer stranger among us, who walked solitary at all hours of the night in the still quadrangles of the college'.[24] They became close friends (although, Richards later confessed, not as intimate as he would have liked) and began to dream of things they might do after Oxford, one of them being printing. Neither of them had any experience of presses, but they were young and so had more conviction than caution, more understanding of dreams than of reality. They had, at least, been sufficiently practical to talk through how the press might proceed. Lawrence would provide the money while Richards had the energy, inspiration and design, and would see to the construction of a forty-foot hall to house the press, as well as to the running of it. The problem – the first of many – was that Lawrence had no money of his own yet, so had asked his father to advance £30 against the grant coming from Magdalen. When it became clear that all funding would come from Lawrence and all legal documents were to be in Richards's name, his father objected. The extent of Lawrence's trust, and of his idealism, can be gauged by his reply to his father's objections: 'to rate this [inequality] as important would be to stultify our ideals in the outset'.[25]

Lawrence's parents did not share his idealism. Nor was his brother Will convinced by Richards, and wrote to say as much. Lawrence did not refute Will's objections – 'your character of him seems to me very apt and fairly complete'[26] – and went further to say that 'he is a most complex and difficult personality, and I do not think he will get any better on acquaintance'. But he still thought this collaboration would work. 'He will do his best for the press, and I also . . . I am most fortunate to have found a man of tremendous gift to whom craftsmanship is at once a dream and an inspiration.'[27]

Richards understood the Lawrence family's objections to their partnership and admitted that 'it would be hard to imagine two more diverse minds than his and mine'. And yet they did find common ground: after Lawrence's death, Richards remembered the night they first met, when they sat in front of the fire in his rooms, and 'talked and talked and he unfolded what seemed then the extraordinary thought that the world stopped in 1500 with the coming of printing and gunpowder.' Then, late that night, 'some deep and quick affection took hold upon us whose vividness stirs me still after thirty years have passed away'.[28]

Perhaps Lawrence's family also sensed, as parents can do and as Lawrence himself did not, something that Richards only admitted to late in life: that he was in love with his friend. 'It was love at first sight. He had neither flesh nor carnality of any kind; he just did not understand. He received my affection, my sacrifice, in fact, eventually my total subservience, as though it was his due. He never gave the slightest sign that he understood my motives or fathomed my desires.'[29]

Another letter written during this period was to Leonard Green, with whom Lawrence had previously discussed the idea of a printing press. Green had written to Lawrence for material for a lecture he was giving on the Crusades. Lawrence's long reply is an extraordinary feat of recall for someone who had neither reference books nor notes to hand. More impressive than the memory is the depth of analysis of the issues of fighting on that terrain: 'What I felt most in Syria, put shortly, was the extreme difficulty of the country. Esdraelon, and the plain in which Baalbek lies are the only flat places in it. The coast road is often only 50 yards wide between hills and sea, and those hills you cannot walk or ride over . . . for heavily armed horse operations in such country are impossible.'[30] Hattin, where some 17,000 Crusaders had lost their lives in the great battle against Saladin in 1187, was like a dead lava-flow. Lawrence had preferred to walk between Antioch and Aleppo, but even his mounted guard, who had wanted to ride, found they were unable to because the surfaces were impossible for horses.

He then explained the logic behind the Crusader building programme, where they had built castles, and why – which passes and river crossings they protected, which cities they kept in check. 'The whole history of the Crusades was a struggle for the possession of these castles,'[31] he understood, because with the castles came possession of the land. But not possession of the people. Lawrence also recognised that the Crusades failed, ultimately, because 'the native population of Syria very much sympathized with the Arabs, except the Maronite Christians and the Armenians . . . Any counter stroke in the nature of ambush against the Arabs was impossible, since half their people were spies.'[32] Not only had Lawrence grasped the issues of fighting pitched battles in this part of the world, but, more important, he understood that even if the land could be won in battle, it could be held only by winning what today would be called hearts and minds. And the population would invariably side with their co-religionists. As a military debriefing it was complex, wide-ranging and brilliantly perceptive. It also showed that the bright young scholar from Oxford was good at more than long marches, taking photographs and eclectic reading. His analytical, strategic mind would prove extremely useful were he ever involved in war.

The day before the winter heat broke, 21 January, Lawrence saw snow on the hills. The next morning a storm covered the beach in snow, the whole way down to the waves. Nine days later, it was still blowing. 'Your weather has not been worse than ours this week,' he wrote home. 'I never saw such storms: and no way of heating the house either.' Two weeks later and the coast was still under snow, as was the land beyond the mountains. The Beirut–Damascus railway was closed for a record forty-three days. Further east, the formidable Gertrude Bell, travelling across the Syrian desert towards Baghdad at this time, had woken in the night 'in surprise and putting my hand out felt the waterproof valise that covered me wet with snow . . . it had drifted into my tent a foot deep'.[33]

It was the most severe winter for forty, fifty, perhaps even seventy-five years, a claim that Reginald Campbell Thompson would not have disputed. Thompson, on his way to meet Hogarth and Lawrence, was boarding ship at Port Said when the storm hit and his description of what happened matches the drama of the scene: 'A great gale, blowing to burst itself, sprang up from the south, hurrying clouds of sand from the deserts and whipping a flurry of racing spindrift from the waves at the [Suez] canal mouth . . . The skipper held to harbour until four the next morning the wind unabating, and then put forth, meaning to sail by the coasts of Asia, but . . . on a sudden came a great flash and explosion as though a gun had been fired in the between decks . . . but it was a flash of lightning which had struck the foremast.'[34] The sea was so rough when they eventually reached Haifa that the captain gave up trying to land passengers and continued up the coast to Beirut.

Thompson was a London-born, Cambridge-educated scholar of Oriental languages, specialising in Aramaic and Hebrew. Twelve years older than Lawrence, he already had considerable experience of both travelling and digging in the region. He had spent the winter of 1904 working on the excavations at Nineveh, the great Assyrian capital by the Tigris River in Mesopotamia (now Iraq). After two years teaching at the University of Chicago, he had travelled in the Middle East – this was the summer that Lawrence walked around the castles – and had then returned to London to work at the British Museum. Now he was making his way towards Aleppo, where he would meet his new colleagues.

Lawrence packed up at Jebail in the middle of February. Miss Holmes had discovered that he was good with his hands and had set him to mending windows, shutters and other things around the house – necessary with the storm – and his last days were particularly busy. His eyes had recovered from the strain of reading in poor light so he had also been studying Arabic again. On Saturday 18 February, he travelled down to Beirut with Miss Holmes and Emily Rieder, when he heard that snow had closed the railway between Beirut and Aleppo. They would have to wait for it to be cleared or look for another way to reach Jerablus. He also heard that Thompson had been in Beirut. Newly engaged and hoping to bring his fiancée out to Aleppo to marry in the spring, he had looked for a piano he could ship to their new home, prompting Lawrence to note that 'we are not going to rough it in Carchemish'.[35]

Hogarth arrived in Beirut on 20 February and, as always, brought a sense of calm efficiency to the proceedings. He also brought Gregorios Antoniou, the foreman on all his digs since the two men had first worked together, in 1888, the year of Lawrence's birth. Gregori, a native Cypriot, had been a tomb-robber before working for archaeologists and he was now valued for his experience and his unerring judgment. Hogarth had described how, over many years and at a dozen sites, Gregori had 'never yet stopped short of the bottom or refused to follow a likely lead'.[36] He had become so important that Hogarth was prepared to ship him to Beirut and pay him over the usual rates to work at Carchemish. But at sixty Gregori was neither as agile nor as resilient as he had been, so instead of trying to cross the snowbound Lebanon Mountains to reach Damascus, Hogarth decided to sail down the coast to Haifa – where Thompson's ship had failed to land – to take the longer railway route to Damascus.

Thompson and Lawrence left conflicting descriptions of that journey. Thompson, who had travelled a couple of days ahead of the others, remembered clattering 'across that muddy cataract stream, the Jordan, and over the desolate steppes beyond, where endless showers of snow were whirling, to the frost-beleaguered city Damascus'.[37] Lawrence had a very different recollection, waking Hogarth from his slumbers each time they passed sites with biblical connotations or which the young man had visited on his walk the previous year. Often there was little to see, but Lawrence knew that 'he more than shares my admiration'.[38]

Lawrence's admiration for his mentor was already clear in his letter describing the journey. The three men had the compartment to themselves and, while old Gregori slept and shivered, Lawrence relived his epic walk. 'Mr Hogarth of course knew all the country by repute, and by books, and we identified all the mountain peaks and wadies and main roads . . .'[39] and whatever else they could see from the carriage window. As they crossed the great haj route from Damascus down to Mecca, which Lawrence knew of from Doughty's *Arabia Deserta*, the threads of his life seemed to be pulled closer together. The sun even shone when they stopped at Deraa, the junction of the Haifa and Hejaz railways.

Deraa looms large in Lawrence's story for it was there, six years later, that he was beaten and sexually assaulted by Turkish troops, an incident that stained the rest of his life. But on Deraa platform in February 1911 there was a joy and innocence about him. 'We had a French *déjeuner* in the Buffet, where Mr. Hogarth spoke Turkish & Greek, & French & German, & Italian & English all about the same as far as I could judge: it was a most weird feeling to be so far out of Europe: at Urfa and Deraah I have felt myself at last away from the Renaissance influence, for the buffet was flagrantly and evidently an exotic, & only served to set off the distinctiveness of the Druses & their Turkish captors.'[40] They continued north by train via Damascus to Aleppo, where Thompson huddled around the Baron's Hotel's only wood-burning stove, in a city he described as 'clemmed with cold and famine'.[41]

'At last my chief came,' he later wrote, 'and with him Lawrence, and Gregori, a kind and portly man, long celebrated as a tomb finder, a dowser of graves with iron probe instead of hazel twig.' They had a couple of busy days in Aleppo, first paying a visit to the British Consulate. Kenyon at the British Museum had already written to His Majesty's representative, Raphael Fontana, the British Consul in Aleppo, to request 'all possible assistance'.[42] Kenyon had also asked Fontana 'to move the proper Authorities at Aleppo to be ready to provide adequate police protection (not troops) for Mr. Hogarth's party'. Licences had also been granted for each of the archaeologists to carry firearms – including one for 'Mr. George Lawrence'.

'There were yet to be procured spades and picks,' Thompson continued, 'which the smiths made to pattern; there was hired a caravan of ten camels and eleven horses for the tents, tools, materials and food boxes . . . thus set forth our cavalcade over the undulating brown lands of the Hittites.'[43]

It took three days to reach Jerablus and, while the others rode, Lawrence went on foot. A large mud house had been reserved for them in the small village. They needed the space, for behind the horses and camels there were mules and donkeys, bringing a small fortune in stores that included nine flavours of jam and three varieties of tea, piles of pistachios, for which the region was famous, small mountains of Turkish delight and sweetmeats bought in Aleppo, some tools and even more books. The two nights en route had been rough and the new house was cold. Exhausted but happy, Lawrence lay down and slept early.

Hogarth had described the born antiquary as someone with 'the type of mind which is more curious of the past than the present, loves detail for its own sake, and cares less for ends than means'.[44] Along with this came his observation that many born archaeologists had some sort of infirmity, which helped 'to detach the man for the study of forgotten far off things'. Thompson had another view, that 'a fit man who travels solitary in the Near East with design of long sojourn for great discoveries in digging old cities will apply himself beforehand to learn the manifold needs of his expedition'.[45] Among these needs were the ability to speak to his workers, and to use a camera – photography he thought was 'a most necessary art'. Curiosity about the past, a love of detail, perhaps a physical infirmity, at least a passing knowledge of the language and skill with a camera: of the three foreigners who had just arrived at Jerablus to excavate the ancient site of Carchemish, only Lawrence fulfilled all these conditions. And the junior member of the team was also the only person, foreigner or native, not being paid a wage by the museum.

8

The Apprentice

Foreigners come out here to teach, whereas they had much
better learn, for in everything but wits and knowledge the Arab
is the better man of the two.

T. E. Lawrence to his mother, Carchemish, 24 June 1911[1]

Spring 1911

'WORK BEGINS AT sunrise (6.0 a.m.),' Lawrence wrote with
enthusiasm of his first days as an archaeologist. 'We breakfast
first & walk down [to the *tell*] a little later. Thompson is surveying
the site . . . Mr. Hogarth does the writing up of the results: I
do the squeezing* & drawing the inscriptions and sculptures, & (with
the great Gregori . . .) direct the men. Work goes on (with an hour
for lunch) till sunset. Then home: write up journals: & catalogues:
feed, & go to bed!'[2] This description is not very different from what
might be said of a twenty-first-century dig, with one notable exception: the amount of responsibility handed to the junior member of
the team. An archaeologist straight out of university today would
not be left to run a dig especially if, like Lawrence, they had no
training. It says something about the early state of archaeology and
also the lack of skilled workers that he was allowed to do so much.
Most of all, it shows the faith Hogarth placed in his young protégé.

Of the unlikely threesome, Hogarth was the leader by character
as well as appointment, his extensive experience, reading and language

---

* A squeeze was a copy of an inscription made by covering it with wet paper or
plaster. When the paper or plaster was dry and could be peeled off, it would have
a mirror image of the original.

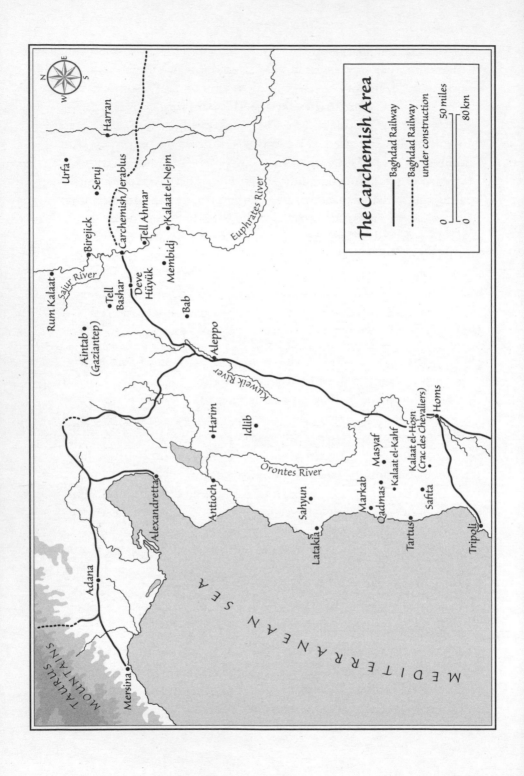

The Carchemish Area

Baghdad Railway
Baghdad Railway
under construction

50 miles
80 km

N
W E
S

TAURUS MOUNTAINS

Mersina
Adana
Alexandretta
Antioch
Latakia
Sahyun
Markab
Qadmas
Kalaat el-Kahf
Masyaf
Safita
Tartus
Kalaat el-Hosn
(Crac des Chevaliers)
Tripoli
Homs

MEDITERRANEAN SEA

Orontes River
Harim
Idlib
Aleppo
Kuweik River

Rum Kalaat
Aintab
(Gaziantep)
Tell Bashar
Birejick
Salur River
Deve Hüyük
Carchemish/Jerablus
Tell Ahmar
Kalaat el-Nejm
Membidj
Bab

Urfa
Seruj
Harran

Euphrates River

skills setting him apart from the younger men. He had first learned to dig with two of the greatest archaeologists: in Egypt with Sir Flinders Petrie, and in Greece with the Minoan expert Arthur Evans. He had acquired sufficient experience of administration and diplomacy to run the British School at Athens and then the Ashmolean Museum in Oxford. And as Lawrence had already observed, he was multilingual, widely read and just as widely travelled: altogether what Lawrence called 'a most splendid' man. He also had a reputation for writing books that managed to be both informative and entertaining: he acquired the information, while the humour came naturally.

Thompson risked looking bland in Hogarth's presence and yet he also had already achieved much. The thirty-four-year-old had travelled extensively in Egypt and Sudan, had taught in the United States, worked for the British Museum and excavated at Nineveh. He had also been published, although the titles of his papers – *On Traces of an Indefinite Article in Assyria* is typical – suggest that he had not yet learned the light touch of scholarship that had brought Hogarth success.

Early on, Lawrence decided that he liked Thompson 'very much',[3] as much for his enthusiasm for music as for his 'tremendous' knowledge of Semitic languages, although the piano never arrived (presumably because the fiancée stayed away). He also liked him because they had common interests beyond work, including shooting and walking although, being older and a different character to Lawrence, Thompson had no need to punish his body. Most surprising was Thompson's passion for the trapeze: he gave a public performance on the ropes each year. He was never to earn Lawrence's admiration in the way that Hogarth had done, but then Hogarth had become a role model as well as mentor and, over the coming years, would become the most ardent supporter of this young, enthusiastic, excited historian.

It was important that the three of them got on because there was little alternative to each other's company and no way of escaping, especially at the beginning of the dig when the weather kept them inside in the evenings. The days were full and busy, but night time could be taxing on the nerves, as Lawrence recognised when describing how 'from the roof little bits drop all day and all night:

and it is full of birds that baptize the bald heads at their leisure'.
Later there were rats, fleas and mosquitoes. 'Then there are the cats:
Father (who is only suffered, not encouraged) . . . comes in at the
holes in the roof and walls by night, and offends lewdly in our beds.
Then D.G.H. throws a boot towards it and hits Thompson, and
plants it in the bath, or knocks the light down: and when he has
got out and repaired damages he finds the cat in his bed when he
lies down again.'[4] Lawrence had the excitement of a first job to
carry him through these days. For nights, 'the power of sleeping
through anything, which I acquired in my little house by aid of late
hours and a telephone bell, is standing me in excellent stead. I am
the only one of the three who gets any sleep at all at night.'[5] One
wonders what he dreamed about those first days.

Each morning, sometimes in company, sometimes alone, he walked
through the village of Jerablus and fifteen minutes along the path
to the ancient city of Carchemish. The archaeological site covers a
huge area, divided into a walled inner city and the larger outer city,
both hemmed in on the east by the Euphrates River. The focus of
their efforts was the city centre, the *tell*, a vast artificial hill a hundred
feet high, literally a blot on the landscape. Somewhere beneath that
accumulation of sand and mud, and the many layers of later buildings, lay the remains of a Hittite capital city. Among those ruins,
they hoped, lay the key to uncovering the lives of a people lost to
history.

Many empires had risen and fallen in the broad sweep of desert-
hemmed farmland that stretches from Egypt in the south up to
Carchemish and then curves east and south towards the Persian Gulf,
the Fertile Crescent. The Hittites were notable among these empires
for having been so completely overwhelmed that, with very few
exceptions, traces of their existence, understanding of their language
and even memory of their culture had disappeared as completely as
melted snow. Forty years before Lawrence arrived at Carchemish,
an encyclopaedia entry stated nothing more enlightening than that
'an independent Hittite tribe under a monarchical government
lived . . . near Syria'.[6] Yet the Hittites were one of the great powers
of the ancient world. At their height, they ruled over much of Asia

Minor, conquered Babylon and posed so serious a threat to the Pharaoh's people that the story of the conflict was the predominant war narrative of ancient Egypt, carved into the façade of many of the temples along the Nile. The inner walls of Ramses II's most extraordinary structure, the temple at Abu Simbel, for instance, tell the story of the final battle and how it needed the personal intervention of the Pharaoh to save his army from utter defeat. What is most extraordinary about the Hittites is not the extent of their power at its height, but the completeness of their disappearance.

Scholars and archaeologists threw much light on the ancient world at the end of the eighteenth century and throughout the nineteenth – Egyptian hieroglyphs, for example, had been translated in the 1820s. But the Hittites remained in the shadows, no more significant than the Amorites, the Jebusites or the many other lost tribes and forgotten nations listed in the Bible. Some clues were thrown up in 1812 when the great Swiss traveller Jean-Louis Burckhardt recorded what he called a 'nail script' in Syria that did not conform to any known language but that was the Hittite cuneiform script. More clues were thrown up in 1834 when a French traveller, Charles-Félix-Marie Texier, stumbled on the ruins of an ancient city near Boghaz Köy, in central Anatolia. Their gods, he knew, were neither Roman, nor Assyrian nor Egyptian.

The Hittites remained in darkness until 1876 when George Smith, the British Museum's brilliant thirty-six-year-old Assyrian expert, stopped near Jerablus on his way out to excavate Assurbanipal's library at Nineveh. Smith noted that he had seen a 'grand site: vast walls and palace mounds: 8,000 feet round: many sculptures and monoliths with inscriptions: site of Karchemish [sic]'.[7] Encouraged by this, and with backing from the British Museum, Patrick Henderson, British Consul at Aleppo, made initial excavations between 1878 and 1881. Before he had finished, an announcement from Archibald Sayce, Professor of Assyriology at Oxford, that the ruins at Boghaz Köy, the *tell* at Carchemish and the inscriptions Burckhardt had seen in Hama all came from the same lost civilisation, the Hittites, was picked up by the press. A nation that had been lost for thousands of years suddenly became headline news, with *The Times* describing them as 'that great ancient people . . . whose wide sway in Western

Asia, stretch[ed] at one time from the Euphrates to the Dardanelles'.[8] Sayce went further with his theory and suggested that the 'Great King of Khatti', mentioned on the walls of Egypt's temples as the rival of Pharaoh Ramses II, was a Hittite. Tablets found at Amarna in Egypt soon afterwards confirmed this theory.

At the start of the twentieth century, all of what had been the Hittite empire fell under Ottoman administration and permission to excavate was granted in Constantinople, where Britain, France and Germany all vied for favour. When Kaiser Wilhelm II appealed directly to the Sultan, the German Orient Society was granted a permit to dig at Boghaz Köy. Other German missions were allowed to dig at a variety of sites across Mesopotamia, including the Assyrian ruins of Kalaat Shergat on the Tigris, and the Aramaean site of Tell Halaf. The British Museum secured the right to excavate at Carchemish. This might have seemed poor consolation because Carchemish looked less interesting than Boghaz Köy from an architectural point of view. But there was one overwhelming reason why the British Museum wanted to dig there: it sat on the edge of the Hittite empire, bordering land that had been ruled by Assyrians, Egyptians and others, on what Hogarth called the frontier of two scripts, the Hittite and the cuneiform.

The Hittites had written texts in three different scripts. Some were written in the Akkadian language using cuneiform signs: this could be read and understood. The 'lost' Hittite language was written using two different systems. Like ancient Egyptian, it was sometimes written in cuneiform, which could be read, although no one as yet was able to understand what the words meant, and it was sometimes written in a form of hieroglyphs, which could not yet be read or understood. The same problem had faced scholars of ancient Egypt until the Rosetta stone presented an official decree written in three different scripts: Greek, ancient Egyptian written in a flowing cursive script called demotic, and the same words written in Egyptian hieroglyphs. Hogarth hoped that Carchemish, sitting on the edge of empires, would give up an inscription written in two or three different systems of writing. The prize he hoped to capture was a Hittite Rosetta stone.

★

'When excavations are successful,' Hogarth had told his assistants, 'there is never a moment to spare.' Thompson agreed with him: 'T. E. Lawrence and I, acting as his idle apprentices, learnt [the truth of this saying] in watching the progress of raking the mountain of Carchemish. For you may dig for week after week, a weary and indefinite time of waiting, finding nothing, and then on a sudden the most glorious treasures will be revealed, tasking your time from dawn to sunset. So was it in the first year of excavations at Carchemish.'[9]

The layout and function of the stones was as confusing as the work that went into digging them up. At the end of his first month at Carchemish, Lawrence wrote that they were moving massive blocks.

> The remains of walls & houses are buried about 2/3 of their height in fairly clean earth, but the upper four feet are filled up with rubble, and small rocks, with the ashlar masonry and concrete of the late Roman town. Whenever we break fresh ground, dozens of these large blocks have to be moved. Some of them weigh tons, and we have no blasting powder or stone-hammers with us. As a result, they have to be hauled, prehistoric fashion, by brute force of men on ropes, helped to a small extent by crowbars. At the moment something over 60 men are tugging away above, each man yelling *Yallah* as he pulls: the row is tremendous, but the stones usually come away. Two men out of three presume to direct operations, and no one listens to any of them, they just obey Gregori's orders, and their shouting is only to employ their spare breath. Now they are raising the 'talul', the curiously vibrant wail of the Bedawi [Bedouin]. It is a very penetrating, and very distinct cry; you feel in it some kinship with desert-life, with *ghrazzus* [raids] and camel-stampedes.

And having constructed this romantic, Orientalist vision in which the young Englishman watches his Arab workers, he breaks the spell with a typical moment of Lawrentian bathos in which 'the stone has slipped & fallen back into the trench'.[10]

With no archaeological training beyond skills acquired as a schoolboy prospecting for treasures and undergraduate volunteering at a museum, Lawrence accepted that this primitive method of shifting stones was how archaeologists worked. Elsewhere, he was to discover before long, they used winches and tackle, and engines strong enough to propel flying machines over the English Channel. But in Carchemish they used muscle and rope, and for the simple reason that Hogarth had chosen for it to be this way. 'I was certain', the Director wrote by way of justification, 'that the site would yield interesting results to simple means, but I was far from sure that it was sufficiently rich to justify heavy expenditure on the purchase and transport of elaborate digging plant.'[11]

As the spring broke, sunshine melted snow on the Taurus Mountains, which Lawrence could see from the *tell* on a clear day. The broad Euphrates began to rise, swift and cold, and the rolling countryside came into wild bloom, lit by clumps of white-blossomed pistachio trees. The air was rich with promise. Lawrence, whose eyes were used to the muted colours of English gardens, the soft green of an English field, found beauty in the harshness of the ruins, the river and fields. He made a point of picking wild flowers for the house, just as he liked the idea of having books and fragments of antiquities in the sitting room – eventually there would be side-tables made out of ancient columns and vases of ancient glass. For now, at this early stage when everything was fresh and exciting, there was a joy in becoming accustomed to a morning walk, the call to prayer, the smell of cumin and cardamom, the sight of a hundred men busy on a hillside, a thrill to stepping into a high-bowed Euphrates boat, steered by a massive oar, instead of the flat-sided Cherwell punt, pushed by a single pole – a fascination in every aspect of every day.

Within a month, a routine had set in, work was under way and it was clear that only one archaeologist was needed on site most of the time. The three archaeologists took turns to sit on the mound. Back at the house, Lawrence logged fragments of pottery. He had the patience and the steady hand needed to spend hours piecing them back together, as he had done years earlier with things bought from Oxford road diggers. On the mound, he measured stones, copied inscriptions, made squeezes and took the occasional photograph. 'Digging', he wrote at this time, 'is tremendous fun, & most exciting, & interesting.'[12] The mornings were his favourite time, when the sun was up but the air still cool, especially if he was there when the hundred or more workers – Kurds, Turks and Syrian

Arabs – stopped for breakfast. 'From all the villages below us on the plain there come long lines of red and blue women & children, carrying bread in red-check handkerchiefs, and wooden measures full of leben on their heads. The men are not tired then, and the heat is just pleasant, and they chatter about and jest & sing in very delightful style. A few of them bring shepherd's pipes, and make music of their sort.'[13] What they made of their young master in his baggy shorts, a big red Kurdish sash round his waist, the tassels hanging on his left hip, the sash partly hidden beneath a Magdalen College blazer, is unrecorded.

Working on the site, with Hogarth and Thompson up at the house, and Gregori keeping the men focused, Lawrence had time to think about himself and the way his life was shaping. In this, as in so much else, he was influenced by Hogarth. By any measure, Hogarth was a successful man. He held an important museum post, had a wide readership for his books, an ability to attract large audiences for his lectures and an impressive record of excavations. Yet unlike many people in archaeology at the time, Hogarth was driven by the need to earn his keep. He was one of eight children of a Lincolnshire clergyman and, although his father had managed to send him to a good school and then to Oxford, there was neither inheritance nor benefactor on hand to make up his shortage of funds. Constantly aware of the need to support his wife Laura and their young son, he had insisted that the British Museum pay money into his bank before he left to look at Carchemish in 1908.[14] In spite of limited funds, he had travelled widely, read even more widely, and acquired a name for himself. Lawrence and he had much in common, including the need to earn a living. But unlike Hogarth, Lawrence seemed least concerned about financial necessity.

'Mr. Hogarth has been most exceedingly good to me all through,' Lawrence gushed like a schoolboy, and 'taught me a tremendous lot about everything from digging to Greek erotic verse'.[15] He had also been discussing what Lawrence might do next, a necessary precaution seeing that the future of the Carchemish digs depended on what they found in the coming weeks. So the older man is likely to have heard then, if not before, about the plan to set up a printing press with Vyvyan Richards in a big hall somewhere in the English countryside. He is also likely to have heard of Lawrence's desire to expand his thesis into a book on the Crusades, and to write about his travels in the Near East in *Seven Pillars of Wisdom*. But another idea was now taking shape. He had written home earlier asking his parents to send out a copy of Doughty's *Travels in Arabia Deserta*. In a letter written at the end of March, he mentioned that when the book arrived, he might bind it in camel hide to help preserve it, 'for I must know it by more than library use, if I am ever to do something of the sort. Mr. Hogarth thinks my idea of patronizing the Soleyb [a tribe in the desert between Syria and the Hejaz] instead of the Arab promising both in security, & novelty. They are an interesting people . . .'[16]

No doubt the Soleyb – the Bani Slayb – were and are very interesting. Hogarth was certainly familiar with what little was known about this most elusive of tribes, for he had mentioned them in a book he had written some years earlier.[17] Lawrence's parents were less happy with the idea of his travelling in Arabia, both for the risks involved and because a journey into Arabia might jeopardise the demyship from Magdalen College to continue his Crusader work. His mother accused him of trying to rival Doughty (which probably sounded worse to them than it did to their son), something Lawrence vehemently rejected. 'You remember that passage [in Doughty] that he who has once seen palm-trees and the goat-hair tents is never the same as he had been: that I feel very strongly.'[18] To support his case, he pointed out that many of the people he most admired, and particularly Doughty, had been shaped by journeys they had made. He also restated his reasons for wanting to travel with this tribe, who were 'pagan, and by common consent the original, pre-Arab inhabitants of Arabia. They go on foot, often, by preference, since some have wealth and baggage-camels: are great hunters of gazelles, hospitable simple folk, in no way fanatical. They are much despised by the Arabs, who as you will see in Doughty are feather-brained and rampol-witted. He always had a good word for the Soleyb, but told me he thought their way of life would be very primitive.'[19]

Doughty was one of the few people to have written about the tribe: 'The Solubby household go then to settle themselves remotely, upon some good well of water, in an unfrequented wilderness, where there is game. They only (of all men) are free of the Arabian deserts to travel whithersoever they would; paying to all men a petty tribute, they are molested by none of them. Homeborn, yet have they no citizenship in the Peninsula. No Beduwy, they say, will rob a Solubby, although he met him alone, in the deep of the wilderness, and with the skin of an ostrich in his hand.'[20] The tribe stayed out of the Egyptian deserts, but pushed up through Mesopotamia, and were occasionally seen in Damascus and more so in Baghdad, where they went to trade. 'A spring and summer with them (which is what I was thinking of) would be a fresh experience: but I have no intention of making a book of it.'[21]

The idea was a good one if, like Lawrence, you had survived walking in the summer through Syria and Palestine, were gaining confidence in your abilities, improving in your fluency in Arabic and looking for material for a book you are planning, *Seven Pillars of Wisdom*. Lawrence knew his parents would reject his plan to travel if it was merely to research a book. But going for the experience, to shape himself . . . that was something else. Yet he should have known it would meet with a negative response. Perhaps he did know, which was why he wrote that there was 'no hurry about that'. The desert would still be there and the time would come for him to travel in it.

Permissions to excavate ancient ruins were not the only concessions being fought over in Constantinople. British foreign policy had long recognised the need to protect access to the eastern parts of the empire, notably India. The British invasion of Egypt in 1882 had been driven by the need to secure the Suez Canal. So when, in 1903, the Ottoman Sultan granted a German-led consortium a concession to build a railway from Constantinople to Baghdad to link up with the line that already existed between Constantinople and Berlin, the British were concerned: running close to the Mediterranean, it could become an alternative route to the East. It might also threaten British interests in the Persian oilfields. The rise of the Young Turks in 1908 gave Britain hopes of renewing its influence in Constantinople and of gaining control of the Turkish

Asian rail network. But when the British government turned down a Turkish request for a loan, the Germans stepped in (Deutsche Bank provided the money), and relations between London and Constantinople cooled again.

A few days after Lawrence had started work at Carchemish, the Baghdad Railway Company and the Ottoman Ministry of Public Works announced that the line would cross the Euphrates at Jerablus. Two days later, the railway's chief engineer was celebrating in Aleppo. In a confidential report sent to the British Ambassador in Constantinople, Raphael Fontana, the British Consul, described how there had been 'a great influx into Aleppo of German engineers and employés connected to the Baghdad Railway'. The German company had also announced the opening of a factory, expected to employ up to 500 men. 'This factory', Fontana added, 'will serve also as a means for introducing machinery into the country, as the mechanics employed therein will be able to set up and repair machines of all kinds.'[22] He also reported that their Royal Highnesses Prince George and Princess Maria Immaculata of Saxony had been in Aleppo, where the Baghdad Railway's chief engineer, Meissner Pasha, had given a banquet for them. The Vali and the German Consul had attended, but Fontana had not been invited. The inference was clear: German influence was on the rise.

Lawrence, in his youthful enthusiasm, described excavating as being 'like Pandora's box, with Hope in the last spit of earth'. By the middle of April 1911, the Carchemish *tell* had given up a quantity of decorated stone slabs, including four chariot scenes, two with warriors holding prisoners and severed heads – which were familiar from the decorations of Egyptian temples – and a figure of a man adoring a palm. But they had found no bilingual or trilingual inscriptions, and while a young man might be maintained by hope, Hogarth needed something more substantial. He knew that his decision not to invest heavily in the site had been the right one and he returned to London prepared to say as much to Kenyon; it would be difficult to justify continuing much longer, or coming back for another season. In Aleppo on 24 April, he wrote to Kenyon that 'you have got and will continue to get quite enough Hittite sculpture and inscriptions . . . to justify the dig',[23] but the linguistic key they had hoped for had not been found and a second season could not be recommended. Instead, he suggested that they continue digging as long as possible into the summer at Carchemish and that the following year they turn their attention elsewhere: he had told Lawrence that he thought they should move further down the Euphrates to Tell Ahmar, another promising Hittite site.

Many writers have spun a web of intrigue around the British Museum dig at Carchemish, citing, among other things, the fact that Hogarth had arrived with letters of recommendation from the British Foreign Secretary, Sir Edward Grey. Why would the foreign secretary interest himself in the movements of a museum director and his small-scale, poorly funded archaeological dig? Conspiracy theorists conclude that the British government wanted eyes on the ground, to spy on progress of the German-built railway, to gauge the popularity of the Turkish government and to report on the activities of agents of Britain's so-called friends, the Germans and Russians. Given the future wartime activities of Hogarth, Thompson and Lawrence, all of whom worked in intelligence, it is tempting to conclude that they were already on assignment. But for whom? Lawrence joined Military Intelligence soon after the outbreak of World War I, but if Military Intelligence were involved in Carchemish, they would not have employed these Oxford archaeologists without military personnel on hand. One of the most compelling points against the Carchemish team doing intelligence work is this: if the British government had an interest in the progress of the Baghdad Railway, or the activities of Germans or Russians along the Euphrates, why would Hogarth recommend closing the digs?

As soon as he reached England, in the middle of May, Hogarth refined his opinion, and recommended that Thompson continue at Carchemish 'throughout the coming summer, so long as he is able to keep it going economically, or until he has proved that neither the Acropolis nor the ground near its landward feet and on the West of the site is likely to yield adequate return to your expenditure'.[24] But he also kept the door open, pointing out that 'a site, so extensive and so notorious as Jerablus, demands, I think, a very full trial, which can hardly last for less than a full season'. Thompson was being paid £1 a day, Lawrence was only working for his keep and the reduced workforce was paid pennies. As there was still plenty left in the budget, Hogarth now wrote to Thompson instructing him to dig through the summer.

The instruction was received with mixed emotion in Jerablus. Lawrence, delighted, wrote to say 'the idea of digging on is glorious, for there is really hope of several parts of the digs'.[25] Thompson's dismay can only be imagined. His main interest at Carchemish was as a translator of Assyrian and Semitic texts,* none of which had been found. Added to this was the disappointment that his fiancée had not come out: he wanted to go home and be married. None of this was reflected in the message he sent to Kenyon to let him know that 'both Lawrence and I are delighted at the prospect of continuing, however long . . . Lawrence tells me that he is in no wise troubled by the heat of this country, as he walked continually throughout last summer through Syria.' As for his own response to heat: 'I spent a year at Mosul [in Iraq], six months in the Sudan and two summers in Chicago.'[26] So at least the heat would not be a problem.

The dynamic between Lawrence and Thompson changed as soon as Hogarth left. At the beginning of the season, Lawrence had written warmly about him, but now that Thompson was his superior, letters home were coloured by a rising note of criticism: 'Thompson is one of those unhappy mortals who cannot or will not read French – but then he is a scientist[27] . . . Thompson has given up testing the site (perhaps a little too soon)[28] . . . He is a restless body at night . . . any little thing upsets Thompson[29] . . . Thompson is not a digger[30] . . .' And, just a few weeks after Hogarth's departure, there was this: 'Thompson feels his dignity as chief too much, & weighs his words.'[31] This last comment was written on the May day when Gertrude Bell had paid a visit.

Bell had visited Carchemish in February 1909, before the archaeologists had moved in. Now on her way back from Baghdad, she decided to visit Hogarth and to see what they had done with the *tell*. At Birejick, the Kaimmakam told her that Hogarth had left, but

---

* Later it would be discovered that Hittite was an Indo-European language.

that Thompson was still on site. 'Accordingly I went there – it was only 5 hours' ride – and found Mr. Thompson and a young man called Lawrence (he is going to make a traveller) who had for some time been expecting that I would appear. They showed me their diggings and their finds and I spent a pleasant day with them.'[32]

The meeting reveals Lawrence's anxiety at their lack of achievement at Carchemish. Writing to Hogarth the evening of Bell's visit, he noted that Thompson 'has dressed tonight, & something of the sadness of the last shirt & collar is overtaking him, for Gerty has gone back to her tents to sleep. She has been a success: and a brave one. She called him prehistoric! (apropos of your digging methods . . .).'[33] To his parents, he described how they had shown off their learning:

> She was taken (in 5 minutes) over Byzantine, Crusader, Roman, Hittite, & French architecture (my part) and over Greek folk-lore, Assyrian architecture, & Mesopotamian Ethnology (by Thompson); Prehistoric pottery & telephoto lenses, Bronze Age metal technique, Meredith, Anatole France and the Octobrists (by me): the Young Turks, the construct state in Arabic, the price of riding camels, Assyrian burial-customs, and German methods of excavation with the Baghdad railway (by Thompson). This was a kind of hors d'oeuvre: and when it was over (she was getting more respectful) we settled down each to seven or eight subjects & questioned her upon them. She was quite glad to have tea after an hour and a half, & on going told Thompson that he had done wonders in his digging in the time, and that she thought *we* had got everything out of the place that could possibly have been got: she particularly admired the completeness of our note-books. So we did for her.[34]

Part of his sensitivity at Bell's 'prehistoric' comment was his awareness that she had recently visited the German Orient Society's excavations at Ashur (Kalaat Shergat), the ancient Assyrian capital on the banks of the Tigris River (in what is now Iraq). To read her response to that visit – something Lawrence was spared until later in life* – is to understand that he had good cause to be anxious: 'I

---

* Bell's letters were published in 1927, the year after her death. When he read them, Lawrence wrote that they 'are very good, and well display her eagerness and emotion' (DG p. 543).

spent three enchanting days at K. Shergat and would gladly have stayed longer.' She particularly enjoyed the company of the dig leader, Walter Andrae, a handsome man seven years her junior. A photograph of the two of them at the dinner table with three other German archaeologists shows the men in high collars and buttoned-up jackets, and Bell looking composed and relaxed. She enthused about Andrae, whose 'knowledge of Mesopotamian problems is so great and his views so brilliant and comprehensive . . . He put everything at my disposal, photographs and unpublished plans, and his own unpublished ideas. I don't think many people are so generous.' She ended by saying that 'K. Shergat was looking its best. I love it better than any ruined site in the world. The only drawback of my visit was that I was so reluctant to go away.'[35] A couple of days later, she was at Carchemish and making it clear that the British lagged behind the Germans both in historical expertise and in personal charm.

Lawrence's opinion of the German techniques was less flattering. 'They lay down gravel paths, wherever they want to prove an ancient floor, & where they pile up their loose stones into walls of palaces.'[36] The Carchemish dig might not be so good to look at – and it was to get worse over the coming weeks – but everything you could see was original Roman or Hittite or Assyrian, not a Teutonic reconstruction of what might have been. 'So we showed her that and left her limp, but impressed.' Then he dealt another blow: 'she is pleasant: about 36, not beautiful (except with a veil on, perhaps)'.[37]

Archaeology can be dull plodding work, especially the kind of 'primitive' archaeology they were engaged in and on a site that had yet to be proved. Thompson tried to talk it up when he wrote that 'the digger shall know good days when the basket-men carry out the dust of forgotten palaces, disclosing their glories, and that compelling eagerness, leashed to restraint lest haste should be a spoiler, spying the sampled corner of a chiselled monument all delicately carven, bared by an Arab pickaxe, and the sweet delights of prying out its secret runes'.[38] He had also written about 'long days under a blazing sun or in bitter cold, a little king in Babylon ruling his feofs, ever measuring, scribbling, drawing'.[39] Lawrence was developing a less rosy view and at the end of April, after Hogarth's departure, confessed that 'we have found nothing Hittite but large sculptures, & fragments of such. Never a Hittite stratum, or even a Hittite building. For all this place so far has taught us about them we might as well never have come.'[40] Yet while he was frustrated that their discoveries had revealed nothing significantly new about the Hittites – and certainly nothing to help decipher their hieroglyphs – he had learned a great amount from the people he was overseeing.

Eighty men were retained on the Carchemish dig after Hogarth and Gregori had left. 'Will [his brother] asks after the ethnology of this place,' he wrote after he had been there for seven weeks. 'I am afraid I do not know what it is. There are Kurds, a few Tcherkers [Circassians] (of course heaps in Membidj), Turks, and Arabs.'[41] Some of these people were beginning to stand out and were already being referred to by name in his letters. Among them was Haj Wahid, a cook with a passion for firearms. Thompson had employed him on the journey he had made through the area in 1904 and described him as 'a handsome, black-moustached man, speaking Arabic, but perhaps with Kurdish blood in his veins; down his shaven skull was the ancient suture of a wound received in some brawl'.[42] Others who knew him found him vain-glorious and a lover of finery, yet both honest and faithful. Haj Wahid had had a reputation as a heavy drinker and dangerous man who, by his own admission, had spent five years as a sergeant in the Sultan's pay, followed by five years in the Sultan's prison. When he was freed, he married, and opened a café in Aleppo, which was where Thompson had found him back in March, on his way to Carchemish with Hogarth and Lawrence. The Haj – the name identifies someone who has made the pilgrimage to Mecca – had been employed as cook (and taken his wife and child with him) and he served the Englishmen breakfast each morning, several courses for lunch, and dinner around 7 p.m. And while he might not have been the most refined cook – Lawrence found him 'not original, except in the matter of cakes that are half custard and half rubber sponge',[43] which he made without an oven (he didn't have one) – he could produce a feast of soup, fish, meat, vegetable, omelette and a dessert, using just a single small spirit lamp. Occasionally there were mishaps, as when he emptied an entire tin of curry powder into a pilaf: Hogarth and Thompson complained about their livers for days afterwards. But most of the time the Haj was as reliable in the kitchen as he was when they needed a threatening presence to scare off local officials or to pull a gun on robbers.

Lawrence found the Haj and the other workmen 'very curious and very simple, and yet with a fond directness and child-humour about them that is very fine'.[44] More than their openness, he appreciated how they had welcomed him into their lives, recognising that he had more than a little 'child-humour' about him. So, too, did Thompson, as became apparent that spring after they had dismissed the son of one of the local elders, Sheikh Ibrahim. The Sheikh's son was happy to be paid but reluctant to work, and after several warnings about his sense of entitlement, he was dismissed. The Sheikh was furious when he heard the news and went immediately to the mission house to tell Haj Wahid that he would put a spell on him, the Englishman and the overseers if his son were not reinstated. 'The Haj came to us a little perturbed,'[45] Lawrence wrote home. In the version of the story that Lawrence wrote later, clearly intending it for publication (though it was never published), when Hamoudi the Hoja (overseer) heard about the plan:

[his] hand doubtfully touched his lips and forehead. 'Yes sir, but . . . he is a son of Ibrahim Mul'Ali . . . the Moghreby (magician) . . .?'

'No matter, Hoja.'

Late in the afternoon we lay limply on our beds, listening gratefully for the dying-away of the two-hour tumult always born of pay day, when on a sudden a new voice, surcharged with anger, took shrill mastery of the babble. It rose till it compelled all to a hush that stayed unbroken after itself had ceased. A minute later the Hoja intruded, white and trembling, crying out, 'The Moghreby has cursed the digging: we must not go on till you have taken back his son or death will come of it. O Sir what are we to do?'

'No matter, Hoja: do you not know we are greater magicians than he?'

The Hoja went out half-comforted, but we turned to one another and consulted what we might do. The crisis was grave, for if unallayed, fear of the magician would rob us of half our men next week. At last, 'Haj Wahid,' called my friend to our servant, a Kurd,

Happy families: six-year-old T. E. (Ned) Lawrence sitting on the steps of the family's house in the New Forest with his mother and three of his four brothers

The Crusader castle of Sahyun, to which Lawrence walked in August 1909. He thought it 'perhaps the finest castle I have seen in Syria'

SAHYUN. *The South-East Corner.*

Lawrence's photograph of 'wonderfully picturesque' Carcassonne, visited on his cycle tour of France in August 1908

Fine young men. The Lawrence brothers in 1910: (*left to right*) Ned (who graduated from Oxford that summer), Frank, Arnold, Bob and Will

Lawrence at the Oxford
University Officers Training
Corps camp, summer 1910,
looking considerably younger
than twenty-one and already
averse to wearing full uniform

Lawrence bought a
bronze replica of Hypnos,
the god of sleep, when
he passed through Naples
in 1909, a treasure for his
Oxford bungalow

Janet Laurie, a friend of the Lawrences,
who claimed that Ned proposed to
her in 1910. This portrait shows many
similarities with the bronze Hypnos

Fareedeh el Akle, the Arabic teacher at the American Mission School in Jebail and one of Lawrence's confidantes

David (D. G.) Hogarth, curator, archaeologist and author, who taught Lawrence 'a tremendous lot about everything from digging to Greek erotic verse'

Central Aleppo, where Baron's Hotel was Lawrence's first port of call from his earliest visit in 1909 to his last, in the summer of 1914

Lawrence's sketch of the mound at Carchemish where he worked from 1911 to 1914, the happiest years of his life

Sarah Lawrence, Ned's mother, with whom he had a troubled relationship as a child and a distant one as an adult

The earliest known image of
Lawrence in Arab dress, and a
rare picture of him grinning

Dahoum, the young man Lawrence
took as his assistant and protégé, and
in whom he recognised the potential
and the rights of Arabs

Leonard Woolley in hat and Lawrence in shorts and blazer,
in front of a Hittite chariot scene at Carchemish

James Elroy Flecker, enthusiastic poet and reluctant British consular official in Beirut. Photograph by Lawrence

The 'strange boy who tramps Syria on foot and digs Hittites for Hogarth': Flecker's description and portrait of Lawrence

Gertrude Bell dining with German archaeologists at Ashur on the Tigris. To Bell's left is Walter Andrae, whose company she particularly enjoyed

proud of his fighting ancestry, 'go out and bring a hair of this fellow.' 'From his clothes, sir?' 'No, from his head.' In a few minutes, a cry and a burst of excited query proclaimed the insult achieved. Haj Wahid returned in triumph with a short grey hair.

'From his beard, Khawaja,' said he, expectantly [using a word that can mean *master* or *foreigner*]. 'Good: Haj Wahid, tell the people we are making a wax image, and in it we are putting the hair. Then when we drive a pin into the heart, the Moghreby will straightway drop dead. But if we melt it before your fire, his life will run away from him to Gehanum [hell], even as the drops of hot wax fall into the fire and are consumed.' Haj Wahid's eyes sparkled, and in a few minutes, his kitchen was busy with the hum of voices, and loud expressive '*wallahs*' of amazement and delightful expectation.

To watch the triumphal dying of the sun – radiating surges of unimaginable rose, blush-like, to the heart of the dust-clouds which ever in the evening whirl over those desolate plains of the upper Euphrates – I stood that evening in the door of the house, when a figure in dusky white rushed from behind a wall, and almost threw itself at my feet.

'Effendi, Effendi,' gasped Mul'Ali, 'they lied to you, indeed they did lie: I am a poor man, I said no harm of you: Effendi, dismiss all of my sons if you will; only in the Name of Allah the Merciful, the Compassionate, give me back that hair.'[46]

Mul'Ali also offered them a hen as part of his peace-offering; they, in turn, refused the hen but gave him back the hair. The bluff worked well for, as Lawrence reported home, their 'renown advances in the Arab-speaking world'.[47]

Their renown as magicians spread further towards the end of June, this time in relation to policemen. They were obliged by the terms of their agreement with the Turkish authorities in Constantinople, and according to Kenyon's request, to have one or two *zaptieh* – policemen – on the site. These men were paid and fed by the expedition, but they often turned out to be more nuisance than help. If they made any problems, the Englishmen tried, usually successfully, to have them transferred elsewhere. In June, for instance, they had had a 'sour' *zaptieh* moved, but in his place had come a man who was 'continually interfering, & malingering, with demands for brandy. We got rather tired of this, and so when he produced a preposterous fever, we promised him his medicine, and invited him into the kitchen. Thompson put on a pulpit face, and recited the Hebrew Alphabet and "the House that Jack Built" in a solemn voice, waving a cabalistic scroll in one hand, the other on the man's pulse: the whole village crowded round the door to see.'

The ailing man was then given a glass of water, into which Lawrence poured some Seidlitz powder, an effervescent mix used as a laxative. The *zaptieh* never discovered the efficacy of that particular cure because as soon as the powder hit the water, with Thompson intoning a long, loud amen, it burst into a spume that terrified the policeman. 'The Zap. dropped the glass & leapt back with a yell, and in a twinkling there was not a man but ourselves in the room: some of the onlookers did not feel themselves safe till they had put the corner between themselves and the devil visibly striving to void himself from the glass in white smoke.'

'Am I not your friend, your *raffik*?' the *zaptieh* asked after finding the courage to return. 'Why did you give me that from which I might have died? What have I done to you which was not good?'[48]

To convince the policeman that the powders would not have killed him, Thompson and Lawrence forced their two young water carriers to drink half a glass each. When they survived, the *zaptieh* retreated upriver to Birejick in shame, while one of the water boys walked around the site the following day declaring, 'I drank some of their sorcery . . . it is very dangerous, for by it men are changed suddenly into the form of mares and great apes.' 'Our fame as nigro-mancers [exorcists] is gone abroad to Aintab & Membidj,' Lawrence concluded. 'The powder now foams a tall man's height from the glass with the noise of a dust-filled wind.'[49]

This particular water carrier was called Ahmed, an Arab name although he claimed his family had lived on the *tell* for as long as anyone knew. Lawrence liked to think that Ahmed was descended from the Hittites, an idea supported by his resemblance to some of the ancient carvings. He was no more than fifteen years old and had very pale skin, which explains why, to tease him, he had been given the nickname Dahoum, Darkness. Dahoum was exceptional for reasons other than the shade of his complexion. Most workers on the Carchemish excavation thought of little beyond buying a(nother) wife, feeding their families, paying off debts, acquiring a donkey or more land with the cash they earned. But Dahoum wanted to go to Aleppo, the nearest thing he knew to a big city, and get himself an education. In the meantime, as there was no school in the district, he tried teaching himself to read and write some words in Arabic: only one other person in the village could do so. 'Altogether', Lawrence wrote home, when first mentioning Dahoum, 'an interesting character' and 'has more intelligence than the rank & file. He talks of going into Aleppo to school with the money he has made out of us. I will try to keep an eye on him, to see what happens.'

Ten days later, at the beginning of July, Lawrence wrote about Dahoum to Emily Rieder, his French language teacher at Jebail. 'I have had quite a success with our donkey-boy, who really is getting a glimmering of what a brain-storm is. He is beginning to use his reason as well as his instinct . . . I had very exceptional material to work on but I made him read & write more than ever he did before.'[50] Dahoum, Lawrence suspected, was another dreamer of the day, with the necessary drive to make his dreams reality.

The problem, as far as Lawrence could see, was how Dahoum would progress, or to where he could progress. His plan to put himself in school in Aleppo would be good for the teaching, but Lawrence thought Dahoum would be both happier and safer in the village. At home, however, there was 'the hideous grind of the continual forced labour, and the low level of the village minds':[51] village conversation rarely strayed far from the practical, the religious or the immediately historical of who did what, when. Then there was the problem of access to books. They had been having impromptu classes using the dust of Jeralbus, but, as Lawrence noted, 'you cannot do much with a piece of stick & a scrap of dusty ground as materials'.[52] The best available education was at the American mission schools, but that brought the danger of conversion and of learning a way of thinking that would be foreign to him. 'Remember,' he told Emily Rieder, 'he is to be left a Moslem.'[53] Lawrence had approved of the mission schools on his first encounter with them, but he had become concerned by the effects of foreign influence: 'if only you had seen the ruination caused by the French influence,

& to a lesser degree by the American', he wrote home, 'you would never wish it extended. The perfectly hopeless vulgarity of the half-Europeanised Arab is appalling. Better a thousand times the Arab untouched. The foreigners come out here to teach, whereas they had much better learn, for in everything but wits and knowledge the Arab is the better man of the two.'[54] The apprentice now had his own apprentice, another dream to nurture on the ancient slope beside the Euphrates.

9

The Wanderer After Sensations

This is the house, venerable stranger, which you asked me to
point out. Within it you shall find kings.
>   Homer, *The Odyssey*, Book VII, translated by Lawrence[1]

Summer 1911

'MR. HOGARTH SUGGESTS 6 weeks more dig,' was the news he
sent home at the end of May. They had dug test pits around
the mound, hoping to justify a second season, and had found that
the great wall of the Hittite palace turned a right angle. Lawrence
understood the significance of this discovery: instead of just coming
to an end, or having been demolished, the wall enclosed something.
'There might be something inside,'[2] something such as a bilingual
inscription. Hogarth also understood, and on 8 June he instructed
them to continue working until August. Five days later, the end
date had been pushed back further still: 'Mr. Hogarth said, "Go on
two months" which will take us into the grapes and water-melons:
we have just arrived at the apricots.'

Because Thompson had given up on the test pits (a little too
soon, Lawrence thought), they had chosen three promising places
to excavate. It was slow, heavy work, digging up and carrying away
the upper levels of earth and debris, work made slower by a heat
so intense that the stones glowed in the afternoon. He had written
that it might be a fortnight before he had anything more to report,
but in that he was wrong: a few days later they uncovered the basalt
base of a Hittite column and the lower half of a man holding a lion
cub by its hind-legs. These were unique and interesting pieces,

although perhaps not earth-shattering, game-changing or even season-justifying to the penny-pinching money-minders at the British Museum. 'What on earth personal news is there to write? I shave three times a week, and yesterday darned a hole in a sock – nothing more.' He reminded his people back in Oxford that 'we are only existing and digging',[3] although he soon proved that there was more to life than work.

The temperature rose further – the mercury could climb to over 43 degrees Centigrade (110 degrees Fahrenheit) – the river fell and the fleas in the house became so aggressive that he moved his bed to the mound. It suited him better to be out, and away from Thompson, although he implied that there was more romance than practicality about the move. 'It is very pleasant in the moonlight, to look down, on one side to the rushing Euphrates, & on the other to over the great plain of Carchemish, to the hills of the Salt Desert on the South. Our diggings are certainly in one of the loveliest spots in the world: and in one of the most memorable.'[4] He now had an extraordinary amount of responsibility as he ran the workforce (Gregori had gone home and Thompson's Arabic seems not to have been good enough for that), photographed the finds and reconstructed fragments back into pots. The heat helped him win the battle to give up eating meat, which 'kept on going off'.[5] So now they ate 'a chicken once or twice a week, a fish or two from the river', provided by a man who caught them with his sword, and 'there is rice, and bread and leben which are better'.[6]

More than the practical arrangements, he was enjoying his position with the men. 'You would be amused at our workmen,' he wrote to Florence Messham, his childhood nurse,* 'and the curious tricks they play, to deceive us or to please us. Of course Thompson & I have to be doctors and fathers, & god-fathers and best men to all of them, and last week one man asked us to be good enough to pay the price (£12) of the wife he wanted to buy. She was a girl of the town, and so of course was a fearful extravagance for him, for he was quite poor, and could have got a girl from the villages

* Florence Messham disapproved of his friendship and printing-house plans with Vyvyan Richards.

round about for two pounds quite easily. And for that two pounds the girl would be very fat (a sign of beauty here) with lots of tattoo-marks on her face, and able to make bread and knead dung-cakes for fuel.'7 More than as match-makers, they had a reputation in the district as doctors, for they had a chest of medicines and their treatments were free: after Lawrence washed one man's scorpion bite with ammonia, he reported that 'I have a fame above Thompson as a hakim [doctor].'8

But however good the summertime living, the digs were less successful. Even Lawrence, the optimist, reported that they had found nothing more than a few shards of pottery and a section of classical moulding. But he was learning that their fortunes as archaeologists could be made or lost on the turn of a spade: dig here and find a treasure that makes you world famous, or dig a few feet to the left, find nothing and sink into obscurity. In late June, it looked as though the gods were smiling on their perseverance when they began to uncover what looked like more rooms in what they now thought was a lower palace, and two Hittite houses that appeared to have some walls still standing. Inside one of the houses they found an unusual collection of ancient terracotta horses. These discoveries threw light on the development of Carchemish, even though they might not advance knowledge of Hittite archaeology. Even the excavations were looking promising.

Yet it was with concern that Lawrence watched a dust trail on the horizon. As it rose out of the heat haze, it composed itself into a messenger sent by Fontana in Aleppo and he carried a telegram from Kenyon. Hogarth had failed to persuade the British Museum to keep the digs open longer. 'When palace with north acropolis and houses and tombs well tested stop work. Kenyon.' Thompson sent one back by return – 'Closing fortnight'9 – and allowed himself to dream of home and marriage.

Lawrence wrote home by the same courier to say that they would 'clear out as soon as possible: so in a fortnight we will shut down the digs. By the terms of the telegram from the British Museum they are so disappointed at our results that there will be no second season. It is a great pity for we had on the strength of our former orders, just begun important clearances. We will leave the site like a warren, all disfigured with rubbish heaps and with all the work only half done: altogether about the most unsatisfactory job that one can imagine.'¹⁰

Thompson was relieved, Lawrence dejected, and Hogarth critical – first of Kenyon for giving up so easily, and then of Thompson for moving so quickly, especially when the new finds included 'limestone lined graves with bronze axeheads and scores of "champagne" cups'.¹¹* A week later, Hogarth came out fighting, with a report on the excavations in *The Times* that spelled out the significance of the site – 'under its walls . . . Pharaoh Necho met Nebuchadnezzar' – before explaining their achievements: in a short season of digging, they had found the longest and one of the most perfect Hittite texts, and 'for the first time a long series of Hittite narrative sculptures', although his 'reasonable' hope of finding a bilingual Hittite-cuneiform text had not yet been fulfilled. Although his report admits to less than spectacular results, it ends with a comment that Hogarth intended as a plea to the museum for a second season: 'a more fortunate cast than those made so far may yet strike remains of the city's archives, collected into some single spot on the Acropolis or near it'.¹² Archaeology still had a hold on the public imagination and, as many *Times* readers would have known, it relied on luck as well as judgment. The Germans under Winckler had been lucky at Boghaz Köy, and perhaps the British would be if they returned for a second season at Carchemish.

Kenyon remained sceptical and, in spite of Hogarth's very public plea, he wrote to inform the Standing Committee of the British Museum Trustees that 'after consultation with Mr. Hogarth, he had come to the conclusion that enough had been done to show the general character of the Jerablus site, and that a discussion of the results was necessary before carrying the work further'.¹³ On the same day that Kenyon made this report, Lawrence and Thompson left Haj Wahid, the Hoja, Dahoum and the rest of the excavation team and moved fifteen miles south along the Euphrates.

When Hogarth had done his reconnaissance of the region in 1908, he had noted the size and location of Tell Ahmar, the 'Red Hill',

* Pottery cups shaped like champagne bowls.

another mound on the Euphrates worth excavating. He had asked his two assistants to drop down the river to inspect the ruins before leaving the area, so 'a great barge was sent down for us from Birejik', Thompson later remembered, 'and awaited us near the [Carchemish] mound. These boats are moved with two long sweeps, and swing and twist in the eddies of the current as they go down . . . A contrary wind arose, so that we moored to the bank after nightfall and bathed in the dark, warm waters and wrestled on the sand; these Arabs are poor at grips and know naught of locks or holds. Again a little, and the moon being now near its full, we pushed off and floated down to Tell Ahmar at midnight, past the great high-prowed ferry-boats.'[14] They spent four days at Tell Ahmar, reading and recording inscriptions, taking photographs and making squeezes. Then, on 12 July, Lawrence wrote that 'today in the afternoon I am going off to Urfa'.[15]

He had long been planning to walk around the region when the dig finished, intending to look at the Crusader castles as part of his Magdalen College research. 'The men here say it is best to go along the carriage road as far as Seruj (about 2 days) and then take another road south. This route I may vary of course as I get later information.'[16] If he sounded unusually cautious, it was with good reason: he was in the area where he had been violently attacked and robbed two summers before and he would have known that the mention of Seruj would have alarmed his parents, especially as the region was more unsettled now than it had been two years earlier. He had already assured them that 'people seldom or never get ill out here: fever is not a serious ailment: it only at the worst involves resting half a day; small-pox I should be proof against, & typhoid is rare in *the country*: one is much more likely to get it in Aleppo, or even at Jebail'.[17] To calm nerves at home, he did his best to plan out his route – Harran, Urfa, Birejick, Tell Bashar, Aleppo, Jebail – which he thought would take a month. He then planned to spend the winter in the region, partly because the British Museum only paid his travel expenses to the coast and the boat home was expensive, while it would cost him little to 'winter either in Jebail or in one of the villages in the plain here: the latter would be the more interesting: and certainly as comfortable: an empty fireless marble-lined hall does not add to one's natural heat. If I can find someone here to teach me Arabic I will probably stay.'[18] There was someone who could teach him Arabic: the same person he had been helping to educate, the fourteen-year-old donkey-boy, Dahoum.

He was also enjoying his perceived status in the region. 'We are such kings in the district', he wrote home, 'that it would be a pity to spoil all our good work by abandoning it finally. It is quite extraordinary to see the difference our stay has made in the workmen.'[19] There is a surprising naivety about this comment. Experience should already have taught him that they were treated as kings because they provided cash employment in a country where many people had no cash and barely survived off barter. They were welcome because they employed hundreds of people and because they paid well. They were appreciated because they treated people well, cared for their sick and cheered their successes. But he was not a king and his experience of being attacked two summers earlier near Seruj, when he had a pistol and an *iradé* from Constantinople in his pocket, should have reminded him of his vulnerability. He was a young man, a wealthy one by local standards, and an extremely unusual one for being wealthy and still wanting to walk alone, in remote countryside, in the summer.

'At Carchemish in 1911 the casual visitor to the dig met a frail, pallid, silent youth. The shut-up Oxford face, the down-cast eyes, the soft reluctant speech, courteous, impersonal, were impressive, disturbing and disagreeable.'[20] So remembered Ernest Altounyan,* the Irish-Armenian son of Aleppo's most respected doctor, who visited Carchemish while he was home from his medical studies at Cambridge. 'For here obviously was someone cleaving through life propelled by an almost noiseless engine.' Altounyan was writing after Lawrence's death in a motorbike accident in the English countryside, and this last comment, in the light of what Lawrence went on to achieve, has a touch of hagiography about it. But his

---

* Altounyan's children, on holiday with him and his wife in the English Lake District in 1928, inspired Arthur Ransome to write *Swallows and Amazons*.

observations about the young archaeologist's manner – shy, soft-spoken, retiring – are convincing, as is his assertion that 'by 1911 he had spun his cocoon but had not yet the assurance that enables the full-grown man to leave it when required'.[21] Altounyan thought that although Lawrence was aesthetically mature, in many other ways he was not.

The humiliation of the attack that had ended his Crusader castle walk was far behind him. He had come out of Oxford with an impressive degree and, more important, with the backing of some very influential people, foremost of whom was Hogarth – Altounyan calls the older man 'robust and pagan'. Lawrence had just spent seven months in the region, improving his Arabic and learning how to be an archaeologist, and by his own admission he was now feeling like a king, on top of a beautiful world of great plains, mighty rivers, grand ruins, a world inhabited by people he was beginning to understand better than most Europeans had done. Now, the claim he had made to the head of his Oxford college more than two years earlier rings true, that 'living as an Arab with the Arabs, [he had] got a better insight into the daily life of the people'.[22] He had learned to see the difference between Arabs, Kurds, Turks, Armenians and all the many other peoples who lived alongside each other in the region. He also knew, as he had written from Carchemish, that 'digging in any case would always be a thing I would try to do, & the more I know of it the better'.[23]

Yet it was also a time of introspection, enabling him to think of himself, and his plans. Perhaps, if the dig did not resume after the summer, he would travel with the Slayb tribe in Arabia and follow Hogarth's example by writing a book about his journey. Perhaps he would set up the press with Vyvyan Richards. A few weeks earlier, he had considered the way he and his brothers were turning out and had realised that none of them would be able to support their parents in their old age: 'One a missionary: one an artist of sorts and a wanderer after sensations: one thinking of lay education work: one in the army, & one too small to think. None of us can ever afford to keep a wife: still the product of fairly healthy brains and tolerable bodies will not be all worthless in this world. One of us must surely get something of the unattainable we are all feeling after.'[24] It was a perceptive appraisal. The wanderer after sensations looked the most likely to touch the unattainable, although Thompson might not have thought so as he watched his colleague walk away from the mound they had been inspecting for Hogarth. He went alone, with a small bag and no water or food, in the heat of a summer afternoon.

'On a Wednesday about July 12 I left Tell Ahmar, and walked about an hour: there, feeling thirsty I went to see some Kurdish tents, in which the villagers of some houses close by were staying, and got leben and barley bread; no money accepted.'[25] This first sentence of Lawrence's journal from the summer walk picks up from the good days of 1909. There is a sense of joyous freedom, of the endless possibilities, of the pleasures of the open road. He was young and strong, far from the complications and implications of home, at ease with himself, the people and the place. What's more, he had a sense of purpose.

Whatever else Lawrence burned in August 1914, he did not burn the diary he kept of his walk that summer. What survives of the handwritten account of the 1911 walk gives an insight into another significant milestone in his development. Arnold Lawrence, his youngest brother and literary executor, who prepared the diary for publication in 1939, four years after Ned's death, described it as filling 'a block of centre pages in a small canvas-bound notebook, the rest of which contains personal memoranda (expense accounts and addresses), data on the ancient East, translations of Arabic fables, etc. Each day's happenings were described that evening and on the following morning.'[26] The suspicion that this might look very similar to the notebooks of many contemporary travel writers is confirmed by Arnold's assumption that 'he intended to rewrite the whole, for it would seem that he must have had a literary motive for the unusual exercise of keeping a diary and for persisting in so doing under such physical difficulties'.[27] The difficulties became more apparent as the days went by.

When he reached Urfa after a walk through the dusty, burned-out countryside, he settled into the great khan, as he had done two years earlier. Then in spite of the immense heat, which turns Urfa, trapped by cliffs, into an oven in the summer, he went to photograph the looming ruins of the castle that sit high above the old town. It is typical of Lawrence's sense of purpose, his single-mindedness, that he failed to mention, if he even noticed, two of Urfa's main attractions: its souks, and the sacred pool filled with carp which has a connection to the story of the patriarch Abraham. Instead, he climbed the hill up to what had been the seat of a Crusader count when the place was known as Edessa, and spent days observing, measuring and photographing the ruins, even though he had decided that almost everything that survives had been put there after the Crusaders were chased out.

A policeman was waiting to see him that first evening, when he returned to the khan. This time, he asked to see his papers and inspected the renewed *iradé* and his passport, which had an effect, although probably not the one Lawrence wanted because the next day the chief of police came to warn him against going out alone: 'Boys might throw stones.'[28] The following morning there were police scattered around the khan, waiting for him. Bowing to the inevitable, Lawrence agreed to the protection, but he negotiated his way into taking just one man with him. The policeman was not used to walking in the sun and soon 'complained of the heat, so I sat him under an arch with some snow [ice] and a bowl of water and tobacco, and he was happy'.[29]

The problem was solved, but Lawrence was less happy. The previous night he had slept badly, troubled by a wisdom tooth, which he had soothed with iced rose-petal sherbet. On Monday 17 July, when he left Urfa for Harran, some thirty miles away, the tooth was 'rather worse: an abscess and face painfully one-sided'.[30] The following day, 'feet very tired, tooth much worse. Side of face all sore and swollen.'[31]

It is clear from this section of his diary that he must have suffered similar levels of pain on his previous walk and on the French bike rides. But because he kept no private journals on those earlier journeys, the letters he sent home are the only testimony we have as to how much he punished his body, how far he pushed himself, not something he wanted his parents to know. The letters home tell only one side of the story, the part that would not alarm his parents, the part that reflected well on him. The diary is a very different record. Raw and unedited, it gives a more rounded account of what he did, what he saw and, on occasion, what he thought.

The first impression is of the extraordinary willpower needed to overcome such intense physical challenges. The journey was arduous, the heat intense, the distances long, the surfaces uneven, the nights mostly broken, the risks to his safety still huge in spite of his assurances otherwise. His diet also remained spartan: mostly bread, leben and fruit – plums were in season – and occasionally some vegetables, eggs or cheese.

His writing style had also matured over the two years. Even though it was no more than a traveller's journal, an aide-memoire written in moments snatched from a day's journey, there are descriptions of people and landscape that, while still far from the high-flown style of the post-war *Seven Pillars of Wisdom*, are also a long way from the laboured descriptions of his early letters from France or indeed his Crusader castle thesis. There is this description, for instance, of his arrival at the Kurdish town of Harran, his first stop after Urfa:

> I found the sheikh in the castle, which he has made his house. There was a huge stone vaulted polygonal tower, with deep embrasures and an earth floor. In this he with seven or eight others was reclining, discussing the loss of a key. When I came in he greeted me, and called for rugs and cushions, and then I sat down. He was a young man, perhaps eighteen, with a sharp, rather rapacious and mobile face, and dark curling hair: very broad and tall; of course thin. He had been sheikh only one year, since his father died. We talked a variety of things (they were astonished that I was there so early from Urfa) and he rather strained my Arabic by asking for a description of English local government, and our marriage customs. He was also curious as to the dignity of sheikh in England. His manners were excellent, very unlike the common people, for he did not snatch at my things, but waited (eagerly) for me to show them him. Some of his men had heard of Jerabis (or Gerabis as they said). They were interested in the coming of the railway.[32]

The sheikh did everything he could to make his unexpected guest comfortable. He fed him eggs, cucumbers and wheat-bread. At sundown, he brought out a good quilt to keep him warm, even though it was a hot summer night. The following day there was a grand coffee ceremony which forty people attended and where Lawrence answered the many questions that were put to him about himself, his equipment – they were particularly intrigued by his tape measure – and his reasons for being there. Lawrence, in turn, learned much about the young sheikh. He was standing in for his elder brother, who was detained at the pleasure of the Constantinople government to ensure his good behaviour. 'They are old régime and Ibrahim Pasha men,'* Lawrence noted, adding that although the Milli federation had fractured since the old pasha's death, the young sheikh of Harran could still count on 2,500 houses. 'This means a force of 10 to 12 thousand men; enough to constitute a danger to central rule.'[33] What Lawrence did not record, perhaps because he understood it would bring trouble if his notebook fell into the wrong hands, was the cache of eight to ten thousand rifles that the sheikh showed him in one of the castle's underground vaults.

They sat up and talked politics that night, until the sheikh fell asleep with his head on Lawrence's knee. The next morning, his second at Harran, it became clear that the sheikh would like him to stay longer, perhaps even for ever, and, thinking it might help persuade him, had offered Lawrence two 'first-class wives' as a present. Another man might have found this offer tempting, especially as even Lawrence noticed that 'the women here are extremely free, handling one's clothes, and putting their hands in one's pockets quite cheerfully. Also they never pass one without speaking.'[34] To someone so shy and reserved, this was not always a good thing: one can imagine his discomfort at having the sheikh's women put their hands in his pockets.

The following morning, he politely declined the sheikh's generosity and left Harran.

Two weeks after leaving Tell Ahmar – by which time Thompson was in the arms of his fiancée – Lawrence walked back into Jerablus. He had visited Urfa, Birejick, Harran and the 'most glorious'[35] castle at Rum Kalaat, had slept in the houses or tents of Turks, Kurds, Armenians, Yezidis and Arabs and, as was always his intention, had

---

* Ibrahim Pasha, leader of the Milli-Kurds, had remained loyal to Sultan Abdul Hamid II even after he had been deposed by the Young Turks, and he was killed by regime assassins.

returned to Jerablus at sunset on 28 July, tired, happy, full of observations and new information, and was cheered as he walked back
into the village. 'The women of the Hoja began to sweep and clean
all the place as soon as they saw me over the hills. He himself [the
Hoja] rushed from the end of the village, and for an hour I held a
levee of all the people in the village . . . Their greetings were
something to hear.'[36]

There were two reasons for the welcome. The first was to do
with their tradition of hospitality, and the friendship Lawrence had
encouraged during the season's dig. The other was to do with the
work that Lawrence and his colleagues had brought them. At Birejick
some days earlier he had received a message to say that 'the Kelaat
[at Carchemish] was sad',[37] which was to say that it was empty and
the workers were sad. None of them had worked beyond their own
fields since Lawrence and Thompson had closed the digs and, if
they did not return, there was little prospect of any other paid work
in that remote corner. But he was to discover that there was a limit
to their welcome.

'I am very well,' he wrote home the next day, 'and en route now
for Aleppo . . . I am probably going now to stop wandering in
Ramadan. I dare hardly ask for food from a Mohammedan house,
and Christians are not common enough.'[38] As so often with his
letters home, there was more to the story than he wanted his mother
to know. She would have guessed as much, had she known that
Ramadan was still four weeks away. So why was he stopping now
and heading to Aleppo?

That evening, he settled into the house of the Hoja, Hamoudi.
Sheikh Hamoudi ibn Sheikh Ibrahim el Awassi of the tribe of
Damarkhan, to give him his full name, was the thirty-year-old son
of a man who, in that region, was considered wealthy. Like Dahoum,
the young water carrier, Hamoudi stood out from the other workers:
there was something commanding in his manner, which had made
him the obvious choice for Hoja or headman on the excavations.
Now, when he brought Lawrence a dinner of bread, eggs, yoghurt
and *ayran*, the salted yoghurt drink, the young man was touched by
the gesture. 'The Hoja (refusing to eat with me) went out and closed
the door after him: this is the highest politeness I have ever met

from an Arab.'[39] No doubt Hamoudi wanted to show respect to one of the 'kings' who had brought – and he hoped would continue to bring – work to his family and the village. Perhaps the Hoja was also already aware of something that would be unmistakable the following day.

Lawrence admitted to having a headache all evening, although he slept well on Hamoudi's roof and was up before sunrise, along with the rest of the village. He left some instructions about stores and then set off for the mound, intending to measure the floor of the palace, which they had exposed just before closing the digs. 'Hoja started with me,' he later wrote in his journal, 'but my distemper of the past two days increased suddenly, so I went on alone. Then it developed unexpectedly in a sharp attack of dysentery.' He was seriously ill. One of the biggest risks with dysentery, if that was what he had (it might have been typhoid), is dehydration, and in the heat of July in Syria the risk would have been greater still, especially with someone so determined to test their body as Lawrence. But even he now realised that this was a problem, so he found a quiet spot on the mound and lay on his back through the morning and midday. 'About 3, I sat up and tried to dress, but fainted promptly for about an hour, and again when I made a second try. Under the circumstances,' he wrote without a hint of irony, 'I was afraid to go near the edge of the pit with the measuring tape, so could not work.'[40]

However rudimentary his medical knowledge, he knew he was seriously ill, so when he finally made it back to Hamoudi's house, he gave himself a dose of arrowroot, mixed with milk; this ought to have soothed his stomach. He also sent someone to Birejick to bring a carriage because as he finally admitted, 'Cannot possibly continue tramp in this condition. Can hardly lift hand to write this.' If his strength had gone, at least his sense of humour was still intact, as he confessed that he had 'dreamed when fainting of milk and soda! Sublime.'[41]

Hamoudi tried to keep the young Englishman indoors the following day, but failed. When Lawrence did go out, mid-morning, he fainted again and gashed his cheek on a stone. 'A good deal of internal trouble,' he recorded that day. 'Up three four and five times in the nine hours and had headache besides.'[42]

On the second day of his confinement, Lawrence wrote that the Hoja had been 'awfully good all these days, with me making quite unprecedented demands on his time and patience. But poor man, a most dreadful bore as well, does his best by five or six repeats to get every idea of his into my thick head, which usually understands before he speaks.'[43] The seriousness of his illness can be gauged by a story Hamoudi later told Ernest Altounyan: 'when it appeared that he [Lawrence] would be very ill, the neighbours came around and advised me to put him out, lest he should die and his family should suspect me and the government put me in prison. I refused to listen; but before he lost consciousness he called me and said, "Don't be afraid, Hamoudi. See, here on this paper I have written to my father to say that if I die you are not the cause." So I fed him with milk and nursed him till he was well.'[44]

One person Lawrence seems not to have found boring during his illness was Dahoum, who came to look after him on each of the four days he was in bed. When, on 3 August, he felt strong enough to leave, albeit on horseback, Dahoum went with him. Before then, something occurred which Lawrence either did not understand or chose not to record, even in his own notebook. What he did note was that 'the bottom fell out of the Hoja's hospitality on a sudden'.[45] It 'fell out' when Lawrence asked to borrow Hamoudi's horse to ride to the next village, Membidj. Hamoudi not only refused, he even suggested that Lawrence move to Dahoum's house and stay there until he had recovered. Why would he do this? What had upset the Hoja so much? Was he still worried that the *khawaja* might die and bring trouble to his house? This kind of illness can turn your mind when the fever grips, so was Lawrence delirious? Was there a problem of payment for the care he had received, or a lack of payment? Or had Hamoudi understood and taken offence at the fact that the foreigner was more interested in the teenager?

In the end, Lawrence hired a horse from someone else in Jerablus and rode to Membidj. Dahoum went with him on the pretext that Lawrence had no small change to pay for his services. They parted at the river crossing on Friday morning, 4 August. The following night, he was at Baron's Hotel in Aleppo, well fed and looking forward to a good bed. Perhaps he would also have time to consider the fact that both of his 'tramps' had ended badly – he had been attacked and robbed on one, seriously ill on the other. Both had involved him lying to his parents and both had been cut short. He had described himself as 'a wanderer after sensations', but he now knew that there were some sensations he could do without.

The following morning he was awake at 5. Feeling 'not very well',[46] he decided to stay at Baron's until late afternoon, reading and writing. In a letter to Hogarth that morning he announced that 'I have reached civilisation at last, and am vastly content with its beds.'[47] He exaggerated the length of his walk – he had managed just over two weeks, not the month he mentioned to his mentor. He did at least admit to having gone down with dysentery and having put an early end to his walking plans for the summer. Other plans, however, were looking more promising, for a letter had come from Hogarth with the news that, even if there were no second season, there was still work to be done at the site. Lawrence replied that 'if there is a second season (and there should be I am certain, if only to save the B.M.'s face) try & have Gregori sent to us. He would have, I am convinced, saved us a lot this year: the Hoja is no use as a digger, and we (pianissimo) weren't very brilliant either.'[48]

He spent four nights in Aleppo and, although still extremely ill – his last night was one of 'high fever, great sweating and delirium. Worst night have ever had'[49] – he did visit Raphael Fontana and his wife, made enquiries about the camera stolen two years earlier and went to the souks with Haj Wahid to look for antiques and embroideries. The Haj put him on the train to Damascus, with a watermelon. He stayed in Damascus long enough to find an authentic chainmail shirt for his brass-rubbing friend Charles ffoulkes, and continued to Beirut with the twenty-nine-pound 'shirt' in a sack. In Beirut he checked into the Deutscher Hof, the German hotel, and from there, still weak, feverish and occasionally fainting, wrote three notes that have a bearing on this story.

The first was to Noel Rieder, the six-year-old son of his French teacher at Miss Holmes's American School. In it, he announced that the British consular official James Elroy Flecker was on his way to Jebail. Flecker had been languishing in the British Embassy at Constantinople, struggling with his consular examinations, until a staff shortage forced the authorities to send him to Beirut. On the way out, he had married an intelligent, strong-minded Greek woman, Hellé, who would need to be resourceful as well, for her newlywed husband, whom she called Roy, was a man with an ability to annoy people and attract trouble.* Flecker, at twenty-six, had already contracted TB and was often sick. He was also far from happy to be in Beirut. 'It's a long way away,' he wrote to a friend in England, 'a filthy town, pleasant country, camels, palms, missionaries.'[50] With Oxford and literature in common, he and Lawrence quickly became friends, with Flecker calling him 'a strange boy who tramps Syria on foot and digs Hittites for Hogarth'.[51] Lawrence, in spite of the dysentery, noted that he had 'been doing little but talk to Flecker and his wife.'[52] Lawrence ended his note to the boy by telling him that he had been crying crocodile tears, and telling him to brush his hair.

The second note Lawrence wrote from the Beirut hotel was to Noel's mother, Emily Rieder, to share the news that he would be in Jerablus for the winter – 'not for the joy of fragments of antiquity (mostly reburied by us) but for the buying of stolen ones'.[53] There was also news that the German team of engineers laying the railway to Baghdad had decided to run their track through ancient Carchemish and to ford the Euphrates right in front of their excavations at the *tell*. So he was also going back to curb 'the stone-loving instincts of the railway builders. If I can manage it not a cut stone of Carchemish shall decorate their embankments.'[54]

The final note from Beirut, written in his canvas-covered book on the morning of Sunday 12 August after another fever-addled night, simply says, 'Left Beyrqut about 11 A.M. All over.'

---

* On arrival in Beirut, for instance, the consular cavass (an armed attendant), 'a magnificent, though elderly Druse, as fierce-looking as one could wish, with his large curved sword', came to clear their bags through customs but ended up in a fight with an official who suspected that they were smuggling tobacco.

10

If the Italians Permit . . .

He just has the faith to let him walk in the dark without tripping.

Will Lawrence writing about Ned, 11 June 1914[1]

Winter 1911–12

'I AM DUE IN Beyrout Dec. 10 [1911]. My orders are to go on as quick as possible to Carchemish: inspect it: return to Egypt: go to Mr. Flinders Petrie for a month, get back to Syria: go and build me a house on the mound: get back to Aleppo: bring out Woolley (new chief), and the stores, and dig for three months. Mr. Hogarth comes out early May. If the Italians permit, this programme will be.'[2] There was so much information in Lawrence's letter to Emily Rieder, written from Oxford in November, that it was clear his adventures in the East were far from 'all over'.

He had reached home in the second half of August and retired to bed with what he described as malaria complicated by lingering dysentery. 'But don't imagine I am ill,' he wrote in his typically obtuse manner to Vyvyan Richards, who had complained about not seeing him, 'merely a hopeless weakness that sits me down after a hundred yards is done on foot, and also I cannot go upstairs save crab-wise.'[3] If he lacked the strength to visit Richards or to work on his Crusader castles book, he was at least able to write to *The Times*. The paper had published Hogarth's report of progress at Carchemish the previous month. On 6 August, Harry Pirie-Gordon, who had lent Lawrence a map of Crusader castles for his 1909 walk, wrote to the editor reporting 'lamentable proceedings in Upper Syria

133

and Mesopotamia',[4] where the citadels at Aleppo, Urfa and Birejick were at risk of demolition. Lawrence followed up the next day with his first piece of writing in a major publication, accusing the Young Turk government of vandalism:

> Every one who has watched the wonderful strides that civilization is making in the hands of the Young Turks will know of their continued efforts to clear from the country all signs of the evil of the past. They may not know, however, that this spirit is gaining ground in the provinces. All visitors to Aleppo will have seen the great castle that rules it from every part, with its ring of battlements and its memories of prehistoric, Hittite, Assyrian, and Roman dominion. This great mass is now to be cleared away and levelled, and one of the prominent Levantine financiers of the town has the project of constructing there a new quarter for the poorest inhabitants on the lines of the London East-end. The property will soon be put up to auction, and there are strong hopes that the end will be achieved.

The letter then mentioned the threat to the castle at Urfa, where 'a beginning has been made by the clearance of the old Greek town walls; as these were one of the largest as well as one of the most complete circuits in the Turkish Empire, there can be no two opinions as to the improvements effected'. Finally there were the castles at Birejick and 'Rum Kaleh'. 'It is hoped the coming of the Baghdad Railway may mean its final conversion to modern uses. If so, this will be the second benefit of the sort conferred by the railway, since the ruins of Carchemish are to provide materials for the approaches to the new iron girder bridge over the Euphrates. Everybody will sympathize with these latest and most worthy efforts of the Constitution Government to let a little light into the darker provinces.'[5] Lawrence did at least have the sense and the discretion to sign his letter 'the Traveller, Aleppo', but Hogarth knew who had written it and he was unimpressed – not with the sentiment, which he shared, but with so public an attack on people who had the power to stop their work. Yet it was Hogarth, patron and mentor, who had offered Lawrence a way back to the Middle East.

Hogarth had suggested to Kenyon that they move their attention to the mound at Tell Ahmar, but the Imperial Ottoman Museum in Constantinople – the organisation that controlled archaeological work in the empire – had written to Kenyon to say that they hoped the team would return to Carchemish. From this it was understood that the authorities in Constantinople would issue only one permit and that would be for Carchemish. More than this, there was another pressing reason for the British team to return in the winter, as Lawrence was to discover several days later.

Hogarth had been impressed with the way Lawrence had taken to archaeology with no previous training or background knowledge, and he would need the young man's expertise with pottery for the coming season. Thompson, however, had impressed him less, and Hogarth was disappointed that he had agreed to wrap up the dig so quickly. As he was unwilling to leave his newlywed wife behind, he was obliged to back out of the excavations,* which left Hogarth free to approach C. Leonard Woolley to take over the dig.

Woolley was an Oxford graduate, and former Assistant Keeper of Antiquities at the Ashmolean,† known to both Hogarth and Lawrence. His problem, when Hogarth approached him, was availability for he was part of a University of Pennsylvania team excavating in Nubia. In this winter of 1911, he was expected to work with them until the following February. Hogarth persuaded the thirty-year-old to travel to Carchemish after the Nubia dig. Once this was agreed, Hogarth wrote to Kenyon that Woolley had plenty of experience of running an excavation and 'we have Lawrence who knows people and place'. Kenyon was persuaded, which left the lingering problem of lack of funds, and even that Hogarth was about to solve, although quite by chance.

Walter Morrison is one of the shadow figures of this story, which is a strange comment to make about a man who had graduated from Oxford with a first-class degree in classics, had inherited a fortune (worth the equivalent of £30 million today), developed business interests around the world and was a member of Parliament. It would

---

* Thompson stayed in Surrey for the next two years, excavated in Egypt in 1913 and fought in Mesopotamia in World War I.

† Woolley's reputation today rests on his work in the 1920s at the Sumerian city of Ur, where he discovered the royal cemetery, and earned himself a knighthood for services to archaeology.

be hard to hide in the shadows with that sort of profile and yet that is what he did. He made significant donations to his old university, including £30,000 for a readership and £50,000 to the Bodleian Library, but always on the understanding that the gift would remain anonymous. He also put considerable money into some of his other enduring passions, one of which was the study of the Holy Land and Near East: he was the founding benefactor of the Palestine Exploration Fund, bought them their London headquarters and sat on their committee for decades, encouraging the mapping of the Holy Land, which he thought 'was so obviously a duty for the English nation to undertake'. Morrison had personally chosen Lieutenant Horatio Kitchener of the Royal Engineers, the man who would become British Secretary of State for War at the outbreak of World War I, for the 1874 survey team. By 1911, the great benefactor was seventy-five years old, but still very active and very low profile. He was still generous too, as he showed that autumn when he attended Hogarth's lecture about the work at Carchemish and the challenge of Hittite archaeology: at the end of it, he handed over a cheque for £5,000 to ensure that the excavations continued.

'You may have guessed who he is,' Hogarth wrote to Kenyon. 'If so don't, please, communicate your guess to anyone at present.'[6] The anonymous nature of the donation has encouraged speculation that Morrison was a 'front' and that the British government was funding the excavations as a cover for an intelligence-gathering operation. But ten years later, soon after Morrison's death, Kenyon wrote in The Times that 'it is a duty to say now, as it would have been a pleasure to say in his lifetime, that it is to him [Morrison] that scholars are indebted for the successful excavations on the site of the Hittite capital, Carchemish'.[7] When Kenyon added £2,000 of museum funds, the excavations at Jerablus were assured for several years.

All Lawrence knew was that work would resume and, on 9 November, he wrote to Emily Rieder to explain that 'I am very busy, for it is the *pottery* (O the despised pottery!) which is the reason for our second year's dig. I am in the seventh heaven or thereabouts as a result.'[8] With Woolley unavailable until February, Lawrence assumed he would spend the time building a house on site, so they would be closer to the digs. But the great organiser had other plans for Lawrence and had written to tell Professor (and later Sir) William Flinders Petrie about this 'very unusual type'.

At fifty-eight years of age, Petrie was already a legend. Self-taught, physically imposing and with a number of eccentric habits, he was the first professor of Egyptology at the University of London. He had done more than anyone alive to turn what until the end of the nineteenth century had been the amateur hobby of antiquarianism into the science of archaeology. Hogarth had worked with Petrie in Egypt in 1894–5, and the Professor valued Hogarth's opinion. So he would have been intrigued to read about a young man 'whom I feel quite sure you would approve of and like. He has very wide and exact archaeological knowledge, though not of Egyptian things, and, in view of his being employed in the future by the British Museum or others, I should very much like him to get some experience of your School, particularly in tomb digging. I think if you put him to help, for example, on a prehistoric tomb site you would not regret it . . . for I can assure you that he really is worth-while.' Hogarth mentioned three other points he thought Petrie should know about his protégé: that he spoke 'a good deal of Arabic', although his Syrian dialect would have mystified some Egyptians; that he would probably come down from Syria on foot (a slight exaggeration); and that 'he is extremely indifferent to what he eats or how he lives'.[9] How could the Professor refuse?

Lawrence arrived not on foot but by boat from Beirut, having first made a brief visit to Carchemish. When he finally sailed from Beirut, storms and quarantine delayed him and he did not reach Cairo until 14 January 1912. He may, as Hogarth had claimed, have been indifferent to how he lived, but he was not averse to comfort and he checked into the Bristol Hotel, which boasted the 'finest situation in the centre' of the city and 'famous cuisine'.[10]* Facing the large expanse of Ezbekieh Square, within sight of the more famous Shepheard's Hotel, the Bristol was described around the time Lawrence stayed there as suiting 'people to whom the rigid observance of

* In an earlier incarnation, as the Hôtel d'Orient, the hotel had hosted the novelists Gustave Flaubert and William Thackeray.

formalities is irksome':[11] evening dress was not obligatory for dinner. It also charged about half the Shepheard's rate. It then took him two days to find the Professor.

Petrie was in a boarding house at Helwan – Hélouan-les-Bains as it was grandly called at the time – a suburb a half-hour train ride south of central Cairo. Helwan had been famous for the curative properties of its sulphur springs for at least 3,500 years, so it appealed to a famous archaeologist suffering from gout, a hernia and a cold. They had a brief meeting at the hotel, after which the Professor sent Lawrence back to the city.

His first glimpse of Cairo was brief and specific. Instead of visiting the Egyptian Museum and the Pyramids, he walked around the old city and visited the Museum of Islamic Art, which impressed him. The streets of the old city might not compare with his memories of Aleppo, but they did have 'the most glorious architecture'.[12] After two days, he left for Kafr Ammar, fifty miles south up the Nile. Hilda Petrie, who followed with the Professor some days later, described seeing 'the pyramids of Abusir, Gizeh, Saqqara, and Dahshur . . . then Lisht pyramids where the Americans have worked. Lastly we stopped at Kafr Ammâr, and were met by cook-boy Mohammed and two other men to carry baggage. Two travelling dealers showed us many antiquities in a lonely little courtyard among palm-groves, and later we rejoined our men and tramped with them across three canals by bridges, and the cultivation, and crossed the muddy bottom of another canal and joined the dry desert.'[13] The bean fields were in flower. Petrie's three assistants, Mackay, Engelbach and Elverson, were staying in mud huts, while tents had been set up for Petrie and his wife. 'Here too is Lawrence, a very good man,' wrote Hilda Petrie, a woman Lawrence found insufferable, 'arrived from Carchemish to put in some weeks' training with Flinders for workmen, tomb-work, bakhshish [sic] system, and returning to Carchemish next month to dig.'[14]

The site, called Tarkhan, was a burial ground within sight of several pyramids, but although there were remains from the beginning of history, Lawrence was started on eighth-century BCE tombs and within days he was unhappy:

we go out every morning about 8 a.m. after breakfast, and look at tombs. About 15 men and 20 boys are digging for them: they find them in sand and flint soil, the edge of the great desert of Africa, where it dips down in flats to the cultivated lands bordering the Nile. They scrape the soft sand with hoes – one's feet sink in it each step – and where they do not feel rotten stone at the tool depth, they hollow out. In a few minutes, if they disclose a rectangular form of 4' by 3'6", they know they are at the top of a well-tomb. They then dig down from 8 to 15 feet in the same soft sand, filling of the shaft, and at the bottom find a room, still clear of debris, unless the roof has fallen. In these rooms are piled up three or four mummy-bodies, in rotting coffins with great store of bead-nets along their length, and amulets, and sometimes pottery . . . It is a strange sight to see the men forcing open a square wooden coffin, and taking out the painted anthropoid envelope within, and splitting this up also to drag out a mummy, not glorious in bright wrappings, but dark brown, fibrous, visibly rotting – and then the thing begins to come to pieces, and the men tear off its head, and bare the skull, and the vertebrae drop out, and the ribs and legs and perhaps only one poor amulet is the result.[15]

He found these methods crude and even shocking. He knew that archaeology was still in its infancy, and was practised in many different ways. But the issue here, for him, lay in the different nature of the two excavations. At Carchemish, he was exposing a city. They had found few human remains, so his imagination had been free to inhabit the place with people of his own construction. At Kafr Ammar, there were no ancient palaces or houses, just a pyramid in the distance, on a clear day, and the dead, which he was finding beneath his feet and bringing to the light. He spent the first days watching the digs, stringing rows of ancient beads and copying texts. 'Even our firewood comes from 24th dynasty coffins,' he wrote home, 'and our charcoal brazier first performed that office in the days of the fall of Carchemish.' He had already decided that he was not cut out for what he considered body snatching. He had also decided he did not like Egyptians and called them:

horribly ugly, very dirty, dull, low-spirited, without any of the vigour of the self-confident independence of our men [in Carchemish].

Besides the fanaticism of the country is deplorable, and the treatment of women most un-European: most of the Petrie workmen have several wives, and have had many more, and one could not stand or work close to them for a few minutes without catching fleas or lice. Nor would one talk to them with the delicious free intimacy of the men at Carchemish, They either got surly, or took liberties. They were frenetic, and querulous, foul-mouthed, and fawning . . .[16]

He was looking forward to being back in Syria, until Petrie arrived and Lawrence's mood changed.

Petrie's presence transformed the excavations, which he now found enjoyable, even though their first on-site meeting was far from auspicious. When Lawrence arrived wearing his Carchemish work gear – football shorts and Magdalen blazer – Petrie took one look and said, 'They don't play cricket here.'[17] Lawrence, remembering this some twenty years later, noted: 'he seemed to think [blazer and shorts] was better for cricket. He meant football, I expect.'[18] But however much he was put out – still unsure of himself, Lawrence hated to be criticised – he soon displayed the same mixed emotion for Petrie as he had for Hogarth, profound respect and gentle mocking. So although he thought his new patron was 'intensely self-centred and self-standing', he admitted to his parents that 'I like him exceedingly, but rather as one thinks of a cathedral, or something immovable but by earthquake. He is a quite inspired archaeologist.'[19] Petrie's eccentric rules amused the young man: why, he wondered, insist on banning pens, even for letter writing? To Hogarth, Lawrence described Petrie as 'enormous fun, with systems of opening tins and cleaning his teeth and all else', and wondered 'why hasn't he died of ptomaine poisoning?'[20] from his habit of scraping mould off half-eaten tins of food. But the best account of the venerable archaeologist went into a letter for Emily Rieder. 'No one but I would have achieved a letter at all from a Petrie dig. A Petrie dig is a thing with a flavour of its own: tinned kidneys mingle with mummy-corpses and amulets in the soup: my bed is all gritty with prehistoric alabaster jars of unique types – and my feet at night keep the bread-box from the rats. For ten mornings in succession I have seen the sun rise as I breakfasted, and we come home at nightfall after lunching at the bottom of a 50 foot shaft, to draw pottery silhouettes or string bead-necklaces . . .'

Then, having revealed why he had time to write – he had had another malaria attack – he described:

> the great man of the camp – He's about 5' 11" high, white haired, grey bearded, broad and active, with a voice that splits when excited, and a constant feverish speed of speech: he is a man of ideas and systems, from the right way to dig a temple to the only way to clean one's teeth. Also he only is right in all things: all his subs. have to take his number of sugar lumps in their tea, his species of jam with potted tongue, or be dismissed as official bound unprogressists [sic]. Further he is easy-tempered, full of humour, and fickle to a degree that makes him delightfully quaint, and a constant source of joy and amusement in his camp.[21]

No wonder Lawrence liked him.

Contrary to his suggestions, it was not all play. With Petrie there, they were digging a new site and soon hit what Lawrence described as 'probably the richest and largest prehistoric cemetery in Egypt'.[22] They opened one hundred graves in the first week, each packed with grave goods. There was no Tutankhamun-style gold – that was ten years off and hundreds of miles to the south – but they soon had a hoard of coffins and beds, jars and pots, delicate ivory spoons and heavy bronze tools, baskets woven more than four thousand years earlier, shrouds and, of course, mummies.

Petrie was clearly impressed by his young guest's potential as an archaeologist because, although they spent only a couple of weeks together before he returned to Syria, Petrie asked if he would be interested in running his own excavation in Bahrain. Petrie believed that these early Egyptians whose tombs they were now opening at Tarkhan had travelled through the Red Sea and into the Indian Ocean, and he was confident that Bahrain, as one of their staging posts, would turn up interesting discoveries.* For someone of Petrie's standing to make such an offer to a twenty-three-year-old archaeologist with one season's experience is a sign of just how exceptional Lawrence appeared, even at this early stage of his development.

Lawrence was flattered, especially as Petrie explained that the

---

* Petrie's hunch about Bahrain was sound: in the 1950s, Danish archaeologists found one of the world's largest ancient cemeteries at Dilmun.

funding was assured for Bahrain, and he wrote to Hogarth to ask for his opinion, at the same time assuring his mentor that he would commit to dig at Carchemish for as long as the work continued. He left for Cairo on 30 January 1912.

The plan he had shared with Emily Rieder in November – Egypt with Petrie, then Carchemish to build an expedition house at the *tell*, Aleppo to collect Leonard Woolley, the new Director, followed by three months' digging – had one proviso: 'If the Italians permit'. The reference was to the conflict that had broken out between the Italians and Turks over control of what we now know as Libya, the North African *vilayets* of Tripolitana, Fezzan and Cyrenaica.

The Turks had ruled this part of North Africa since 1551, but the Italians cited various rights granted to them by the 1884 Congress of Berlin, at which Europe's powers had agreed to areas of influence and control on the African continent. The Italians were being opportunistic: they could sense the weakness at the heart of government in Constantinople following the fall of the Sultan. Claiming that the majority of Libyans were anti-Turk and therefore, by some dubious deduction, pro-Italian, Rome had issued an ultimatum on 27 September 1911 that Turkey must cede Libya or face a fight. To back up the threat, an Italian fleet appeared off Tripoli the following day.

The Young Turk government immediately capitulated by offering Italy control of Libya while maintaining nominal Turkish sovereignty. A similar situation had existed in Egypt since 1882, when a British army had invaded; Egypt was still nominally part of the Ottoman Empire, there was an Egyptian ruler or khedive, Abbas Hilmi Pasha (himself of Albanian origin), but British officials ran the country. The Italians rejected the offer and attacked Tripoli on 3 October. The ensuing war saw Libyans fight alongside Turks against an Italian army of some 100,000 men. Before Lawrence left Egypt for Syria, two things of note had happened: the Italians had made the first use of aircraft in wartime and, in the process, had invented aerial bombardment.* The Turks, lacking anti-aircraft weapons, became

---

* Lieutenant Giulio Gavotti was the first to use aerial bombardment when he 'decided to try to throw bombs from the aeroplane' at a Turkish position on 1 November 1911.

the first to shoot down an aircraft with conventional rifles. More significant than this was that while Libyans continued to fight along-side Turks against the Italians, people elsewhere in the empire observed Turkey's military inefficiency and what looked like a lack of political will. When Italy declared sovereignty over Libya in November 1911, many of the Sultan's subjects dared to dream of independence.

Lawrence had described Egyptians as deplorably fanatical, a verdict with which many foreigners in Cairo would have agreed. Two years earlier, in February 1910, the Egyptian Prime Minister, Boutros Ghali, had been assassinated in Cairo. The assassin, who was caught and sentenced to death, explained that he had killed Boutros Ghali because he was helping to continue British control of Egypt. The killer belonged to a secret cell called the Society of Fraternal Solidarity (Jam'iyyat al-Tadamun al-Akhawi), whose slogan was 'Egypt for Egyptians'. Following the assassin's confession, a new Egyptian Secret Service Bureau was created, al-Qalam al-Siyari.* By the time of Lawrence's visit to Egypt, the Bureau had compiled a 'strictly confidential' report on twenty-six secret nationalist societies and admitted that there could be many more. 'The enclosed statements', the report made clear, 'have been drawn up with the greatest difficulty.'[23]

Lawrence could not have known about this confidential briefing – not even the conspiracy theorists who believe he was already engaged in intelligence gathering for the British government go so far as to suggest that he was in touch with al-Qalam al-Siyari. But there was no secret about the tense state of Egyptian politics and he would have heard more about it during the days he spent in Cairo after leaving Petrie, although his focus in the capital was on the past, not the present or future. 'Cairo is glorious,' he wrote from the Bristol Hotel. 'I have spent in all now six days here, and have been four times to the mosque of Sultan Hassan, once to the bazaars, three times to the Arab museum, twice to the Khedival Library. [The fourteenth-century mosque of] Sultan Hassan is amazing. I must come back to see it again some time, and as well to go out

* This organisation was later enlarged by Presidents Nasser, Sadat and Mubarak and still exists as the Muhabbarat, the secret police.

to see the Pyramids and the great Museum of the Egyptian things. But the real matter is that the Arab architecture, faïence, and manu-scripts are so fine that one has no time for sight-seeing.'[24]

He reached Aleppo on 2 February, expecting to find money from Kenyon to pay for the building of the new expedition house at Carchemish. But as he wrote to Flecker, 'when I got to Aleppo I found that the British Museum idiots had sent me orders to buy the site and build the house, and had forgotten to provide the funds'.[25] A week later, still in Aleppo and clearly frustrated by the delay, he complained to Hogarth. 'Seriously, I hope the money will roll up soon, because it is now Feb 10 and the house will not be built in a fortnight.'[26] Ten days later, still in Aleppo but much calmer – it was, he decided, 'a splendid place to spend a week in'[27] – after days trawling the souks with Haj Wahid, he had 'all the curio-dealers of Aleppo' calling for him all day – 'simply a queue by the time I have finished breakfast'. By then he had bought a heavy camel-hair mantle 'such as Bedouin sheikhs wear: Baghdad made: very warm and beautiful. With this, if I sat on the North Pole, it would melt.'[28] When the money arrived – £50 – he left for Carchemish.

Lawrence left Haj Wahid to attend to the heavily laden mules while he went ahead, covering the thirty miles on foot and stopping for the night in a town called Al Bab, where he took a room in the old khan. Haj Wahid and the mules finally arrived at 9.30 p.m. He set out alone again the following morning and this time met several people he knew, as well as two groups who did not know who he was. 'They both abused me as an Italian ('talian and Talaman–Italian & German, are the same out here) and apologized profusely when they learnt I was English.'[29] Clearly not everyone in the prov-inces was happy that the Italians had the upper hand against the Turks.

The war took a dramatic turn the next day when two Italian cruisers appeared off Beirut at dawn with orders to clear the harbour of Turkish naval vessels. The two Turkish naval ships, a torpedo boat and an antiquated corvette, were outgunned and knew it. At 8.30 a.m., the Italian admiral sent an ultimatum to the Vali of Beirut demanding that the two ships surrender within half an hour. The Governor was aware that he had no alternative and sent a message agreeing to their demands. But the Governor's reply did not reach the Italians until after 9 a.m., by which time they had already opened fire.

It was one of the least glorious of the many naval encounters staged in the Mediterranean. The Italian destroyers were far offshore when they first opened fire, at a distance that made them both untouchable and unreliable in their aim. Flecker, who was in Beirut, later wrote that 'the report of a cannon – a single and extremely noisy shot of warning – roused me from sleep. The dreaded Italians had come.' The Italian ships seemed so large, the Turkish torpedo boat so small, he thought the Italians could have winched the latter on deck and used it as a launch. 'The Italians sent five shells over the town by mistake, and one each through two banks. About a hundred interested spectators on the quay, struck by the bursting shells, paid the penalty of their rashness. As for the Turks, no watch had been kept on the boat; the officers all slept on shore and only a few reached the ship in time.' While the Italians were sinking the ships and killing bystanders on the quay, Flecker himself was in a carriage. He reported:

> in the centre of town, things were, as the French say, 'well otherwise serious.' At the first shots the Arabs fled howling indoors in senseless panic; recovering, they looted the barracks and attempted to murder all Christians, myself included, and the Governor only just succeeded in restoring order at the risk of his life . . . As for me, an extremely unpleasant crowd, having just succeeded in looting rifles from the barracks, stopped my carriage, and sticking their bayonets uncomfortably near my stomach, swore I was the Italian Consul. I said no, but that I was a splendid Englishman. At that moment the cannon of the cruisers began to roar again, making everyone more excited and dangerous than ever. I cocked my revolver in my pocket determined to shoot through my coat at one particularly horrid fat man.

Deliverance came in the form of a Turkish soldier, and Flecker made it to the Deutscher Hof Hotel. To Lawrence, he told it slightly differently that he had been driving to the hotel with the Finnish Vice-Consul when they were stopped. 'The mob took us for Italians, and would have lynched us, but for the driver who stuck to his box, and a splendid police fellow, who came across to our rescue.

The Russians rewarded him with fifty pounds. Our Embassy sent him a silver cigarette case.'[30]

Later, when he thought back on the day, Flecker understood that 'it was a paltry affair of a few hours, but while it lasted it seemed like the end of the world. Unforgettable the thunder of the guns shaking the golden blue of sky and sea, while not a breath stirred the palm trees, not a cloud moved on the swan-like snows of Lebanon.'[31] Flecker's wife Hellé agreed with his apocalyptic view: 'That Italian attack marked the end of our happy days at Beyrut.'[32] It also carried severe consequences. One of them emerged a few days later, when orders came from Constantinople to expel all Italians from Aleppo, Damascus and Beirut *vilayets*. Among the sixty thousand people forced back to Italy were many families who had lived in the area for generations, including the Marcopoli family from Aleppo. Originally Greeks from Chios, they had been trading and banking in Aleppo for a century, acting as consuls for Portugal since 1866 and widely trading in antiquities.*

The Italian bombardment, and the expulsions, led to talk of the fall of the five-hundred-year Ottoman rule. When Lawrence crossed the Sajur River by the footbridge, still far ahead of Haj Wahid and the mules, he fell into conversation with 'an Armenian of Urfa, who didn't care what or who took the Government, so long as they ousted the Turks. He was more bitter against the Mohammedans than anyone I have met out here.'[33]

There was no shortage of problems waiting for Lawrence at Jerablus and for the first time he had to face them alone. Not the least of these was the challenge of buying the land on which the ruins of the ancient city of Carchemish stood. To do this, he needed to identify the owner, which took some time, but he turned out to be someone called Hassan Agha. When Lawrence approached him to buy the land, he was told it would cost £180. The young archaeologist knew the government was intending to expropriate it and would pay no more than £18 as compensation. He had also

---

* Lawrence and Woolley both bought cheaply from Marcopoli 'the day before they were expelled' (HL p. 195).

learned enough about haggling for antiquities to know that this was Hassan Agha's opening offer and he was confident the price would come down. More worrying was the behaviour of the officer in charge of the troops sent to protect the excavators and whatever they uncovered, because Lawrence now discovered that he was forbidden to excavate or to start work on building an expedition house until his credentials had been checked with the authorities in Constantinople. At the same time, German engineers had arrived to work on the next section of the Baghdad Railway. Although Lawrence managed to stop them laying track through the excavations, he reported that 'the railway has brought a horrible crew – all the sweepings of Aleppo'.[34] It also brought his new director, Leonard Woolley.

The two men had already met when Woolley was Assistant Keeper at the Ashmolean, so Lawrence knew there would be no clash of characters. But there would be a delicate balance between them that would need some tact on his part if it were to be maintained. Because while Woolley would be running the dig, would have the authority and had far greater experience of archaeological excavations, it was Lawrence who knew the Carchemish site well and the workforce better, who had a wider knowledge of Hittite history and antiquities, and now even had a rapport with the engineers laying railway track along the side of the ancient city and an understanding of the politics of the region. During the fortnight he waited for Woolley and for permission to start work to arrive from Constantinople, Lawrence had made peace with the German engineers. He had realised that they needed stone and soil to build their railway embankments. He also knew that in spite of the increased excavation budget, there was still no plan to lay a track to remove the spoil from their diggings: it would be carried out on men's backs. So Lawrence offered the stone and rubble to the railway company, on the understanding that they remove it from the site. The Germans agreed, and both sides were happy.

The army officer at Carchemish was proving harder to appease. Even after Woolley arrived, on 13 March, he refused to allow work to resume, informing them that the Kaimmakam of Birejick would not allow it: the permit to dig had been issued to David Hogarth, who was not there. The officer did not know who Woolley was, and nor did he care. The reason for this difficulty lies in something mentioned by Consul Fontana to Kenyon at the British Museum. Kenyon had written to inform Fontana that they were intending to resume work at Carchemish early in 1912, to which Fontana had replied with the news of administrative changes. 'Unfortunately the Sanjak of Ourfa, within which Jerablus is situated, has now been detached from and made independent of the Vilayet of Aleppo, so that the Governor General now can no longer take direct action in connection with Jerablus.'[35] In other words, the archaeologists were at the mercy of the local officials, and their friends at the British Consulate could do nothing to help them.

Photographs of Woolley show a refined man in his thirties, his thinning hair swept back – none of Lawrence's shaggier locks – a straight nose and a soft jaw. He looks the archetype of a man of learning and culture. Woolley was the third of eight children born to a clergyman in London's East End and, like Hogarth, he needed to earn his keep. He had studied hard at school and won a scholarship to read theology at New College, Oxford, which was a significant achievement: very few from his type of school were ever accepted to Oxford, even fewer with a scholarship. But something went wrong at Oxford and he finished with a mediocre degree. His final interview with the Warden of his college deserves recording. The Warden was the Reverend William Spooner, a man best remembered not for his formidable divinity and philosophy scholarship, but for the linguistic slips to which he has given his name.* It was from this pink-faced, short-sighted man that young Woolley heard he would not be offered the Magdalen College fellowship that he coveted (not even a demyship, which Lawrence was later given). Nor would he be able to fulfil his original intention of taking holy orders. When Spooner asked what he proposed to do, Woolley explained the future he had decided on: 'I want to be a schoolmaster; I've done a little at odd times and I like it awfully, so I think of going for it permanently.'

* The Reverend's habit of playing on words, only sometimes intentionally, is known as a spoonerism.

'Oh, yes,' said the Warden, 'a schoolmaster, really; well, Mr Woolley, I have decided that you shall be an archaeologist.'[36]

Like Lawrence, Woolley had learned to balance his lack of height with a physical forcefulness. This became apparent the day after he arrived at Carchemish, when he, Lawrence and Haj Wahid rode horseback to discuss permission to work at Carchemish with the Kaimmakam of Birejick.

The Crusader castle at Birejick is a huge brooding presence along the summit of a steep cliff about the river. The town spreads below it and around its lower gates. Here, at the government building, Woolley observed form by sending in his visiting card to the Kaimmakam. When there was no reply, he sent in another and waited a little longer before marching into the office to find 'an elderly man with grey hair and pointed beard, sly eyes, and flabby figure, ignorant and hardly more than literate'.[37] The old man seemed to have had an equally low opinion of the Englishmen who had stormed, uninvited, into his office and so, contrary to local custom, he did not invite them to sit. 'Lawrence and I made ourselves comfortable on the divan that ran along the walls close to his chair, and Haj Wahid stood by the door.'[38]

The Haj could be a threatening presence, but the Kaimmakam remained unimpressed. When he finally deigned to hear why they had come, he refused to allow the dig to restart. In this, he was merely following the letter of the agreement between the British Museum and the authorities in Constantinople: Woolley wished him to adopt its spirit. But, as the Kaimmakam pointed out, the permit was in Mr Hogarth's name, so unless that gentleman showed himself, work could not resume. Then he relented slightly, and said that he would accept a letter from the British Museum, in Turkish, appointing Woolley as Hogarth's deputy. Woolley, realising that this would take weeks, ran out of patience.

'I *shall* start tomorrow,' he assured the official.

'I have forbidden it, and I shall give further orders to the soldiers to stop you.'

'You have only ten men at Jerablus and I have a hundred and twenty who want to work: I shall start tomorrow.'

'If necessary I shall send more from here, but it will not be necessary.'[39]

Lawrence found it 'too funny for words to hear Woolley explaining to the Kaimmakam, that he did not mean to declare war on the Turkish Empire, but only on the Kaimmakam of Biredjik [sic]'.[40]

Woolley was now getting angry: he had not travelled out from England to be stopped by a local official. 'I only hope', he told the old man, 'that you will come at the head of your soldiers, and I shall take great pleasure in shooting you first:– for I shall certainly start tomorrow.'[41]

It was at this point that Woolley earned Lawrence's admiration because he stood up, took his revolver out of its holster and put the muzzle against the old man's left ear. 'I shall shoot you here and now unless you give me permission to start work tomorrow.' The Turk 'absolutely collapsed'. With Woolley's pistol still at his head, he wrote a note granting permission for the digs to reopen.

'Woolley came out exceedingly well,' Lawrence wrote home. But while there was no disguising his admiration for the new Director, his arrival had created problems: 'with Woolley a stranger to the country, and the language and the antiquities, I have to act as interpreter for him, always, though he is fairly fluent in Egyptian: I have to do the bargaining, and keep the accounts, for he does not know the coinage: I have to choose the workmen, for he does not know them, and to settle our plans, for he has no idea of what we can get in the country and what we cannot: and to coach him, meanwhile in things Hittite'.[42] But there was a service Woolley would soon perform for Lawrence.

The Kaimmakam of Birejick might have been forced to concede in the matter of permission, but he was far from defeated. A man who had been humiliated needed to take his revenge, and a summons was soon delivered, ordering Lawrence to appear in court charged with stealing stone from Hassan Agha, the owner of the land they were excavating. Hassan Agha had seen the Germans taking stone for their railway and, assuming that some financial deal had been done, was annoyed that he was not part of it. So he was suing Lawrence for theft, and loss of revenue.

Under a system called the Capitulations, Europeans were not

answerable to local courts in the Ottoman Empire, but could only be tried under the laws of their own countries. Lawrence would have been within his rights if he had refused to attend, but hoping to clear things up quickly he chose to present himself at the first hearing, which was to be held in the court of the Cadi.* He returned to Carchemish dismayed, having been summoned to a second hearing. Woolley attended the second hearing alongside his assistant and quickly realised that the Kaimmakam was behind the charges. Before the proceedings had gone far, Woolley interceded, reminding the Cadi that he had no jurisdiction over Lawrence. When the Cadi continued to hear the case, both archaeologists pulled their revolvers – on the Cadi and the Kaimmakam – while Haj Wahid held off the guards at the door. With such eloquent persuasion, the case was dropped and the Englishmen's reputation spread further afield.

Not everyone was impressed, however. The local government minister went so far as to complain to Raphael Fontana at the Aleppo Consulate that:

> 'these English of yours at Jerablus . . . they are doing impossible things – perfectly impossible: why, they tried to shoot the Governor and the Cadi of the Province!'
> 'Did they really shoot them?' the Consul replied.
> 'Well, no, they *threatened* to, but they did not actually *kill* them.'
> 'What a pity,' the Consul remarked gently.[43]

News of the incident even spread to Constantinople: when Woolley was next in the imperial capital, he noted that 'my reception by our then Ambassador [Sir Gerard Lowther] was hardly convivial: he seemed to think that our action had been altogether too drastic, and told me that Turkey was a civilized country'.

As a result of this trouble with Hassan Agha, the Turkish War Office claimed that the Carchemish site was a fortress or citadel and, being of strategic value, it automatically belonged to the state. Woolley pointed out that there had been no stronghold at Carchemish since the Roman legions marched north. The British Museum was allowed to continue its excavations, but Hassan Agha had his land

---

* Cadi: a judge in Islamic law.

confiscated.* Woolley later remembered that 'when all was settled above our heads we made Hassan a present of the sum for which he had originally offered to sell us the whole site'.⁴⁴

If they had been unable to buy the land, they did now have permission to continue with their excavations. They were living in tents on the site while the new house was being built – and there was a kitchen tent for Haj Wahid, which very soon had ten bullet holes through its goat-hair roof, a souvenir of the Haj's celebration of the Englishmen getting the better of the Kaimmakam. 'Carchemish is very beautiful these days,' Lawrence wrote a couple of weeks after they had settled in, 'and today we found the Hittite level in the mound-top, a pot-burial, and two sculptures. So we are very happy.'⁴⁵ Woolley also sounded happy, both with the life there and with the work to be done. From him, we have one of the clearest and most accessible descriptions of what Carchemish looked like at this time:

> To the primitive castle-builder this was an ideal site. Defended on two sides by water, with difficulty accessible from the land, it needed but little in the way of walls to make of it a fortress impregnable, and as such it was early chosen and continued long in use. Starting at the top of the mound, we have dug down over fifty feet through the accumulated debris of the ages, and still human remains meet us. Arab huts, only just hidden by the grass, give place to Armenian; beneath these are Byzantine ruins, stratum below stratum, three or four building periods to be distinguished in a few feet's depth; then the scanty remains of the Roman fort which one of the legions built to secure Europos ford; then Greek things dating from the Roman time back to the second century B.C. Below these comes Carchemish of the Hittites, again marked off into distinct levels and periods, of which the latest is the fort built or remodelled by Sargon the Assyrian when in 717 B.C., after nearly half a century of war, he had captured the capital of the Hittite Empire, and the earliest may date back to 2000 or 2500 B.C. Four thousand years of history, of sieges, and of changing population, and yet we are only some twenty feet down in the great mound.⁴⁶

* The Carchemish site remains a Turkish military base.

Beneath these levels, he knew, were the remains of Stone Age people who had also recognised the strategic value of a high vantage point over the river and surrounding flatlands.

But Carchemish was about more than identifying levels, as Lawrence had discovered. There was a beauty and much romance about the place, and if one had a lively imagination the old stones might speak as they were dragged back into the light.

> You stand there on flagged pavement or cobbled court whose polished stones have not known the tread of man's feet since Carchemish went down in smoke and tumult two thousand five hundred years ago, and about you and above are the long rows of sculptured figures, gods and beasts and fighting men, and inscriptions in honour of forgotten kings; statues of old deities; wide stairways and gates, here the ashes of doors still lie in the corners of the threshold; column-bases whose shafts were of cedar and their capitals of bronze wrought in patterns of nets and pomegranates – and the scarlet anemones push up between the stones, and the lizards sun themselves on the walls of palace or temple, and the spring wind drives the dust over the ruins of the imperial city. Very magnificent must Carchemish have been when its sculptures were gay with colour, when the sunlight glistened on its essential walls, and its sombre brick was overlaid with panels of cedar and plates of bronze; when the plumed horses rattled their chariots along its streets, and the great lords, with long embroidered robes and girdles of black and gold, passed in and out of the carved gates of its palaces, but even now, when it lies deserted and in heaps, it has perhaps in the melancholy of its ruin found a subtler charm to offset the glory of its prime.[47]

Except that it was not deserted, for the workforce was now digging, scraping, heaving six days a week – Fridays were off – and another team of men were working on the railway beyond the ruins, and building a bridge that would allow the track to cross the Euphrates and move into Mesopotamia and east towards Baghdad.

Lawrence was much relieved as Woolley eased into the job, writing that his new boss 'is getting on very well – goes down with the workmen, is dropping Egyptian hauteur and ruling-race fantasies, likes Syrian cooking and sweetmeats, and (*mirabile dictu*) our dialect! It is a pretty hard piece of work for him.'[48] This left Lawrence free to begin building somewhere for them to live.

He had said that the new house would not be finished in a fortnight, but he had originally allowed little more than a month to
build before Woolley was due out. One might be forgiven for
thinking, therefore, that he was planning nothing more than a small
stone shack for them. But this was Lawrence, dreamer of the day,
and what he planned and built was a compound with an inner
courtyard, a 'very large' sitting room, kitchen, bathroom and store
rooms, three 'museum' rooms to display exhibits from the digs, a
darkroom for Lawrence to develop photographs, bedrooms for
Woolley, Lawrence, Hogarth and Gregori, as well as one for Haj
Wahid and his harem, and others for visitors. The WC had a long-
drop that lived up to its name – forty-nine feet to the bottom. 'You
would like our stone-house,' he wrote to his mother in mid-April,
'with its wood-beamed ceiling, flat roof, Roman-mosaic floor of
birds and trees and gazelles and peacocks, and Damascus tiles on the
walls, the beaten-copper fire-hood, the beaten-copper bath, the
basalt pillars and door-mouldings.'

The mosaic he had found in a part of the ancient city they were
not excavating, being ploughed over by a farmer. To move it from
the field, he woke before dawn with a couple of helpers – Dahoum
was there – glued cloth over the tesserae and left it to dry. If done
properly (it had to be done before the heat of the day), by the
evening the mosaic should come away attached to the cloth. It was
painstaking work, but he enjoyed the challenge and by the end of
April had laid half of the floor, 'a vase in a decorative circle, with
sprays and fruits of a tree: in the foliage are two peacocks, a pheasant,
a glossy-ibis, and some ducks, geese and doves. The whole about
15 feet by 12. I got it down in one piece, but in parts tesserae were
missing, and we had two days work filling them in. The other half
is a little larger, with a design of gazelles and birds, with a large
orange tree.'[49]* Others might have found the idea of moving a
144,000-piece mosaic more trouble than it was worth, but not
a man who had cycled around England to make brass rubbings and

* Archaeologists now working at Carchemish report that 'The mosaic dating from
AD 300 is still there, with its animals and geometrical motifs, damaged along its
middle axis but fine on the sides' (email from Professor Nicolò Marchetti to author,
9 October 2013).

pieced together shards of glass and pottery recovered from building sites in Oxford.

More than the challenge and the rewarding beauty of laying down the centrepiece for their sitting-room floor, Lawrence was absorbed by an important process. As with the bungalow at Polstead Road, and later at Clouds Hill, his Dorset cottage, he was making a home in a place where he had chosen to live. And that, in turn, was part of a larger process. E. M. Forster, the novelist who became a post-war friend, writing about Lawrence in Carchemish, noted that 'whatever he did [with his hands] he did well for he had deft fingers and an exact mentality. But more important than his archaeology – in view of later developments – was his success as a human influence and a British agent. He liked, and was liked by, the workmen, both Arabs and Kurds, he began to share their lives, crack their jokes, learn about their families and friends, approximate to them in his dress.'[50] Lawrence was interested in more than just learning how to excavate, or in searching for the best *antikas* in the area, although both appealed greatly to him. As Forster was to understand, he was seduced by the place, by the way he was living in it and by the people he was living with. He was liberated by being out of his place and away from his people; and while at home he was seen as an outsider, in Syria he discovered a talent for getting on with workmen and foremen, with *zaptiehs* and even *kaimmakams* (those he did not draw his revolver on) in a way he had not done until now. In return, he was being seduced by the life and privileges he was lucky enough to have found. He had described himself as being like a king in Carchemish. That feeling grew with the arrival of Woolley and with the new responsibilities he had taken on.

The dig would last three months, until the end of June, and would then resume in the autumn, to close again when the winter came. Woolley intended to return to England for the summer and deep winter, but Lawrence had other plans. He was happier staying out of England, and was making plans to visit more Crusader castles for his Magdalen research. He was also raising the possibility of staying in Carchemish for the winter as well, on the pretext that someone needed to watch the Germans and that, if no European archaeologist were present, the railway engineers might try to quarry the site for more stone. He had already planned for the eventuality of a winter in his new house: 'for this', he wrote, 'I had a fire-place built and cold weather arrangements made'.[51] If Hogarth agreed, he would come home briefly in the autumn because the museum needed him for a while in England, and he would stay a few days in Oxford, but spend the winter in Jerablus. Then he announced, 'I would like to bring Dahoum back with me for conversation purposes.'[52] Whatever Lawrence wanted with Dahoum, it was far more than mere conversation.

Dahoum's name had been appearing in Lawrence's letters with increasing regularity since the young man had looked after him through his bout of dysentery. Lawrence had recognised his desire to improve himself, to read and learn, and he had decided to give the donkey-boy a chance. Since then Dahoum had enjoyed a change of fortune. Most days started with him giving Lawrence an hour of Arabic conversation. Although he was officially still only a water carrier, Dahoum helped bring objects to the house and was allowed to clean and arrange them. When Lawrence heard that the sheikh of Dahoum's village was taking thirty of the forty-five piastres he was paid each week, the Englishman set himself up as 'protector-of-the-poor-and-enemy-of-all-the-rich-and-in-authority'.[53] As Lawrence's workload became heavier, so he began to teach Dahoum to use his camera, although he complained that 'you have no idea how hard it is to instil elementary optics into his head in imperfect Arabic. He will put plates the wrong side out.'[54] Forster noted that now 'personal emotion entered: he became intimate with Dahoum, to whom he was passionately devoted'.[55]

Hogarth – 'Mr. Hogarth' – arrived at Carchemish in the hot days of early May. He had travelled out through Constantinople, where he had met Kaiser Wilhelm II. The Kaiser was in the Ottoman capital to broker a settlement between the Italians and Turks over Libya, at which he failed. How Hogarth managed to see him is less certain. From the German ruler he had won an assurance that the Baghdad Railway would not encroach on the archaeological site. So he was feeling pleased with the state of affairs when he arrived at Jerablus, and he wrote a glowing report to Kenyon at the British

IF THE ITALIANS PERMIT . . .

Museum. 'Lawrence is even more useful this year than last, as he has now quite mastered the local Arabic and through his residence here after the dig last year has come to know all the villagers intimately.'[56] A week later he went further and wrote that Lawrence 'now knows the local people and their speech very well, and having had longer training in Hittite things than Woolley, is an invaluable adjutant to the latter'.[57] Because of their progress, Hogarth went on to suggest, both men should be retained for as long as the dig might last. He also felt that Lawrence should be paid for what he was doing. The sum of fifteen shillings a day was suggested and, while only half of what Woolley received, it was in addition to his expenses and his university grant. It would give him enough by the end of each season to pay for his travels, to buy antiquities and carpets, and to put some money towards his printing-press project.

The digs also went well as they uncovered what Lawrence called 'a good little pedestal mounted on the backs of two basalt lions', which he later drew, and 'a memorial altar, with four lines of close-written Hittite linear inscription'.[58] Hogarth called it 'the finest Hittite inscription yet found'[59] and left for England, content.

When they closed the digs for the summer, in late June, Lawrence saw Woolley and many cases of antiquities on to a ship at Alexandretta, and then headed to Aleppo where he installed himself in Baron's Hotel. There had been a cholera outbreak and the city was in quarantine. There was also a sense of panic as the Turkish army suffered one setback after another in Libya. None of this was mentioned in the letter he wrote home from the comfort of his room. Instead, he described 'a feeling of blessed peace in the air at the ending of my immediate digging work. Woolley is off and I am my own master again, which is a position that speaks for itself and its goodness.'[60]

II

Because He Loves Us

Then twittering out in the night my thought-birds flee,
I am emptied of all my dreams:
I only hear Earth turning, only see
Ether's long bankless streams,
And only know I should drown if you laid not your hand
  on me.

James Elroy Flecker, 'Stillness'[1]

Summer 1912

THE SUMMER STRETCHED before him rich with possibilities. Woolley was away until October, so Lawrence had three long, hot months to fill. There were jobs to finish at Carchemish, Arabic lessons to be had, and he was planning another walk, but this time with Dahoum, his constant companion. In Aleppo he collected new *iradés* from the Vali, who described him as a professor of the University of Oxford and wanted it to be known that he was 'an inestimable person, whose work archaeologically and intellectually they [the Ottoman government] were quite unable to express in words'.[2] Beyond the flippancy, the document required all government officials – including kaimmakams – 'to see that I am well lodged, well fed, provided with transport, with guides, interpreters, and escorts, if I express a wish'. The document would be useful if he went on a long walk, although there were obstacles that not even an *iradé* could surmount.

The war in Libya was expected to be a quick one, but it had dragged on, with escalating losses on all sides, and as it continued, it destabilised the Ottoman Empire. There had been several attempts at negotiation between Rome and Constantinople – including the one brokered by Kaiser Wilhelm – and the Turkish government had repeated its offer of allowing Italy to administer Libya, under nominal Turkish sovereignty. This arrangement was important to the Turks because it would allow the Sultan to retain his status as the Caliph or secular leader of the Muslim faithful.

When negotiations failed, Italian ships had bombarded the Dardanelles, the narrow waterway leading from the Aegean to the Marmara Sea. The Russian government protested, increasingly worried that its fleet would be trapped in the Black Sea, a fear that was realised when the Turks blocked the straits leading to the Bosphorus. With international trade to and from the Black Sea brought to a standstill, the conflict threatened to escalate. This did not deter the Italians from invading Rhodes on 5 May 1912 and then moving through the other Turkish Dodecanese Islands soon afterwards. By late June, Turkey had lost control of many of its islands and of the Libyan coast, its army forced back into the Libyan Desert.

'It seems the Turks suffered a defeat the other day somewhere,' Lawrence wrote around this time, adding that 'it won't hurt Turkey'.[3] In this his judgment was sound, at least in the short term, and it reflected the view of Consul-General Henry Cumberbatch in Beirut who had reported that 'It is difficult to tell how far the Arabs of Syria will stir themselves should they be called upon to do so, on behalf of the present Ottoman Government, to which they are by no means attached owing to its policy of "turkification" which they resent.'[4] Cumberbatch predicted that if the government in Constantinople continued its anti-Arab policy, 'there is every likelihood of the conflict between them and that party [the Arabs] . . . assuming grave proportions'.

Italian success at annexing part of the Ottoman Empire encouraged Albanian separatists to shake off Turkish rule, at which point the Balkans looked set to erupt into conflict. Yet Lawrence's only reference to this – at least in writing to his parents – was in a comment lamenting yet more lost letters: 'the Ottoman Post, never very robust, has been knocked dizzy by the stress of war'.[5] Of more interest to Lawrence was the fame that he and his colleagues at Jerablus now enjoyed, in part because of their behaviour towards the local administration, but also because they had money to spend on antiquities. With the Italian dealers exiled, and travel disrupted, there was now more supply than demand. Strangers accosted Lawrence in the streets of Aleppo, while others waited for him at the hotel. One gentleman left a beautiful ancient Damascene tile at Baron's for his approval. 'The compliment is too vast', he wrote home and, realising that they might not understand Eastern ways, added, 'and too intimate for your full comprehension, but it is one of the finest I have been paid.'[6]

In spite of the fun and the compliments, even he knew that trouble was brewing, if not from his own observations then from those of Raphael Fontana, at whose Consulate Lawrence was now a regular visitor. Fontana's wife, Winifred, recalled:

> Lawrence would stroll into the Consulate, his boots thick with mud or dust according to the season, his hair hanging below his ears (but for all that giving an impression of neatness and grace inherent in him) – deposit [borrowed] books gently and in reply to my eager questions say, for example: 'Woolley says the [Joseph] Conrad's movement is too slow. I like it too slow. May I have some more? We are staying to dinner.' Good! The Fellow-Countrymen were staying to dinner! Lawrence told me in after years that he enjoyed the evenings at the Consulate where so many different nationalities met and talked of 'The Situation' (there seemed always to be a situation in Turkey in those days!) or of Travel or the Arts. Lawrence sat there in his ready-made suit and heavy boots, perfectly conscious, I feel sure, of the scandalized looks of the dandified Natives, but indifferent to them – watching quietly for someone intelligent to talk to. I have had it said to me by a Frenchman who afterwards made a distinguished diplomatic career, '*Ma foi*, Madame! I thought I knew something about medieval French history and architecture, but your compatriot Lawrence's knowledge is profound.'[7]

However grave 'The Situation' and however gloomy the diplomat's predictions, with the digs at Carchemish closed, Lawrence was now master of his own time. He reported to Hogarth that 'Fontana has given me leave to do much as I like this summer, (live at

Jerablus etc.), since he found out much of his information about the present state of Syria was rot.'[8] But if the possibility of an uprising had been dismissed, other risks were still very real, not least a worsening cholera epidemic. Some forty people a day were dying in Aleppo, but more worrying than the number of deaths was the high mortality rate: bad sanitation and lack of medical care meant that most people who caught the disease died from it. Lawrence was so worried that the disease might spread to Jerablus, he wrote to ask a doctor in Oxford what he could do to treat patients, asking the doctor not to mention his request to his parents, who would 'go wild with alarm'.[9] With the Consul's blessing and the doctor's prescriptions, Lawrence prepared to return to Jerablus beside the Euphrates to make improvements to the house he had built, to arrange objects in the museum room, to check on the German railway team, to lie on the *tell* on hot summer nights and to dream.

He received two important visitors in July. The first was the Kaimmakam of Birejick, with whom he was now on better terms, perhaps helped by the *iradé* from the Vali of Aleppo. The second was a wealthy German amateur who was excavating at Tell Halaf, a site across the Euphrates from Jerablus. 'Von Oppenheim, the little Jew–German-millionaire,' he wrote with disapproval, 'came about 5 p.m. (sunset at 7.30) stayed till 11 p.m. then went off to eat and sleep: came back at 4.30 and stopped till 10 a.m. and left with a two-hour gallop to his train: a special, so it would wait for him – We have a train only 16 miles away.'[10]

Baron Max von Oppenheim was heir to a large private banking fortune, but had turned away from the family business and from law studies. His mother was Catholic, but the fact that his father was a Jew had excluded him from the German diplomatic service. Oppenheim, undeterred and still committed, told his mentor, the African explorer Gerhard Rohlfs, that he would promote German national interests any way he could. He was sufficiently wealthy and willing for the German government to be interested in using him in some unofficial capacity, and for other governments to watch him. He made an extensive journey through the Arabian desert, became an honorary sheikh of a tribe and wrote a book about his experiences, *From the Mediterranean to the Persian Gulf*. He also spent a couple of years in Cairo, perfecting his Arabic, stirring anti–British sentiment and entertaining the likes of Egyptian nationalist leaders and the Sherif Hussein of Mecca at his house on the edge of the old city. Sir Ronald Storrs, Britain's urbane Oriental Secretary in Cairo (and later one of Lawrence's closest friends), wrote, 'It is true that "the Kaiser's spy", who was attached as Oriental Secretary to the German Agency but described as "unofficial" though enjoying diplomatic privileges, was not, save as a genial host and an enterprising rather than a profound archaeologist, taken very seriously by the British, or indeed by the Germans either.'[11]

The British Levantine Consular Service took him seriously, because in April 1911 Consul-General Cumberbatch in Beirut received a confidential report that the Baron was expected with a party of seven and that arrangements were being made for a two-year scientific expedition out of Aleppo. 'If you wish movements watched, as was Embassy's desire in '99, I will inform Aleppo and Damascus.'[12] Presumably Aleppo was informed, because Raphael Fontana sent a long report to Lowther in October 1911 informing him that 'Baron Oppenheim left Aleppo with a caravan of over a hundred animals towards the end of May, moving East.' Fontana then heard from the Russian Consul that the Baron was 'trying to buy land "for purposes of colonization"'.[13] So Lawrence will certainly have known about Oppenheim, and the suspicions he aroused, from Fontana.

That Oppenheim was a rival for archaeological glory, and for influence among the Arabs and Kurds, was not in dispute: he had a permit to dig at the promising site of Tell Halaf. But it is interesting to see the extent to which Lawrence rejects the man. Oppenheim was fifty-one when he visited Jerablus, and had a considerable reputation as a traveller in the region. Given Lawrence's interest in Arab tribes, and knowing his admiration of Doughty for travelling in Arabia, one might expect him to be more curious about the German and his experiences. Perhaps the Baron could have talked to him about the Slayb, the tribe with whom he wanted to travel. His rejection of the German is out of character. 'He was such a horrible person,' he wrote immediately after the meeting, 'I hardly was polite – but was interesting instead.' The Baron knew this sort of veiled hostility and replied with a backhanded compliment, saying that their work at Carchemish had revealed 'the most interesting and important discoveries he had ever seen barring his own'. Then the Baron turned polite and 'invited me over to his place by his relay of post-horses – 6 days journey in 36 hours! Not for me thanks!'[14] Perhaps Lawrence thought his brusqueness would ensure that he would hear no more of Oppenheim. If that was so, he was mistaken: the two men played opposing roles in the coming war.

By the middle of the July, Lawrence was ready to leave with Dahoum for Urfa and Seruj, intending to copy some inscriptions, but his plans were derailed by the arrival of disease in the village. It was not cholera. 'First of all I had malaria – a short spell of the usual two-day sort. Mrs. Haj Wahid got a new baby, and turned very ill. Haj's boy fell down and broke his head to pieces and had to be tied up; Haj himself went to drink, and collapsed with internal troubles of sorts. So I brought in Dahoum to help Haj's mother in the kitchen and he ungratefully produced malignant malaria (autumn-aestival [falciparum, the most serious form of malaria]) and raved his head off for three days until he nearly died. I had to sit on his chest half one night to keep him in bed.'[15]

When the Haj took his family home to Aleppo, Lawrence was alone with Dahoum. Once the youth had recovered his strength, the two men went upriver to Birejick, presumably en route for Urfa. Lawrence had heard that some French engineers had offered the Kaimmakam of Birejick £2,000 for the right to dismantle the castle ruins and to reuse the blocks for a bridge they were building over the Euphrates. Lawrence's feelings about this can be gauged from the acerbic letter he had written to *The Times* the previous summer. 'I made him squirm,' he now wrote to Hogarth, but predicted that 'they will pull it down all the same'. (In this, at least, he was wrong.) More immediately troubling was the news that he went down with a second bout of malaria. A year or two earlier, he might have carried on regardless, but remembering (or reminded by Dahoum) how illness had almost killed him the previous summer, the two of them returned to Jerablus.

When he recovered, he decided to take Dahoum to Jebail, where he could build up his strength. To get there, they took a train to Aleppo and then on towards Damascus, stopping to visit the ruins of a sixth-century Byzantine compound – palace, barracks and monastery – called the Qasr of Ibn Wardani. The visit inspired one of Lawrence's first pieces of descriptive writing. The story, 'more like the rumour than the reality',[16] captures the ease and happiness he felt that summer, and also shows how far his writing had developed since the dull descriptions of castles and cathedrals of his first French cycling tour. This time, he was writing about the landscape between Aleppo and Hama, 'a monotony of lands, barren to the unskilled eye, but hiding nevertheless in folds villages of clay–domed houses, and black tents of wandering Arabs which from afar look only like larger groups of their herded camels.' Here they found two Arabs, an old man called Khalil and his son. Dahoum recognised the old man as being 'of the kind that know what has been and what will be'. Khalil also had two horses, so he and Lawrence rode while Dahoum and the boy walked beside them for the hours it took to reach the ruins.

> We could see a valley of brighter green, in which were low, brown ruins of thick walls. 'Why,' I said, 'it is of brick, and how sweet the air is here.' Khalil's eyes narrowed with a laugh. 'Did I not know it half-an-hour ago? After rain it is sensible a day's journey off'; and we entered in through an arch whose key-bricks were piled ruinously over the bases of the pillars. The boy then led in speech, and said, 'This is the jasmine court,' and I stood to draw breath and look about its emptiness. I was aware of a soft pervading scent as of half-faded jasmine blossoms. The old Arab took our horses to their stalls in the shadow of the southern wall, and with his boy we passed up a ruinous flight of stairs into the rose-chamber. 'Here,' said the boy, 'was the girst [the heart] of the harem: the rest is swept away': and easily enough over the decayed earthen walls, with their nearly-vanished rose-savour, we could trace in the grass the square outlines of the women's quarters. The lad turned to the right, and led us through a succession of rooms, some with walls levelled nearly to the ground, some with remains of arcades in panelled brick and shattered vaulting, but in all of them were strange, indefinable scents, memories of myrtle and oleander, musk, cinnamon and ambergris.

At last we came into a great hall, whose walls, pierced with many narrow windows, still stood to more than half their height. 'This', said he, 'is the *liwan of silence*: it has no taste,' and by some crowning art it was as he said. The mingled scents of all the palace here combined to slay each other, and all that one felt was the desert sharpness of the air as it swept off the huge uncontaminated plains. 'Among us,' said Dahoum, 'we call this room the sweetest of them all,' therein half-consciously sounding the ideal of the Arab creed, for generations stripping itself of all furniture in the working out of a gospel of simplicity.

And the secret of the place? Old Khalil told us that night over his hearth-fire, that Ibn Wardani was as a king among the Arabs, and the bricks of his palace were kneaded not with common water, but with those precious oils and essences of flowers which of old the Arab druggists could so well compound. 'He made it as a pleasure house for the bride he took of the children of Roum [Byzantium],' and I know no more but that in the ruins was nothing inconsonant with what he said.[17]*

The month at the coast was intended to be one of calm and ease, but although they avoided quarantine Lawrence was robbed of £20 worth of *antikas* on his way to Jebail. And there was news of riots and trouble in Constantinople. 'It is very far off,' he wrote from the coast to reassure his family, 'and here there are no disputes.' Miss Holmes had come down from the cooler hills to reopen the house for them. 'I eat a lot, and sleep a lot, and when I am tired of reading

---

* The *qasr* itself has survived the century since Lawrence visited. Forty-five miles from Hama into what was desert and is now planted with groves of olives and other trees, the three buildings remain. Lawrence missed – or chose not to mention – the inscription over the entrance to the church, which dates it to AD 564, the last year of Emperor Justinian's reign. Nor was he told, as I was, that the technique of using alternated courses of different-colour materials (in this case basalt blocks and brick) was first used here by the imperial architects, but soon became one of the key characteristics of Syrian architecture. The legend has survived at least as well as the structure, for the guardian who came to meet me with a key and the hope of *baksheesh*, after pointing out the buildings' features – basalt blocks, brick vault, inscriptions, upper gallery in the church for women, palace not for a king but for a general – then told me the story of the flower-imbued mortar and urged me to breathe deeply in a vain attempt to conjure the scent of roses.

I go and bathe in the sea with Dahoum.'[18] There was also some work to do after a section of cliff collapsed near by and revealed various ancient tombs. Lawrence, as the nearest archaeologist, went to work. One tomb was early Phoenician – a man placed on his back in a huge urn with a selection of flint tools. Another was a 'Graeco-Phoenician sarcophagus from a rock-tomb. It was white marble, about 8 feet long and pleasant work, anthropoid but Greek-featured.'[19] The grave goods were mostly painted jugs and cups, which he bought there and then for £1. He hoped he would be able to buy the sarcophagus later for the Ashmolean, although he suspected the Turkish government would want it.

Beyond the excitement of archaeological discoveries, there was the pleasure of the sea and the company of friends. Raphael and Winifred Fontana were summering in the hills above Alexandretta, to the north, while the Fleckers had rented a house above Beirut in the small village of Areya. 'There was a fine view over the valleys and mountains,' Hellé Flecker remembered; 'the jasmine shading the entrance to the garden side was in full bloom; as for the pomegranate trees there were several, splashing their bright scarlet touch all over the grounds . . . One day T. E. Lawrence turned up early in the morning. As we enquired how he had got to Areya, there being no train at that hour, he quietly explained that he had arrived by the night train, but not wishing to disturb us had slept on the floor in the station to the scandal of the station-master.'[20]

Their talk was of poetry, literature and Oxford, which Flecker missed very much and would gladly have swapped for Lebanon; he had recently asked Hogarth to see if there was a job for him at the university. 'I hate the East – the Lebanon is Christian thank God,' he wrote to a friend that summer. The contradiction for him was that the East, however much he hated it, was his subject-matter and the inspiration for his work, which he claimed was writing 'the best Eastern poems in the language'.[21] When Lawrence visited, Flecker was working on a long verse drama, *The Golden Journey to Samarkand*, which would become one of his most successful and popular works, so they will have shared the pleasure of these lines:

> We are the Pilgrims, master, we shall go
> Always a little further; it may be
> Beyond that last blue mountain barred with snow
> Across that angry or that glimmering sea.[22]

Always a little further. That phrase would apply to Lawrence as much as anyone, pushing his body as far as it could go.

But not this summer of happiness, which he spent lying on the divan in Miss Holmes's house with a book in hand, or taking Arabic classes with Miss Fareedeh, who had also returned to the coast to be with Lawrence, or heading to the beach with Dahoum, who 'wrestles beautifully better than all of his age and size',[23] but who was more interested in pigs, which he had never seen before.

Dahoum is often difficult to bring out of the shadows in this story, but there is a moment during the summer in Jebail when he steps into full light, in a conversation recorded by Miss Fareedeh. When the two of them were alone, she had asked why he was so devoted to the Englishman. To this Dahoum replied, 'You ask why we love Lawrence? And who can help loving him? He is our brother, our friend and leader. He is one of us, there is nothing we do he cannot do, and he then excels us in doing it. He takes such an interest in us and cares for our welfare. We respect him and greatly admire his courage and bravery: we love him because he loves us.'[24] These comments were echoed later by several people who served with Lawrence in the war, and who believed the Arabs accepted Lawrence, in a way they accepted no other foreigner, because he could do things they could do and sometimes do them better.

Lawrence was also beginning to imitate the ways of these people who so intrigued him. He sent salaams to family and friends in England, had begun to copy the Arab way of introducing exaggerated flourishes in his greetings – 'salaam me to Noël from the knees to the eyes: and down again',[25] for instance – and he had adopted their dress. Until this moment, Lawrence had been recognisably the Englishman abroad in his Magdalen College blazer, or shorts with knee-high socks and hobnail walking boots. But this summer, which he described as 'one of the pleasantest I have ever had',[26] he crossed a line and 'was three weeks walking about Jebail in Arab dress: Excuse was an illness, which found rest only so: but the village made the most of it!'[27] This was about more than mere medical necessity. Lawrence had already posed for a photograph at Carchemish in which he appears to be wearing some of Dahoum's clothes – baggy white trousers, embroidered waistcoat, cropped dark jacket and an elaborate headdress. The photograph is rare not just because it is the first to show Lawrence in Arab dress, but because he is beaming, clearly very amused. Because he is happy.

12

An Old Story

I am gathering a store of Arab News and notions which some
day will help me . . .

> T. E. Lawrence to his mother, Carchemish,
> 22 October 1912[1]

August 1912

THE CENTRE COULD not hold and things were beginning to fall
apart. The empire was crumbling long before Lawrence took
to the beach and yet, as he sat in Arab clothes, enjoying the calm
sea and the company of Dahoum, he felt no tremors. Before leaving
Jebail at the end of August 1912, he reported 'a fine view of an
Italian fleet yesterday: talk of war, which won't be popular here: the
Arabs fancy they are winning. Bulgaria looks interesting but that
will be an old story before you get this [letter].'[2] Flippancy, an airy
sort of carelessness, was the standard tone for his letters. But Bulgaria
'interesting'? It was much more than that.

When the Young Turks had forced Sultan Abdul Hamid II to re-
instate the constitution and hand power to parliament in 1908, the
Constantinople government struggled to control its further reaches and
its European provinces looked particularly vulnerable. Austria-Hungary
exploited this weakness by annexing Bosnia, while the Bulgarians
declared independence. When the Young Turks deposed the Sultan
the following year, the situation became more unsettled, as Lawrence
discovered on his Crusader castle walk. Things became more serious
still while he was in Jebail in 1912, when the Turkish army collapsed
in Libya and an alliance of Turkey's former Balkan provinces – Bulgaria,

Greece and Serbia – created the Balkan League. The League's declared purpose was to offer mutual protection. But as so often with these things, it was more an agreement on mutual aggression. Mixing religion and politics in a way that has become depressingly familiar in our own time, the League stood as the champion of Christian minorities against Ottoman-Muslim tyranny and it demanded that Constantinople grant Macedonia autonomy or face war.

Just how wrong Lawrence had been about Bulgaria – interesting, but soon over – was clear by October. By the time he and Dahoum were back in Aleppo to meet Woolley, the Turks had ceded Libya to the Italians, and Montenegro had joined the Balkan League and declared war on Turkey. Serbia, Greece and Bulgaria joined in and, by the middle of October, Kosovo, Crete and much of European Turkey had been invaded in what *The Times*, with foresight, called 'the first stage of an incalculable war'.[3] Before long, Bulgarian divisions – in greater number and better organised than the Turks – were moving towards Constantinople.

Although the fighting was far from the sleepy *tell* at Jerablus, the threat from its blood-dimmed tide was felt in Syria. Aleppo was 'very disturbed', as Lawrence admitted in a letter home, 'with the Government forcibly levying transport animals, and scouring the country for reservists in hiding'.[4] Anatolian peasants had long made up the bulk of the Turkish army and in *Seven Pillars* Lawrence vividly described how the burden of conscription fell 'heaviest on the poor villages, and each year made these poor villages yet more poor'.[5] With the Balkan conflict going badly, Turkish recruiters eventually reached Jerablus.

To Lawrence's relief they went first to the German engineers and conscripted so many of their labourers that work stopped on the Baghdad Railway. While this was going on, the men working for the British Museum hurried to the Hittite ruins and brought with them their horses and asses. Two hundred men slept at the *tell* that night, perhaps more than at any time since the great city had fallen. Lawrence, who liked nothing better than to play with people in authority, proudly announced that not only did they retain all their men, but the recruiting officers did no more than pop in for coffee and a cigarette. 'This has much enhanced our prestige.'[6]

If he felt able to make light of the troubles, people in England did not. His parents, who had not seen him all year, were now reading about how the conflict was spreading across the region: *The Times*, at the beginning of September, reported 'anxiety in Turkey' and an 'increased nervousness with which the more thoughtful Turkish politicians and statesmen are regarding the situation in the Balkans'.[7] His anxious parents now wrote to suggest he give up field archaeology. Come home, they suggested, and look for a university post. Lawrence knew it would be safer, but it would mean being away from Dahoum and his life in Jerablus, and being home with his mother, with all that that entailed. It would be dull compared to the life he was living. 'I am afraid no "open fellowship" for me,' he replied and then, in his clearest statement of intent, wrote, 'I don't think anyone who had tasted the East as I have would give it up half-way, for a seat at a high table and a chair in the Bodleian. At any rate I won't.'[8] That phrase 'half-way' would have worried his parents as much as anything they were reading in the newspapers, for he recognised – and they now knew – that a process had started in him, a change of taste, of thought, desire and intention, that was transforming the young man.

The decision to stay or to get out before the region burned might not be his: Hogarth and Kenyon were also concerned about the way the conflict was escalating. However serious the situation, Lawrence's letters gave little away and were filled with his usual mix of gossip, details of antiquities excavated and others bought. In early October, for instance, he wrote about his return to Carchemish and how 'the men lit a huge bonfire on the top of the citadel, and fired about 300 shots that evening in our honour. It was the biggest noise ever heard in Jerablus since the defeat of Pharaoh Necho by Nebuchadnezzar in 614, and was seen and heard from Biredjik and Tell Ahmar, and inland for nearly eighteen miles.'[9]

Money was a more pressing concern than security. The British Museum had received some of Walter Morrison's donation, but Kenyon would not, or could not, send it to Woolley. With payday for the two hundred workmen only three days off, and only £40 in hand, Lawrence went to Aleppo to borrow money. Usually this would not have been a problem; everyone in town knew his credit was good. But it was becoming clear, even to this young man, that the war was changing everything, including the behaviour of money-lenders, who were suddenly loath to take risks. His parents might have known more about it than he did, because *The Times* and other papers reported developments. The headlines tell the tale: 'Outbreak of War' (9 October), 'Declaration of War by Turkey' (18 October), 'Turkey Invaded' (19 October).[10] In Aleppo, he knew some of this and, although the news was slow to come through, the effects were immediately felt. This was, for instance, a very good time to buy antiquities: he and Woolley were now the only serious buyers in town and one reason for their own shortage of cash was that they had bought big and had already spent £200. Lawrence was still considering spending a further £400 on an eighteenth-century ceiling, painted in lacquer and gold leaf, which he thought he could sell to the Victoria and Albert Museum, or to a private collector such as Lord Carnarvon. In the end he did manage to borrow £100 and they did pay the workers that week. Meanwhile Woolley urged Kenyon to send more funds.

Lawrence wrote home about the weather: it was still warm enough to swim 'with a frolicking company'[11] at midday, but sufficiently cold in the mission house at night to justify lighting the fire and laying out the Bokhara carpets over the mosaic floor. He wrote about the challenges of running so large a workforce: 'the size of operations we have tackled is becoming more than a little oppressive'. He wrote about the historical challenge of having 'the whole of Hittite history . . . in the melting-pot – or the craftsman's mould – out here'.[12] He wrote about coping with the number of finds for, 'in half an hour [of resuming the digs, we] had uncovered the jambs of a doorway in black basalt, with long and perfect Hittite inscriptions. After our great stone of the Hogarth period, this is the best inscription yet discovered here, and we are correspondingly glad.'[13] He wrote about making jam out of quince, pear and apple, and about finishing the mudbrick dome above the new toilet block. But he did not write about going home.

With the post suspended or erratic, Woolley admitted that they were 'very much in the dark as to what is going on in Turkey'. Occasionally reports did reach them, such as news 'that the Bulgarians have advanced victoriously south of Adrianople [Edirne]. If Stamboul falls, it may be the signal for serious events out here – here perhaps more than in most parts of the Empire.'[14] Lawrence knew from history as much as from personal experience at Carchemish that they were living on one of the region's fault-lines. Where ancient Egyptians had once clashed with Assyrians, where Romans and Persians had faced each other, Turks now stifled the national aspirations of Arabs, Kurds and Armenians.

Woolley and Lawrence were very aware of the possibility of Kurds and Arabs rising against the Turks and they had agreed, as Woolley wrote to Kenyon, that 'should a row come, we shall stop at Jerablus, as being the safest place; possibly we should be all right, but communication would be difficult and you must not, in that case, expect to hear from me'.[15] Whatever anxiety lay behind Woolley's hope that 'possibly we should be all right' will have increased when he read Raphael Fontana's letter 'prophesying the fall of the Turkish Empire'.[16] Lawrence seemed to agree: 'it is obvious that the Balkan states have the better of it' and that 'Bulgaria has every possibility of finishing off Turkey (if the powers let her) because the Turks are such helpless stupids.'[17]

Cut off at Carchemish and excited by this turn of events, Lawrence mentioned to his parents that the Armenians were also preparing to rise against the Turks – and then hurriedly instructed them not to 'jump to the idea that we are in Armenia and are revolting or being revolted. We are in Jerablus (and probably camped out) digging the tombs.' He added, 'We dig and dig, and doctor our men and settle their disputes and talk with them about all things in heaven and earth.'[18] The most immediate problem the war created for them, beyond the shortage of cash, was the hold-up of deliveries: the railway tracks and carts they needed to clear heavy debris from the site had not arrived, nor had food and photographic supplies. For a while they lived off what they had in the house and what they could buy from the villages, which made it all the sweeter when their stores did finally arrive, for they included various brands of marmalade, caviar and even Russian rubber sponges. They slept on linen sheets, had Kurdish carpets underfoot and a boatload of olive-tree roots to keep them warm through the winter. What they still did not have was money, and not even their own cash was enough to keep the digs open. By the second week in November they had to lay off all but twenty of the workforce, but by then they had also heard that Kenyon would not be sending more money. 'It is good business for them,' Lawrence ranted, knowing that the museum was sitting on much of Morrison's donation, 'but we are insolvent.'[19] Woolley was more politic and wrote to warn Kenyon of the consequences of withholding funds: 'if we stop work altogether at the end of the week I shall not have quite sufficient in hand for travelling and salaries'.[20]

Concerns about getting home were irrelevant because they were still at Carchemish and were still digging, although now with only a skeleton workforce. They were not expecting any great discoveries, but archaeology is an unpredictable pursuit and they stumbled upon the ancient city's North Gate, which Woolley described as 'a whole range of masonry fortifications with gateway and protecting towers'. His optimism spilled over into thoughts for the next season and he advised that 'much work should yet be done on a part of the site where we had not expected to dig at all'.[21] But the future was clouded by worries of war. For now, they prepared to wind up the dig, reburying anything important that could not be locked away for, as Lawrence noted, people were taking advantage of the power vacuum, 'tombs [were] being plundered and buildings destroyed every day in the districts round about'.[22]

In this intense period of living, Lawrence was also optimistic. He was 'gathering a store of Arab News and notions which some day will help me in giving vividness to what I write'.[23] Some biographers have seen this comment as further evidence that Lawrence was working more for British Military Intelligence than he was for the British Museum. But if Lawrence was collecting for anything, it was for the book he was already writing about his experiences in the region.

They closed the dig at Carchemish on 21 November and then went to see the leader of the local Kurd tribes, Busrawi Agha, to request his protection for Carchemish should there be trouble in their absence. When they reached Beirut on 9 December, ready to take ship for England, they heard the latest news of the Balkan War. In Carchemish they had been told that the Turkish army had held the Chatalca Line and that the Bulgarian advance, irresistible up to this point, was stopped twenty miles from the capital. Constantinople was saved. In Beirut they heard that Turkish forces had been defeated on almost all other fronts and, having lost most of their European territories, the Young Turk government had been forced to sign an armistice with Bulgaria, Serbia and Montenegro. Hostilities rumbled on with Greece for control of Epirus and Yannina, but the first Balkan War was effectively over, as was Turkey's European empire.

Flecker had already left the 'cursed place' of Beirut by the time Lawrence and Woolley arrived. The diplomat and his wife Hellé had taken ship for England. In his absence, the archaeologists seem not to have gone to talk to his superior at the British Consulate, Henry Cumberbatch. Instead, they went to the American Vice-Consul, Felix Willoughby Smith. Born on the Black Sea, the son of a career diplomat from Connecticut, Willoughby Smith had been in Beirut for two years, which is to say that he was a seasoned observer, and knew the ways and the people of that part of the world. When Woolley and Lawrence arrived with a story to tell, it adds credence to their tale that he believed them.

Much of Smith's long, detailed report concerns news the archaeologists had heard from 'a certain Busrawi Agha'.[24] It also contains the detail – not included in Lawrence's *Diary of a Journey across the Euphrates* from the previous year – that in July 1911 the Sheikh of Harran, the young man who had fallen asleep on Lawrence's knee, had shown him a cache of eight to ten thousand Martini rifles and ammunition that he kept hidden in the vaults of his Crusader-era castle, waiting for the day when the Kurdish tribes would rise against the Turks, avenge Ibrahim Pasha's death and take control of their lands. Smith noted the 'undisguised satisfaction' with which the Kurds were watching the Turkish defeat in the Balkans and reported that, since the Turkish capitulation to Italy over Libya, there had been 'secret meetings of the leading Arabs in Aleppo, Damascus and elsewhere, condemning Turkey's betrayal of the Arabs and proposing to turn out the Turks and take over the Government'. More alarming, because the implications were so wide-ranging, was news of 'a conspiracy into which they [Busrawi Agha and the Milli-Kurds] have entered with the Khedive of Egypt, the Sherif of Mecca, the Sheikh es-Senussi, and Ibn Rashid, whose object is to expel the Turks and to set up an Arab Sultan, apparently at Baghdad as capital'.

There is nothing in Lawrence's or Woolley's papers to verify this meeting, but it seems safe to assume that it did take place and that this is what Smith heard from them. The most extraordinary claim relates to the international conspiracy. 'As long as the Sultan was also the Khalifa [Caliph] the religious bond that held the Kurds and the Arabs to the Empire was strong: but with Abdul Hamid's deposition [1909] this bond was snapped; the only Khalifa recognized is the Sherif of Mecca.' The repercussions of an uprising against Turkish rule, in 1913, by an alliance of Egyptians, Hejazi Arabs, Libyan tribes and Mesopotamian Arabs and Kurds would have been felt around the world. One of the consequences would have been the risk, for Britain in particular, of losing control of the Suez Canal and access to the Persian Gulf oilfields. Smith, who found nothing far-fetched in any of this, added that he had 'long observed the disaffection of the Bedouins and of many city Arabs (Moslems) with Turkish rule'. The main obstacle to the uprising, in his view, was the need for a suitable leader. Sherif Hussein of Mecca, whom he had met the previous year, lacked the qualities to lead an uprising. But among his family were younger, better-educated men with both the character and the ambition to help forge a new world. Lawrence agreed and the first thing he did, three years later when he became involved in the Arab revolt, was to choose a new leader. 'I went down to Arabia', he wrote after the war, in *Seven Pillars of Wisdom*, 'to see and consider its great men. The first, the Sherif of Mecca, was known to be aged. I found Abdulla [one of his sons] too clever, Ali too clean, Zeid too cool. Then I rode up-country to Feisal, and found in him the leader with the necessary fire.' At the end of 1912, as Lawrence and Woolley prepared to sail back to England for a brief Christmas break, that fire was not yet visible.

13

The Happiest Time, the Richest Dig

There is really nothing else to say! Everything is going so well
that nothing else matters.
> T. E. Lawrence to Florence Messham, Carchemish,
> 18 April 1913[1]

Early 1913

NOW BEGINS ONE of the most rewarding periods of his life. He
was returning from a cold English winter to the sunshine of
Syria. He was on his way back to a region that he hoped was settling
after the war. He was twenty-four years old, physically fit, confident
in his work, fascinated by the place in which he was living, optimistic
about his prospects and very friendly with some of the people whom
he had come to know over the past two years. What's more, he had
options. When he had to wait some days at Port Said for the Beirut
boat, he took the night train to Cairo and then 'ran up to Petrie's
dig [at Kafr Ammar] to see what was happening there . . . I was
lucky to find Mrs. Petrie not there,' his low opinion of her unchanged,
'the Professor was as usual.'[2] There was a motive behind this visit to
Petrie: he wanted to know whether the offer to dig in Bahrain was
still available and wrote to tell Hogarth that it was, and that Petrie
was happy to share any Bahrain finds with the Ashmolean. Lawrence
was still not committing to the offer, but it was an obvious alternative, should the British Museum close Carchemish. Kenyon and
Hogarth were waiting for Lawrence's report from Jerablus before
making their decision. Kenyon had tried to impress on him that 'it
is very desirable to avoid serious risk, not merely for their own sakes,

but in the interest of the Museum, and indeed of the political situation generally'.[3] Hogarth had added that the museum would not reopen the excavations 'unless there is a pretty clear prospect of their being able to do a decent spell of work'.[4] They would make their final judgment when he reported back from Jerablus. He knew that closure was more likely as soon as he reached Jerablus and found the country in a state of tension and their villagers living in hardship.

Winifred Fontana, the wife of the British Consul in Aleppo, remembered that 'T.E. and Woolley appeared to believe that Kurds were planning an attack to sack Aleppo (their crops had failed) and persuaded Raff – my husband – to report to the Consulate.' But Foreign Office papers suggest that Fontana had reported on the possibility of an attack while Lawrence was still crossing the Mediterranean. The Balkan War had brought local trade to a standstill and there was extreme poverty and very low food stocks in the Aleppo province. Fontana also pointed out that in some areas – Jerablus was one – Kurds and Arabs had refused the Turkish call to arms. More than being unwilling to help support the empire, Fontana believed many of them wanted to see it fall. 'News of Turkish defeats have been received with satisfaction by various Christian communities, and with satisfaction mingled with regret by the Arabs, who dislike the Turks but regret the fact of Moslems having been defeated by Christians.'[5] In another part of his extensive report to Sir Gerard Lowther, the Ambassador in Constantinople, Fontana noted 'an openly-expressed and general desire, among high and low, both among the Arabs throughout this district and Christians of all sects and races, that the present [Turkish] Government should be finally and summarily done away with, and that England should take over and govern the country'. German diplomats were reporting similar comments, that the people of Ottoman Syria and Mesopotamia longed for the Kaiser to liberate them.

Dahoum had stayed in Carchemish while Lawrence was in England, but now, after a brief visit to the digs, they installed themselves in Aleppo. From Baron's Hotel, Lawrence wrote on 25 January 1913 to tell Woolley that 'the Kurds here are quiet, with no intention of doing anything unless matters get bad in Stamboul.

They are then going all out, and the Arabs have promised to move with them (our men as well!). The richer Armenians in Aintab, Aleppo, etc. are leaving: some are in Beyrout, more in Egypt.'[6] The threat now for people in Carchemish and Aleppo was not from the Balkans but from what was happening in Constantinople. Two days before Lawrence wrote to Woolley, a group of Young Turks had burst into the Sublime Porte while the Cabinet of the Liberal government was in session. Nizam Pasha, the Minister for War and the man most widely blamed for Turkish failure in the Balkans, was assassinated and the Grand Vizier (Prime Minister) Kamil Pasha was forced to resign. Fontana worried that this latest Young Turk coup would spark riots in the further provinces and he wrote to Cumberbatch at the British Consulate in Beirut asking him to send ten rifles and ammunition 'for the defence of H.M. Consulate at Aleppo in view of possible disturbances'.[7]

Lawrence still thought they could have a season at Carchemish 'if Constantinople holds straight', but that was a big 'if', and he was clearly concerned because he went on to say that he hoped the digs would not resume until the autumn. Woolley wished otherwise – presumably out of personal interest – and told Hogarth that Lawrence's comments were 'more cautious than I had hoped, but as you don't believe that Stamboul will fall I take it that this will satisfy you'.[8]

The fast-changing situation and lack of definite news made any appraisal of the situation difficult, any judgment compromised. 'At present,' Lawrence wrote two days after the coup in Constantinople, 'latest news here is of the fall of the cabinet: how or why is not known: it sounds to me like war and the Young Turk party on top again: if so matters will hum.'[9] 'Hum' was an appropriate word to describe the immediate reaction to regime change. The day after the coup, Consul-General Cumberbatch reported that a large gathering of disaffected people had met in Beirut – Muslims, Christians of many cults, and Jews – and had elected a committee to demand, among other things, that Arabic be used as a state language and that a larger percentage of revenue collected in the Beirut *vilayet* be spent locally. In case the significance of the gathering was lost on Lowther, the Consul-General explained that 'this is perhaps the first time that public meetings of the kind have been allowed to take place in Turkey'.[10]

Aleppo lay across the mountains and, while Beirut was vulnerable to the sea, it was exposed to the open steppes and to the desert. Fontana and Lawrence waited there to see what would happen next. Lawrence, who had been in touch with some Kurds (although not necessarily with Busrawi), knew that even if the great Arab-Kurd uprising did not happen, there was a local plan. Busrawi's eldest son and one of the Shahin sheikhs had been seen in Aleppo staking out likely houses to loot. Many Armenians who had remained – and that included the Altounyans – were frantically arming: Lawrence thought there was a fortune to be made selling them weapons, although the trade in weapons was officially banned. For once, Fontana seemed not to be exaggerating when he talked of a 'critical situation' and of 'menace' from 'a Kurdish rising accompanied with an Arab tribal movement'.[11] Fontana was concerned that the Aleppo Consulate building 'is particularly exposed in situation and in construction to attack by a mob. And the presence of Warships at Beyrout and Alexandretta, although a sure safeguard for those parts, cannot be considered as affecting a guarantee for the safety of foreign Subjects at Aleppo in exceptionally critical times.' Under the circumstances, he 'thought it necessary that this Consulate should be provided with arms for its protection and for that of British subjects, who would take refuge therein in the event of an outbreak'.[12]

Cumberbatch contacted the captain of one of the British warships off the Syrian coast, who offered six standard-issue army rifles and a dozen revolvers. As they had no intention of requesting permission to import weapons into Turkey, there was some discussion as to how they would be delivered to Aleppo. Lawrence had a suggestion. As Fontana explained to Lowther, 'Mr. Lawrence, who knows the country well, offered of his own accord to bring the rifles to Aleppo, provided they were landed at a sea-side house in the vicinity of Beirut belonging to friends of his.'[13]

Lawrence and Dahoum took the train to Beirut some time around 3 February. The exact sequence of events, like the justification for them, is obscured by Lawrence's love of opacity, and by a need for tact in case his letters were opened; this was an illegal and perhaps also a dangerous operation along the coast of an unstable country whose government had just been overthrown. In normal times, there would have been a steamer coaling up in Beirut harbour ready to leave on the 190-mile journey up the coast to Alexandretta. But there was nothing normal about these times and, as no boat was scheduled for the next three days, Lawrence went to see Cumberbatch at the Consulate 'and he sent me up in a cruiser, the *Duke of Edinburgh*, which was quick, and comfortable, and big, and quite interesting'.[14] Mr and Mrs Lawrence of Polstead Road, Oxford, might have found it puzzling that their twenty-four-year-old son, a junior archaeologist on an inconspicuous dig in a remote corner of the Ottoman Empire, was being ferried up the Syrian coast by the Royal Navy. Nothing in his subsequent letter, which talks of offloading cases of antiquities held at the British Consulate in Alexandretta, would justify the ride or calm their concerns. 'I had Dahoum with me and he was most impressed, and impressed everybody on board. They all made him offers to come with them permanently, and took him all over the ship and feasted him. His remarks on what he saw were very funny: sometimes very embarrassing for me who had to translate. They blazed off big guns, and searchlights, and had drills and parades and sports for our benefits.'[15]

Lawrence insinuated to his parents that the Royal Navy was there to rescue the antiquities, held up in the Alexandretta Consulate since the previous June, and there was certainly something underhand about having the navy send boats ashore, under cover of darkness, to offload antiquities. From Alexandretta, he wrote a more detailed description to Hogarth of moving what he called 'the spoils' from the Consulate. 'A custom-house guard was a spectator, but an unintelligent one', as he repacked sixteen boxes of antiquities. 'I had to take them to pieces and repack in Petroleum [Company] boxes: the bronze, the Bull's head, and the Chariot I packed very carefully. Some of the others I smashed to make things go in.'[16]

He and Dahoum then had enough time to visit Alexandretta's souks, where he bought a beautiful small cabinet, elaborately inlaid with ebony and ivory. He thought it might be early Italian Renaissance, but it was Syrian work and went to decorate the sitting room of the house he had built at Carchemish. Having smuggled antiquities out past Turkish customs, he then set about smuggling things in.

A couple of weeks later he confessed to his mother that he had been involved in 'the iniquity of gun-running in Beyrout. The consular need of rifles involved myself, the Consul-General in Beyrout, Flecker, the Admiral at Malta, our Ambassador in Stamboul, two captains, and two lieutenants, besides innumerable cavasses, in one common law-breaking. However Fontana got his stuff.'[17] It is not clear where, exactly, the weapons were landed, but it seems that they came off HMS *Medea* at Beirut. Lieutenants Bevan and Watson brought them off, while Cumberbatch's cavass, Abdel Kader Shemli, had a carriage ready to take them to Beirut railway station for the eighteen-hour ride to Aleppo. They had breakfast at Rayak in the Beqaa Valley and lunch at Homs, and found, when they reached Aleppo, that Fontana was too sick to receive them. Lawrence was there to entertain them, which he did for the next six days. 'I had to trot them over Aleppo,' he explained to his mother, 'and we did trot over it all, all day and all night.' Then he took them to Carchemish, entertaining them at the expedition house. When they left, they carried with them 'Babylonian gems, and Greek coins, and Roman bronzes, and Persian carpets, and Arab pottery'. For once, he aired reservations about taking antiquities and antiques, commenting that it was 'all going to a warship, a modern engine of efficiency and destruction . . . what will their Captain say to their stuffed bags?'[18]

Some biographers have seen this 'Aleppo incident' as yet more evidence that Lawrence was working for British intelligence, but I have found nothing to support the claim. Lawrence certainly exceeded what one might expect of a young archaeologist, just as he was to exceed what was expected of a junior liaison officer in Arabia in 1917. H. V. F. Winstone, the biographer of Woolley and of Gertrude Bell, and author of a book on British intelligence operations in the region, questioned why both Woolley and Lawrence took such an interest in the politics of the region, and why some of the papers relating to their activities were locked up for so long. (Some continue to be embargoed.) It is tempting to see the hand of British intelligence at work, perhaps the Secret Service Bureau (SSB), which had been created in 1909, the same year that the British Museum dig at Carchemish was authorised. SSB was charged with gathering intelligence; its foreign branch was subsequently called the Secret Intelligence Service (SIS), more commonly known as MI6. A union of the Royal Navy, British diplomats and the British Museum, working together in a politically sensitive region, on the route of the Berlin-to-Baghdad Railway, on a dig with anonymous funding – conspiracy theorists would point to a profusion of co-incidences, and to the fact that before long Woolley and Lawrence would certainly be involved in intelligence work. Also, these two men, along with Hogarth, Gertrude Bell and others, worked together in the Arab Bureau in Cairo during World War I. But if they were spying for Military Intelligence, it is unusual that they chose to brief an American diplomat in Beirut. A more likely explanation for their interest in regional politics is concern for their safety and for the safety of their work at Carchemish.

Trouble did not come, Mesopotamia did not move against the Turkish government and nor did the Kurds help themselves to the wealth of Aleppo. Perhaps word reached them of weapons smuggled into the city. Winifred Fontana, remembering that 'there were rifles under most of my divans at the Consulate',[19] thought Lawrence had made it known 'so that a rumour . . . might spread through the tribe and decide its leaders to give us a wide berth in the event of the raid being carried out'.[20] The British Consulate received nothing more damaging than attention from other diplomats – the German Consul went to complain that they had stockpiled weapons. The British navy patrolled the Syrian coast. The Young Turks, in power again, went back to war in the Balkans, hoping to hold the enclaves of Scutari, Edirne and Janine. The Kurd and Arab tribes watched, waiting for the moment to move. The objectors in Beirut, Damascus and Aleppo, the members of secret societies and people with a public profile, continued to agitate for reform.

If trouble did not come, the threat did not go away, which is why on 22 February, when he returned to Carchemish after seeing the naval officers on to the Beirut-bound train, Lawrence still did not know if Woolley would come and dig that season, and 'if the Museum doesn't dig, and doesn't pay me a retaining fee, I'll be ruined'.[21]

Woolley came, departing from England at the end of February, but by the time he reached Aleppo, Lawrence had left Jerablus. He had heard from Dahoum or Hamoudi of an ancient cemetery called Deve Hüyük, near the Sajur River and within sight of the Baghdad Railway. Looting was a crime in the Ottoman Empire, and there were still policemen in the area, but as many as fifty villagers were digging the site without a permit. Lawrence sent Dahoum to see what was happening and to buy whatever he could – there were 'some nice pieces of Roman bronze and glazed pottery' – because he knew that even if he went in disguise, the villagers would make trouble and prices would rise. Madame Koch, a German antiquity dealer whom Lawrence described as someone who had been too long in Aleppo and was now 'a very quaint person', had already descended on the site. Lawrence wrote to Hogarth 'garrulous' with excitement at discovering that there were Hittite graves, especially as they had found none at Carchemish. The tombs, from the late period, were filled with great bronze spears, axes and swords. The problem was that Madame Koch had no interest in such things, so the villagers broke them or threw them away as being of no value. 'I got some good fibulae [brooches] . . . some bracelets and ear-rings of bronze, a curious pot or two . . . and as a sideline, some Roman glazed bottles, with associated Greek pottery, and a pleasant little lot of miscellanea . . . tomorrow I return there to gather up, I hope, Hittite bronze weapons in sheaves:– unless the police get there first.'[22]

He was disgusted by the tomb clearing he had done in Egypt for Petrie, but this work, on his own initiative, was different. Perhaps it reminded him of the digging he had done in England, looking for Roman sites with his schoolfriend Beeson. 'It is exciting digging,' he told Hogarth, 'a plunge down a shaft at night, the smashing of a stone door, and the hasty shovelling of all objects into a bag by lamp-light. One has to pay tolerably highly for glazed pottery, so I will probably buy no more . . . glass is found, but very dear . . . bronze is thought nothing of.'[23]

Woolley arrived at Baron's Hotel on 27 February and when Lawrence showed him some of the *antikas* he had found, he was as impressed with Lawrence's understanding of the different ages of the burials as he was with the objects he had collected. In his official report on Deve Hüyük, published the following year, Woolley explained that 'a vast amount of plundering is going on, almost unchecked by the authorities, resulting for the most part in the destruction alike of antiquities and of the information that would make them of real value'.[24] As they could not stop the looting, they sent Hamoudi to take control of the site – it was essential for the archaeologists to know which objects were found together and in which grave. 'Our visit was opportune,' he explained to Kenyon, 'for on the same day three men had been sent out to the place by the agent for the Berlin museum in Aleppo; they were however intercepted by our cook [Haj Wahid] who by the use of his revolver persuaded them to take the next train home. We have arranged for any further objects of interest to be reserved for us.'

There were many 'further objects of interest'. Deve Hüyük had two cemeteries and the Carchemish team secured the best of the objects from both. Some were from the sixth century BC and Phoenician not Greek, which Lawrence knew made them very rare. In the middle of March he wrote that work 'is still going on, and we are getting very nice things out of it'.[25] So many nice things that they filled four or five crates for England. The unusual point about these, as with the cases collected from the British Consulate at Alexandretta, was that they were sent via Cumberbatch in Beirut to be put, in Woolley's words, on 'the first available warship'.[26] They could not pass them through conventional channels because they had no right to be exporting them. A month later, twenty cases of antiquities had reached Hogarth, and Woolley was describing Deve Hüyük as 'played out, practically'.[27] A week later Lawrence described it as 'dead: exhausted, and not sooner than ourselves, since we have masses of stuff from there'.[28]*

★

* Peter Moorey, Keeper of Antiquities at the Ashmolean Museum from 1983 to 2002, described the objects that Lawrence and Woolley collected as coming 'from a known site in a manner which would now be regarded with suspicion', but justified their actions by calling it salvage archaeology: 'To the man who rescued [the antiquities], at the time engaged on a major controlled excavation in the vicinity, the course of action followed was both necessary and fully responsible, in the face of depredations by diggers and dealers with no interest whatsoever in the archaeological significance of their loot' (Moorey 1980, p. 1).

In April, there was a lecture in London on the state of Hittite archaeology, a subject of sufficient importance to be written up in *The Times*. Professor Garstang, who gave the lecture, discussed the German work at Boghaz Köy, his own excavation at Sarcagoze and the digs at Carchemish. Special mention went to the Hittite archive that had been found at Boghaz Köy and to the ninth-century BC palace and walled city that Garstang had uncovered. Carchemish had produced nothing more show-stopping than 'important Hittite sculptures and inscriptions, as well as burials of the bronze age'.[29] Nor was there mention of Hogarth's great hope of finding a 'Hittite Rosetta Stone'. In Garstang's view, Carchemish lacked archaeological significance and neither Hogarth nor the British Museum were happy about that.

While Garstang was passing judgment, two hundred men were scraping at the surface of the Carchemish *tell*. Woolley had divided them into two teams, the majority working with him on the Lower Palace, near the big 'triumphal' staircase, while the others went with Lawrence to dig at the South Gate. A Roman gateway had already been cleared there, but beneath it they found a Hittite structure which Lawrence described as:

> interesting, architecturally, being well preserved, with good polished walls in stone, and a flagged pavement scored with wheel ruts: late Hittite:– The tragedy is that it is only defensive, with no more sculpture than a (or two) horrible lions, standing on the inner edges of flanking towers: we have dug out one tower, and found one lion, badly battered in Roman times when it had stood in the street, and without a head. It had been about 12 feet long poor beast, but is now sad-looking. I think I will cover it up.[30]

The lack of headline discoveries did not deter people from coming to see the excavations, especially now that Jerablus was an easy journey by train from Aleppo. 'We are inundated by visitors,' Lawrence complained after more than a fortnight's work, 'and it makes our day very difficult: we start in the morning early as usual, when it is too cold to do any writing of notes or planning or photography: and then about 10 a.m. comes one batch of visitors, and about 3 p.m. a second. They are usually foreigners or distinguished people, or people with introductions:— and we have to show them all over: such a dull set.'[31] Among the visitors were Raphael and Winifred Fontana and their children. Flecker had called Fontana 'a glorious specimen of high worn out aesthetic Genoese aristocracy',[32] so they presumably were not among the 'dull set'. The diplomat wrote to Hogarth in Oxford after their visit to say that they had 'inflicted ourselves upon them for three days, enjoying ourselves very much. They were very kind and hospitable. Since our visit several more reliefs have been found, it seems, and they seemed pleased with the result of the dig so far. They both seem very fit and well.'[33]

Winifred Fontana was more forthcoming and remembered that 'Lawrence spared himself no pains for this woman's comfort and happiness . . .' The Fontanas were sleeping in tents near the expedition house. 'When the tents blew down in a storm it was Lawrence who emptied the room used as a woodstore by the diggers: carrying out the blocks at furious speed to have ready a dry place for my bedding and that of my children before the rain fell. It was Lawrence, remembering my love of music, who enticed a band of Kurdish musicians to play and sing for us; Lawrence who knew without being told, that happy domesticity does not kill a woman's love of adventure.'[34] He had shipped a canoe from England and he and Woolley often went out on the Euphrates late in the day to shoot birds. Lawrence now used it to take Winifred Fontana to an island near the Mesopotamian riverbank, so that she could collect wild flowers. While there, she was startled by the rattle of gunfire. 'Lawrence laughed at my troubled face and rushed me headlong towards the sound.' He and Woolley had introduced a system to announce new discoveries at the digs: a small fragment was greeted with a single shot, while a large carved slab might be seven or eight. It was fun, and it kept the men motivated for there was kudos in being able to shoot off one's gun, as Woolley remembered when one of the men came to announce that he was quitting work. 'Effendim, I cannot stand it,' the man told Woolley. 'This season so much has been found, there is shooting every day – now it is Hamdôsh, ping-ping-ping, now it is Mustapha

Aissa, ping-ping-ping-ping, now another, but for me not one cartridge since work started. I must go, Effendim, or else you must put me where I shall find something. Honestly, I don't want baksheesh – don't give me money for it; it is the honour of the thing.'[35] This was the sound that had disturbed Winifred Fontana as she picked wild flowers and that had Lawrence paddling furiously across the fast-flowing river. 'We were in time to see a huge Hittite slab hauled by some fifty Arabs with ropes from its ancient tomb of burnt earth.'[36]

Work went well for all of them and, now that they had enough funding to run the dig as they wished, they were confident of results. In March, when they started, Lawrence admitted that 'we have not yet set the Euphrates ablaze',[37] but after a couple of months he described it as 'the richest British Museum dig since Layard's now . . .'* Even Woolley, usually more cautious, was upbeat. They were turning up so much material that Lawrence, with his typical mix of flippancy and enthusiasm, complained that 'we are finding everything, and indeed wish we weren't . . . We were peacefully and quietly finishing the remains of a late Hittite temple; putting everything decently and in order; and then just when we thought ourselves safe, and were folding our hands in sleep, we tumbled over the corner of a new sculptured wall about 20 feet deep in the soil. There were images of monsters and deities.'[38] A carved wall of soldiers, dubbed Herald's Wall, led to a gate decorated with a royal figure, which they called 'the King's Gate . . . because it had to have a name, and we already have about four "palaces" running'.[39] Woolley thought it was 'by far the finest monument yet discovered' at Carchemish. 'It is difficult to overestimate the importance of this gateway,' he wrote to the British Museum, so they would have no doubts about the significance of the Carchemish excavations. 'We now know that outside the ruined area of the Lower palace, in a part of the *Kalaat* [the fortified city] where we hardly expected to dig, there are buildings

---

* Sir Austen Henry Layard, the famous British archaeologist, had discovered the palace of the Assyrian King Assurbanipal at Nineveh, and with it a library of thousands of clay tablets.

of the best period, rich in sculpture, and standing six feet high. Nothing before has promised so well for the site. Clearly our work will have to be extended in that direction.'[40] Happiness would also be extended.

14

Gathering Storm

Everything seems to be quiet at present; but I trust that peace
will be made before the Allies attack the Chataldja Lines. The
Turks don't look like standing fast anywhere now . . .
                                 Sir Frederic Kenyon, 28 March 1913[1]

Spring–summer 1913

THE KURDS AND Arabs had not moved on Aleppo nor risen
against the government in Constantinople, but conversation at
Carchemish was all about affairs in the Balkans. On 5 March 1913,
the Turkish army had been defeated at Yamina. On the 25th, the
garrison at Edirne (Adrianople), as many as 75,000 Turkish soldiers,
had surrendered to the Bulgarians. That same day, the Young Turk
government, whose motto during the coup two months earlier had
been 'Free Edirne!',* was forced to give greater autonomy to six
eastern Anatolian provinces with large minority populations, among
them Armenians and Kurds. On 30 March, they ratified the Treaty
of London, an armistice brokered by Britain and the European Powers,
in which they signed away Turkey's remaining European possessions,
including Crete, the Aegean Islands and the Greek Orthodox enclave
of Mount Athos. The consequences of this diplomatic defeat, following
the military one, were catastrophic in a number of ways. In two years
the Turks had gone from holding an empire across three continents
to an embattled, embittered rump in Asia. The lost revenues from
the ceded territories would have serious consequences for the imperial

* Edirne had been the Ottoman capital in the fifteenth century, before the conquest
of Constantinople.

treasury, as would the need to resettle as many as four hundred thousand predominantly Muslim refugees from the fallen European provinces. The effects on morale were more instant.

The Ottoman government had hoped for a foreign protector as its armies failed and had looked to Sir Edward Grey, the long-standing British Foreign Secretary, and to his counterparts in Russia, France and Austria-Hungary. Turkey had been the 'sick man of Europe' for so long that what was happening was not unexpected: a dozen years earlier even Sultan Abdul Hamid II had admitted that his empire would be partitioned. But the manner in which it was collapsing was unedifying. Britain, long committed to the preservation of the Ottoman Empire, did offer some help, including naval expertise. But the biggest hand of friendship offered from Europe was German and, while the Kaiser did not go so far as to offer a mutual accord or defence agreement (that happened on 2 August the following year, with the Great War under way), the Germans did continue discussions on mutual cooperation and provided German expertise to reorganise the battered Ottoman army.

Few of the effects of these developments were felt directly in Jerablus, or even in Aleppo, but waves of disaffection continued to wash across Anatolia and into Syria throughout the spring and summer of 1913, making worse the local problems, the most pressing of which was the price and availability of food. The winter rains had failed, the price of flour had gone up 50 per cent and other basic foods had also shot up in price. When hundreds of desperate women took to the streets of Aleppo demanding that the Vali intervene to stabilise market prices, Consul Fontana reported that the municipality had no funds for this or any other emergency. He predicted that the lack of rain would bring a bad harvest, and that that would lead to food shortages and perhaps even famine. He conjured an image of mobs pillaging whatever stores of grain and flour were being held in the city. They were better off in Carchemish, where the population was small enough to be supported by the fertile land. But the harvest was important and Lawrence and Woolley knew that when the crops were ready they would lose the majority of their workforce, and therefore would have to close the digs.

More dangerous even than the threat of failed harvest and famine were the consequences of the humbling of Turkish pride. The empire had long been held together by the collective dream of Ottomanism – a vague, inclusive ideal that had at its centre the sultan, who as caliph claimed to be the temporal leader of Muslims while also a fatherly figure to Christians and Jews. That dream was left tattered by massacres of Armenians and other minorities during the reign of Sultan Abdul Hamid II. After the rise of the Young Turks, the weakening of central authority, the deposing of the Sultan, further massacres of minorities and now these catastrophic defeats in Europe and Libya, this central ideal of the empire had fragmented. In the heartland, the most persistent calls were for 'Turkey for the Turks!' while in the Syrian *vilayets*, there was more demand for Arab rights. Raphael Fontana noted that while the French were actively encouraging Christians and Muslims to lobby for a French occupation, the majority of both creeds wanted a British government to rule over them, or, failing that, for their territories to be absorbed into British-ruled Egypt, which would keep them, in name at least, under Turkish sovereignty. To Fontana, the crisis in Turkey gave Britain an opportunity to act in Syria, Palestine and Mesopotamia. Field Marshal Horatio Herbert Kitchener had another view. Kitchener, the British Agent in Cairo and the man who effectively ruled Egypt, warned Sir Edward Grey that 'as soon as the war [in the Balkans] is over, a large number of Turkish troops will return to Asian Minor and Syria. They will be filled with bitter hostility to all Europeans and Christians . . . The presence of these men in Syria and Palestine, coupled with the excitement which I understand already prevails in those provinces . . . must for some time to come be a source of anxiety.'[2] A source of anxiety, but while Arabs called for greater rights, very few were demanding independence from Constantinople.

Lawrence, however, was chanting 'Down with the Turks!' In a letter to Emily Rieder, now teaching at a progressive co-ed boarding school in England, he regretted that 'there is, not life, but stickiness in them yet'.[3] His desire to see the Ottoman Empire give up the Near East derived not from a hatred of Turks, or even of their system of government, but from a belief in the potential of the Arabs and

A doorway in the house Lawrence built at Carchemish, with Haj Wahid, the cook. Many visitors mistook Lawrence's mock-Hittite lintel for a genuine antiquity

Workmen above a row of carved Hittite slabs. Railway carts made it easier to remove the Roman-era concrete laid over the more ancient structures

Carchemish as Lawrence last saw it, from the citadel in 1914, with much of the ancient city exposed

Lawrence's photograph of the Lower Palace area, Carchemish, with some of the 200-strong workforce clearing earth and rubble from the grand ceremonial staircase lined with huge decorative slabs

Carchemish. 'Over 60 men are tugging away above, each man yelling *Yallah* as he pulls: the row is tremendous, but the stones usually come away.'

Gregori, Hogarth's ageing foreman, photographed by Lawrence,
smoking his waterpipe near
the equipment store. A former
tomb-robber, he usually knew
where to dig and how to control
the workmen

The Carchemish foremen: (*from left*) Lawrence's young protégé Dahoum,
Abd es Salaam, Gregori (seated) and Hamoudi

The salon in Lawrence's expedition house, with some of his precious carpets on the wall. He bought the inlaid cabinet (*right*) in the Alexandretta souk in February 1913

Lawrence's portrait of Busrawi (*centre*), Agha of the local Kurds, with two other sheikhs, probably at Carchemish in April 1913 when Busrawi made peace with the Shahins

The wooden Baghdad Railway bridge over the Euphrates at Carchemish where German engineers fought their Kurd and Arab workmen in March 1914

Some of the Carchemish workforce which, at its peak, was 200 strong.
Front row (*left to right*): Gregori (in hat), Lawrence, Woolley, Fuad Bey (the inspector), Hamoudi and Dahoum

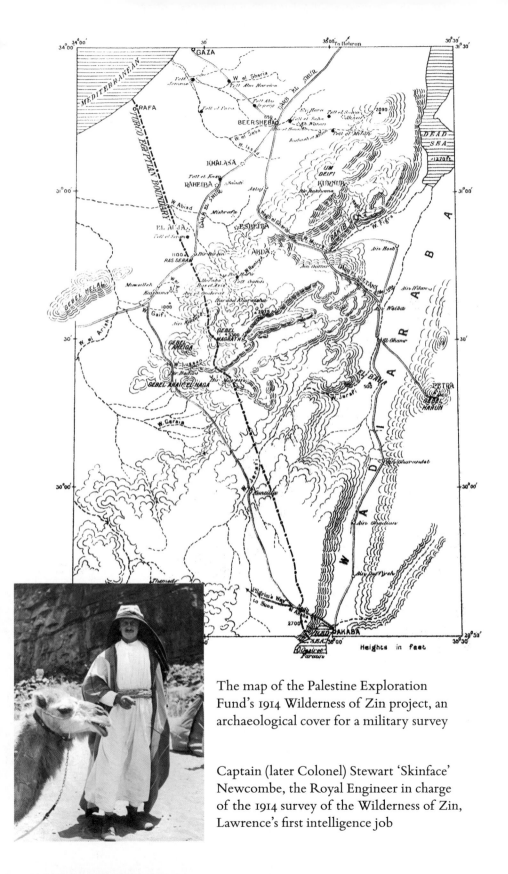

The map of the Palestine Exploration Fund's 1914 Wilderness of Zin project, an archaeological cover for a military survey

Captain (later Colonel) Stewart 'Skinface' Newcombe, the Royal Engineer in charge of the 1914 survey of the Wilderness of Zin, Lawrence's first intelligence job

Lawrence after Arabia, in the Victoria Hotel, Damascus, October 1918.
'Only for me,' he wrote of the fall of the city, 'was the event sorrowful.'

an awareness that the Turks' 'disappearance would mean a chance for the Arabs, who were at any rate once not incapable of good government'. There is no writing from him, or testament from his childhood friends, to support his claim, written almost as an after-thought on the last page of the 1920s *Seven Pillars of Wisdom*, that 'I had dreamed, at the City School in Oxford, of hustling into form, while I lived, the new Asia which time was inexorably bringing upon us.'[4] What we know he had dreamed, this dreamer of the day – and we know this from his friends and brothers – was a world of gentle knights and noble crusade. 'Mecca was to lead to Damascus; Damascus to Anatolya, and afterwards to Baghdad; and then there was Yemen.' This aspiration ran counter to British policy, publicly stated by the Foreign Secretary, to stop the break-up of Asiatic Turkey. It was also against the expectations of Arabs, at least those known to Consul Fontana, who wished for a European – and probably British – administration. But if the wider political picture was one of conflict and confusion, something more harmonious was happening nearer to home.

Kurdish tribes around Jerablus had been divided by a feud that had lasted three generations and had claimed many lives. In April 1913, it was suddenly and decisively brought to an end when Woolley and Lawrence received a visit from two brothers, the Shahins, leaders of one of the Kurdish tribes across the river in Mesopotamia. The visit was entirely unexpected, but Woolley did what local custom demanded and invited the brothers into the expedition house, where coffee and cigarettes were served. While they sat and talked, the house guard, Midai, also a Kurd, came to tell Woolley that another Kurdish leader, the famous Busrawi Agha, had arrived. Woolley knew of the feud between these men and, although he had stared down and even pulled guns on Turkish officials and soldiers, he knew these Kurds could be volatile and he admitted to being 'more than a little nervous'.[5] Unable to deter the rival chief from calling, obliged to invite him in and offer him hospitality, Woolley had no choice but to try to moderate between the men.

Busrawi arrived dressed in an embroidered tunic and his best outer robe, a scarf around his neck and another over his head. His thick beard was trimmed and his moustache worked into horizontal points.

He was accompanied by two retainers and 'a big stoutish Kurd, also well-dressed in Baghdad fashion, a stranger to me'.[6] This was a cousin of the late Kurdish leader Ibrahim Pasha, murdered three years earlier on orders from Constantinople for supporting the deposed Sultan.

As Busrawi approached the sitting room, Woolley feared there would be more bloodshed. 'The two Shahins rose to their feet: Busrawi's party stood silent by the door. I took the bull by the horns. "Busrawi Agha," I said, "I want you to meet my friends the sons of Shahin Bey."' The men faced each other. It was, of course, unthinkable that there would be violence there and then, for no other reason than they were guests in the house of the Englishmen. Then they stepped forward, shook hands, and Busrawi kissed the younger men.

Ibrahim's cousin then spoke and made clear that the encounter was not coincidental. 'He said that this meeting, which was ardently desired by the Milli-Kurd leaders, and was most necessary with a view to uniting Arabs and Kurds against the Turks, had taken place on the only ground where the two rival houses could have met in safety and without loss of prestige, namely, on British soil.'[7] Woolley wrote about this meeting several years after the event – between 1916 and 1918, when he was a prisoner of war in the Turkish town of Kastamonu. Lawrence, who wrote about it on the day of the meeting, noted that 'Woolley cemented the alliance with chocolates, and a photograph, and the whole lot went off to Aleppo with the largest lunch-basket on record, to pay a call on the British Consul there. What poor Mr. Fontana will say to 9 Kurds I don't know. The diplomatic career is not a sinecure in Turkey.'[8]*

---

* This comment about the diplomatic career may have been inspired by Lawrence's friend James Elroy Flecker. Struggling in his posting as consular assistant, he had failed his consular exams and had not endeared himself to his superiors. But the reason he was now leaving for Switzerland had nothing to do with his work: he had had a recurrence of TB. The illness had provoked a storm of creativity and even in hospital in Beirut he had been writing lines:

> Would I might lie like this, without the pain,
> For Seven Years – as one with snowy hair,
> Who in the high tower dreams his dying reign . . .

In a strange moment of synchronicity, at the same time as Busrawi and the Shahins were ending their feud, a thirty-year fight between the ruling houses of Europe was coming to an end with the marriage in Berlin of Princess Victoria Luise, only daughter of the German Kaiser, and Prince Ernest Augustus of Cumberland. The marriage had caught the popular imagination across Europe for two reasons: it seemed to be a genuine love match, and it ended the long-running dispute between the houses of Hanover and Hohenzollern. What would have been most encouraging for an observer of European progress, anxiously watching events in the Balkans – and the wedding was what we would call a global media event – was that on the evening of the wedding, in the baroque opulence of Berlin's Rittersaal, the families gathered to dance. As this was European royalty, it involved the German imperial family, the British King George V, his wife Queen Mary and the Russian Tsar Nicholas II, turning on the dance floor while a range of gods looked down from the painted ceiling. Dancing monarchs, united houses, feuds ended. One might forgive a twenty-four-year-old archaeologist at the end of a successful dig on the Euphrates for thinking that all was well with the world and that life could not have been better.

As the wild flowers were reduced to crisp husks along the paths through the ruins, a rare sense of harmony settled on Jerablus. The wheat and barley crops were brought in and, contrary to predictions, the harvest was a good one. To this satisfaction was added a sense of achievement as the team's most successful season drew to a close. They had made more – and more important – discoveries than in all the previous seasons and 'Mr. Hogarth says they are the best things found archaeologically for many years.'[9] Even Kenyon was 'lyrical' about their work. They had worked hard, too. 'All over!' Lawrence wrote to E. T. Leeds at the Ashmolean, 'Carchemish 4 is at an end, and thank the Lord! We have sweated the last few weeks like fiends, and it has been so hot . . . and now it is become so cool . . . woe is me! for I wanted to bathe.'[10]

When he reached Switzerland, after a hellish journey during which both his wife and a doctor thought he would die, and when it became clear that he would not be returning to Beirut, he wrote to tell Lawrence: 'No more of the infernal East for me.'

Yet even in those calm days of early summer, turmoil was never far away. Throughout May, the Young Turk government in Constantinople, led by the Grand Vizier Mahmud Shevket Pasha, had rolled out its reform plans, which included, among many other things, the acceptance of Arabic in official circles and in schools. Not everyone in government was pleased with these changes, nor with the Baghdad-born Grand Vizier's suggestion (an idea first proposed by a German military adviser) that, as Constantinople was vulnerable to attack from Europe, perhaps the imperial capital might be moved east into Anatolia, even to Aleppo. Conflicting views in government were matched by rivalry in the provinces: Consul-General Cumberbatch reported that government agents were sowing discord in Beirut 'in the hopes of weakening the reform campaign'.[11] Events became more confused and volatile after 11 June when Shevket Pasha was assassinated on his way to his office in Constantinople. The subsequent mood in the empire was captured by *The Times* in an editorial entitled 'A Critical Hour', which noted that few Turkish politicians enjoyed the public's confidence – certainly not the man brought in as interim Grand Vizier, Said Halim Pasha, an Egyptian prince. The assassination had come at a bad time, the editorial continued, because 'differences between the late Allies in the Balkans [Serbia and Bulgaria] appear to be coming to a head'.[12] It also came at what should have been a key moment for Arab dissenters.

The idea of an Arab National Congress would have been inconceivable a few years earlier, but so much had changed so quickly – Turkish decline, growing German influence, a Baghdad-born Grand Vizier, greater Jewish immigration, an increasingly strident Arabic press and some concessions from the Ottoman government. When activists in Paris called for a Congress, the idea seemed less revolutionary than it might have done a few years earlier. The Congress opened at the Société de Géographie on the Boulevard Saint-Germain in Paris a week after the Grand Vizier's assassination. Among the twenty-five official delegates and other guests were people from across the Near East and representing a variety of reform agendas. These included members of the Paris-based Al Fatat, the

Young Arab Society,* the Beirut Reform Society and the Ottoman Party for Administrative Decentralisation. Intriguingly, there were also two Zionists, one of whom was Sami Hochberg, described by one of his colleagues as 'a dubious character'[13] and proprietor of a Constantinople newspaper, *Le Jeune Turc*. A month before the Congress, Hochberg had written a report for the Zionist leadership in which he had argued that Zionists must keep close links to Arab nationalists for the compelling reason that 'we will prevent extremists from leading them'.[14] He understood, as many since then have not, that dialogue between groups with different interests would reduce the risk of conflict.

Although Lawrence in Jerablus was unaware of its progress – and most people in the empire were unaware even of its existence – the Congress was a milestone in the emergence of an Arab political identity. 'A first difficulty of the Arab movement,' Lawrence was to write, 'was to say who the Arabs were.'[15] Must one speak Arabic? come from Arabia? be Muslim? A clear statement on this issue, and on Arab independence, came from Abdul Ghani al-Arisi, a Beirut delegate and another newspaper proprietor. The Arabs, al-Arisi argued, 'have unity of language, race, history, traditions, customs and political ambitions. It is therefore an inalienable right of the Arabs, supported by the full weight of political science, to form a group, a people (*sha'b*) and a nation (*umma*).'[16] But in spite of the assertions of independence and arguments about inalienable rights, nothing in the eleven resolutions agreed by the delegates, and published on 21 June, hinted at a plan to secede from the empire. Instead, pointing out that radical and urgent reform was needed if the empire was to flourish, they called for greater autonomy. However heated the debate inside the Congress, however many people shouted 'Down with the Turks!', the message that emerged from Paris was that Arabs – those represented by this group – were content to remain within the empire, at least for the moment. But however loudly that message was shouted, however extraordinary the Congress, however enlightened the delegates, they had less impact than they

---

* Among their early supporters was Shukri al-Quwatli, later to serve twice as President of independent Syria.

hoped because a week after their announcements the Bulgarians invaded their Balkan League allies Serbia and Greece. The Ottoman government mobilised its newly reformed army, hoping to reclaim lost territory. Then Rumania, seeing a chance for enlargement, sent 150,000 men across the Danube. With the ink hardly dry on the Treaty of London, the Second Balkan War erupted.

15

Eating Lotos

But, propped on beds of amaranth and moly,
How sweet – while warm airs lull us, blowing lowly –
With half-dropped eyelid still,
Beneath a heaven dark and holy,
To watch the long bright river drawing slowly
His waters from the purple hill –

Alfred, Lord Tennyson, 'The Lotos-Eaters'[1]

Summer 1913

LAWRENCE WAS IN no hurry to go back to Oxford, so when Woolley left for England on 14 June 1913 he stayed at Jerablus. He had recently had a rare open disagreement with his mother, who had made a comment about their working on the sabbath, taking Fridays off instead. He had responded by asking, 'Would it be quite considerate to make two hundred workmen miss their day [of rest] for the sake of the two of us? Especially as they are not sophisticated enough to have heard of Julian and Gregorian calendars, or the "first day of the week" theory.'[2] His letters were less frequent after that, and when the excavations closed for the summer, he stayed, revelling in 'the resultant feeling . . . of a most perfect peace: it is midday, everyone is asleep, and the only noise near me is the ticking of a watch on our great table'.[3]

This peace was soon disturbed by the arrival of a stray English consul, en route to Diarbekir, one hundred miles to the east, who needed to be entertained. He wanted exercise, so he dived off the railway bridge into the river, to the consternation of Herr Contzen, the senior German engineer, who thought he was trying to commit suicide. Lawrence showed his visitor around the digs and gave him some shooting practice. When he left, a week after Woolley had gone, Lawrence wrote, 'I'll come to Oxford.' By then he knew there was a chance that his parents might be away at the coast and, if that was the case, he suggested they leave a key at the insurance office in town. He added as a postscript, 'Hope to bring 2 Arabs with me this summer.'[4]

Much has been written about Lawrence's sexual preferences, as it has about his relationship with Dahoum. Even more has been speculated. Dahoum was fourteen years old when they first met, in January 1911, perhaps even thirteen, as his exact birth date is not known. Something about this donkey-boy, bringing water and supplies to the digs, had caught Lawrence's attention and retained it. Their relationship had changed significantly after that first Carchemish season as a result of Dahoum nursing Lawrence through dysentery in the summer of 1911. Dahoum had then accompanied him on the first leg of the journey to Aleppo. Afterwards, Lawrence had looked for ways of repaying the kindness and attention, as well as encouraging the spark he saw in him. He began by promoting him among the workforce – Dahoum became Lawrence's assistant and learned how to use the cameras and to make squeezes of the inscriptions they uncovered. By the summer of 1913, Dahoum, now sixteen, was one of the senior members of the team, although he did not yet have the same status as Hamoudi, the Hoja or overseer.

More important than these practical steps was the help Lawrence provided for Dahoum to improve himself. He had asked Miss Fareedeh at the American School for Arabic history and geography books – nothing 'foreign'. 'I have no wish to do more for the boy than give him a chance to help himself,' although he had already done much more than this, taking him to Aleppo, to Alexandretta, on a British warship up the Syrian coast, and giving him access to the British Consulate and to the houses of the Altounyans and other wealthy people in Aleppo, not normally open to a village boy, however bright. Why was he doing this? In part, because he recognised the boy's romantic spirit. It was Dahoum who had impressed Lawrence the previous summer at Qasr Ibn Wardani, the ruined desert fort where the rooms smelled of roses, all except one, where there was nothing but pure, clear desert air. 'Among us,' Lawrence reported Dahoum as saying, 'we call this room the sweetest of all.'

By his own admission, Lawrence was unable to think plainly. Everything had another level, a parallel meaning. So while the story of Ibn Wardani tells of a love of beauty, he also saw that Dahoum was 'half-consciously sounding the ideal of the Arab creed, for generations stripping itself of all furniture in the working out of a gospel of simplicity'.[5] There was a gospel of austerity here and one that Lawrence, in spite of his compulsive purchasing of Hittite *antikas* and Persian rugs, found seductive. He was interested to see how far this noble young savage might go, to see what he would do, given opportunities. Jeremy Wilson, the authorised Lawrence biographer, describes an 'almost fatherly concern'[6] for the youth. But there was more than paternal care; there was love. Ten years later, when Lawrence referred to his friendship with Dahoum, he talked of it as one in which there was such intimacy and mutual understanding that they had said all that two people could say to each other. This freed them to work or rest together for hours without speaking. Lawrence experienced that sense of calm and trust with very few people in his life. It was not obvious that one of them would be the donkey-boy from Jerablus.

In this summer of 1913, the two of them spent most days and evenings together, working at the digs, swimming in the Euphrates, cleaning and drawing, photographing and cataloguing the finds in the courtyard or large sitting room of the expedition house, even while Lawrence was busy writing of his adventures in *Seven Pillars of Wisdom*, the book he was to burn in Oxford. Woolley was happy with this relationship and had made no objection to Lawrence trusting him sufficiently to let him buy *antikas* in villages – Dahoum was usually offered a lower price, even though Lawrence had refined his haggling technique.

It is impossible to know what Dahoum thought of these changes to his life. He was obviously flattered that the *khawaja* was taking an interest in him, while the extra money and new status helped set him apart in the village. A range of possibilities was opening through his growing ability to read and write Arabic. But only occasionally can we hear Dahoum's voice with any clarity. One moment was at Ibn Wardani, but the most persuasive was his answer to Miss Fareedeh's question, in the summer of 1912, of why he loved Lawrence. He did so, he had replied, because Lawrence was brother, friend and leader, because he could do things better than them, because he was courageous, playful, humorous and, perhaps more important to them, because they knew he cared for them.

This, Lawrence wrote to Hogarth, 'will shock you'.[7] In the event, many more than Hogarth were shocked to see two Arabs, their heads covered in *keffiyehs*, wearing striped, flowing robes over baggy white trousers and embroidered tunics, walking along the High in Oxford or cycling down the Woodstock Road. Lawrence had kept his promise and brought Dahoum and Hamoudi home.

He had spent less than a fortnight there in the past year and a half, and was not planning on staying long this time – ten days in all, and in that time he had work to do. He also needed to look after Dahoum and Hamoudi because they spoke almost no English. The visitors stayed in the bungalow at Polstead Road, Lawrence in the main house, but they spent the days together, several of them at the Ashmolean, where they saw Hogarth, Woolley and Leeds. On 12 August, at the Ashmolean, they also met the painter Francis Dodd; Charles Bell, Assistant Keeper at the museum, had arranged for Dodd to sketch their portraits. As Bell was now on holiday, Lawrence wrote him a description of the meeting:

> Dodd turned up smiling in the morning, and got to work like a steam engine:– black and white, with little faint lines of colour running up and down in it. No. 1 was finished by midday, and was splendid: Dahoum sitting down, with his most-interested-possible expression . . . he thought it great sport – said he never knew he was so good-looking – and I think he was about right. He had dropped his sulkiness for a patch.
>
> No. 2 was almost a failure. Dodd gave it up half-finished.
>
> No. 3, standing, was glorious. My brother came to the door with some people, and Dahoum just at the critical moment looked round a little bit annoyed, to see what the dickens the matter was. Dodd got him on the instant and promptly stopped work.[8]

Dodd gave the first one to Dahoum, and the third one to Bell.

Hamoudi is not mentioned here, perhaps because he was with Woolley that day. (After 1918, Hamoudi became Woolley's foreman and worked at Ur in the 1920s.) But the lack of a portrait of Hamoudi would explain the strange story he told after Lawrence's death when he remembered that 'many wished to photograph us [Hamoudi and Dahoum] as we sat with him [Lawrence] in our customary clothes. And after they took a picture they would come and speak to him and always he said, "No, No." One day I asked him why he was always saying "No, No," and he laughed and said, "I will tell you. These people wish to give you money. But for me you would now be rich."'

'Do you call yourself my friend,' Hamoudi shouted, 'and say thus calmly that you kept me from riches?' It was a rare moment of cultural division between them. It also shows that the Syrians understood the wealth and privilege of their young friend.

Hamoudi remembered that Lawrence had laughed at his anger, and the more he laughed, the angrier Hamoudi became. Then Lawrence said, 'Yes, you might have been rich, richer than any in Jerablus. And I – what should I have been? I should have been the showman of two monkeys.'

'And suddenly,' Hamoudi admitted, 'all my anger died down within me.'[9]

Leeds, who also met them at the museum, described Dahoum 'dressed in picturesque, clean robes, striped in red, black and white'. He thought him 'too spruce and fine for any menial task', and yet when some crates needed moving, he lifted something that would have needed three museum porters to carry. Before they left, Leeds asked them what they would most like to take home with them. They chose two things. One was a water tap, so they would have hot water whenever they wanted, instead of having to heat it in a kettle as they did at home. The other was more revealing of what Leeds called their 'childlike simplicity of incomprehension', for they asked for one of the 'Keep off the grass' signs they had seen on a stake in the University Parks. 'Evidently these hoops possessed magic properties as guards against trespass and might be turned to good account.'[10]

Back in Jerablus, Lawrence wrote that Dahoum and Hamoudi

'entertain large houses nightly with tales of snakes as long as houses, underground railways, elephants, flying-machines, and cold in July'.[11] Later still he noted that 'they are too intelligent to be ridiculous about it. They describe it as a garden, empty of villages, with the people crowded into frequent towns. The towns wonderfully peaceful and populous, the houses very high: the tube railways are to them a source of stumbling.' More important than this was the realisation of their place in the world, for 'they tell the villagers that Syria is a small poor country, very likely to be coveted by us tree-lovers . . . and that the Arabs are too few to count in world-politics. All of this is very proper.'[12]

What Lawrence's parents felt about their house guests is not known; his brothers enjoyed the company of the Syrians. What was clear to the Lawrences, however, was that their second son had grown away from them. Neither the garden bungalow, an academic posting nor even his printing-press plan would be enough to bring him back because – and this he knew and they must have guessed – he had found somewhere that suited him (for the moment, at least) and it was in Syria, not England. That, and the fact that he had Dahoum and Hamoudi to look after, explains why, although Woolley was not intending to return to Syria until the end of September, Lawrence was back in Aleppo on 24 August with plenty of gossip to share.

Writing from Baron's Hotel, he marvelled at having passed from England to the Mediterranean and then by boat to Alexandretta via Egypt without once having had his bag checked by customs. This had particular resonance when he reported that Baron von Oppenheim, now referred to merely as 'the German excavator'[13] – he had dropped the 'little Jew-German-millionaire' epithet, but still called him 'an ass'[14] – had had a cart of antiquities seized by the authorities near Aleppo. 'We know not what will become of him,' Lawrence wrote, barely disguising his pleasure at their rival's discomfort, adding, 'we are very fortunate to have had no check so far in any of our forwarding departments'.[15] Other news included the buying of Hittite seals in Aleppo, the German engineers having built some sheds on the archaeological site (Haj Wahid had taken them over), the weather was hot, the river low, it was Ramadan and the

Turkish army were again requisitioning mules. After the excitement of the digging season and the intensity of his brief visit home, suddenly he was at a loss, 'back in the House of Bondage',[16] as he confessed to Leeds in Oxford, which was where his brother Will found him.

Will Lawrence had graduated from Oxford that summer and secured a teaching job in Delhi. Instead of going straight to India via the Suez Canal, he had decided to pass through the Middle East and to visit this brother. He arrived just a fortnight after Ned had reached Aleppo. Of the five Lawrence brothers, Will and Ned were closest in temperament, age and interests – Will had a love of the classics, studied history at St John's College, Oxford, liked to swim and wrote extremely well. Unlike his elder brother, Will had retained the religious belief their parents had encouraged. One of his Oxford tutors remembered that he 'combined, above any other man that I ever knew, a great love of beauty and a deep religious sense'.[17] He also thought Will was 'perhaps the gentlest, but also one of the strongest; perhaps the most winning' of the young Lawrences.

Will's route took him from Beirut – 'very beautiful, a splendid bay' – to Damascus, which he thought was the most beautiful place he had ever seen. 'I have just come in from seeing moonlight and afterglow and it's simply glorious. Minarets and white roofs . . .'[18] Seduced by the scent of peach, the mix of nations, the industry in the souks, when he reached Ned in Aleppo he described him as 'very well and a great lord in this place'.[19] There is a sense of joy in his description of seeing his brother in Syria, of awe also, because Ned, just a year older, 'is known by everyone, and their enthusiasm over him is quite amusing'. Amusing and impressive, particularly when they happened to meet Busrawi Agha, the great Kurd leader who was visiting his son in hospital, and who invited Will to visit his tents across the Euphrates.

'This Carchemish comes as a surprise,' Will wrote when they left the train at Jerablus. 'The station shows no mound in sight and no river . . . a walk of ten minutes or so over rocky slopes brought us without really any climbing into the Kalaat of Jerablus which is thus low on one side. It is a very wide circle full of old stones and trial pits of the digs dotted about it . . . The Mound is thus impressive only from the riverbank. Then very much so.'[20] But more impressive than the place, and the things they had excavated in it, was the life his brother was living. The day after Will arrived, Dr Altounyan, who had shown them around Aleppo, came to stay with his son (now practising at the Middlesex Hospital, London) and daughter. Among the other people staying at the mission house during these days was Edgar Bonham Carter, Legal Secretary to the government of Sudan,* Charles Cochrane-Baillie, a man with sleepy eyes and a fine, pointed moustache who, as Lord Lamington, had served as Governor of Queensland, Australia, and of Bombay.† There was also an American missionary, Dr Usher,‡ and with him an English officer, Lieutenant Hubert Young – 'an interesting fellow,' Will reported home, 'speaking Arabic and Persian very well.'

Young and Usher were travelling together to Van and had made a detour to visit the Carchemish excavations. 'Neither Usher nor I knew that archaeologists do not dig in the summer,' Young later wrote, 'and we thought it would be fun to combine a visit to the "digs" with a peep at the railway-bridge . . . At Carchemish we found that Hogarth and Woolley were away and the "digs" closed down for the summer, but we were shown over them by a quiet little man of the name of Lawrence, who was for some reason living there alone.'[21] The quiet little man served them coffee, and grapes on a bed of 'snow' (ice) and then gave such a compelling explanation of the site that the two travellers missed their train. The following day, when Lawrence suggested they stay longer – presumably to relieve his boredom – Usher had other obligations, but Young gladly accepted.

'I have seldom enjoyed a week more than that week at Carchemish,' he remembered.

> We spent the days in clambering over the mound, bathing in the Euphrates, carving figures out of the soft limestone, and above all talking. Lawrence was by then twenty-five, though he looked about sixteen, but in many respects he was years older. By his mere

* After World War I, Bonham Carter became Senior Judicial Officer in Mesopotamia.
† Lamington led a British relief mission to Syria in 1919.
‡ Usher helped Armenians in Van in their 1915 uprising against the Turks.

personality he had converted the excavation into a miniature British consulate. His rough native workmen would have done anything for him. Slight and fair and clean-shaven, he was the last person whom one would have imagined capable of wandering about in native dress and passing unobserved among the swarthy and bearded inhabitants, but he had mastered the local dialect and was apparently accepted without question wherever he went as a youth from Jerablus.

Lawrence was less enthusiastic about having so many visitors at Carchemish and admitted, after the Altounyans had left, that he disliked having the house so full. 'Still,' he conceded, 'Will enjoyed them, and the one who is left, one Young, a Lieut. in an Indian Regiment, is a decent sort of person.'

When it was time to visit Busrawi in his tents across the Euphrates, Lawrence was suffering from fever, so stayed at Jerablus: Young and Will Lawrence crossed the river with Dahoum and Hamoudi. 'He sent his sons and some retainers for us, with horses,' Will reported. 'Then we had a ride of about 6 hours through steppes, perfectly barren stony country rolling up and down with only a very occasional well surrounded always by great herds of large black goats in charge of boys with guns.' Busrawi's status was reflected in the number of his followers, in the fighters he could put in the field and in the size of his tent. Both Young and Lawrence remarked that his tent, which they reached after dark, had forty poles. Open sided in one part, with family quarters screened off in another, it was large enough to hold the hundred people who gathered for the feast. 'They laid down a long mat thirty feet or so upon the carpets in front of our mat, placed bread all along the edges of it, and then more than 40 dishes. The old Agha sat between us and gave the signal to start by taking a piece of meat in his hand and putting it in my spoon. Then everyone fell to with eagerness, saying nothing but eating at a great pace simply shovelling the stuff into their mouths. Servants moved behind with mugs of water.' Will enjoyed the food at the time, but suffered for it the whole way to Delhi. After the food there was coffee, cigarettes and entertainment. 'All the while we had been eating,' Will recalled, 'a man had been beating a drum, and another blowing on a pipe, which sounded at times like the reel pipes, but had no bag. After dinner there was a lot of this music, and some dancing, just of men, who capered about waving handkerchiefs and singing, not very exciting.'[22]

There was a horseback game that sounds similar to polo, and a visit from Khalil, the son of Ibrahim Pasha, the late Kurdish leader. They slept in Busrawi's grand tent. Early the next morning, still by moonlight, they rode back to the river with the Agha and a dozen horsemen. Busrawi continued with them to Jerablus, where he and Will caught the Aleppo train. Lawrence, who had recovered from his fever, saw them off. 'When I last saw him as the train left the station,' Will wrote to reassure their mother, who had obviously made a comment about life in Jerablus being uncivilised, 'he was wearing white flannels, socks and red slippers, with a white Magdalen blazer, and was talking to the governor of Biredjik in lordly fashion.'[23] Two months later, from Delhi, Will told his mother, 'You must think of him as a great power in the land for good: the Kurds apply to him continually, as arbitrator in tribal differences, and he has contrived to keep his village, the Hoja's people, sober, while the Germans have made drunken men a common sight in the [railway] bridge builders' cottages.'[24] Some months later still, Will wrote a verse for his brother, worth repeating for the sentiment as much as for the poetry:

> I've talked with counsellors and lords
> Whose words were as no blunted swords,
> Watched two Emperors and five Kings
> And three who had men's worshippings,
> Ridden with horsemen of the East
> And sat with scholars at their feast,
> Known some the masters of their hours,
> Some to whom years were as pressed flowers:
> Still as I go this thought endures
> No place is too great to be made yours.[25]

'I never quite fathomed why Lawrence was still at Carchemish when the "digs" were closed down,' Lieutenant Young wrote, 'but I gathered that it was partly from choice and partly from economy. He used to spend his time wandering about in Arab dress, sometimes for days at a time, storing his phenomenal memory with scraps of local knowledge which came in very useful later on. When he was not doing this he was trying to puzzle out the Hittite inscriptions or target-shooting with a long Mauser pistol. I amused myself by competing with him at both these games.'[26] Some of Lawrence's biographers have pointed out that this time – 'the best life I ever lived'[27] – when he was being treated as a lord, or, as he himself put it, living like a king, was similar in nature (if not in details) to the life his father had enjoyed before he left his wife for Sarah Lawrence. If the theory that Lawrence had overheard a conversation between his father and someone concerned with the financial or legal settlement is true, then he will have known something of his father's privileged, drink-soaked life. And he will have imagined more. It seems hard to find any other credible explanation for his response, on hearing of his father's intention of going to Ireland around the time that Will was in Carchemish: 'Don't go . . . even to play golf. I think the whole place repulsive historically: they should not like English people, and we certainly cannot like them.'[28]

Young mentioned that they spent time that week carving sculptures from the soft limestone, which Lawrence described as 'gargoyles for the better adornment of the house. He [Young] managed in limestone an ideal head of a woman; I did a squatting demon of the Notre-Dame style, also in limestone, and we have now built them into the walls and roof, and the house is become remarkable in N. Syria. The local people come up in crowds to look at them.'[29] If Leonard Woolley is to be believed, the local people came to do more than look at the sculptures. Writing after Lawrence's death, Woolley described how Lawrence had had 'Dahoum to live with him and got him to pose as model for a queer crouching figure which he carved in the soft local limestone'. There is an insinuation in this, that Lawrence was having a sexual relationship with the youth. Woolley then spelled it out: 'To make an image was bad enough in this way, but to portray a naked figure was proof to them of evil of another sort. The scandal about Lawrence was widely spread and firmly believed.'[30] It has been even more widely spread since Woolley wrote those lines and there continues to be a widespread belief that Lawrence was homosexual, either in practice or in thwarted desire.

Homosexuality was illegal in the UK until 1967, even in private and between consenting adults, so Woolley's suggestion of 'evil of another sort' would have had a greater impact in the 1930s than now. He must have realised the power of what he was writing for, having cast his aspersion, he then hastened to add that it was unfounded. If he believed that the rumour was unfounded, then of all the things he might have written about the man he had worked with for so many years, why say this? Perhaps he remembered the moment the two of them were in a Kurdish village, when Lawrence was approached by a group of girls drawing water at a well. 'One bold hussy pulled open his shirt to see if his skin was white all over; and soon, with shrieks of laughter, they were all about him determined to see more, until he escaped almost stripped. He could not take it as a joke.'[31] Perhaps, for Woolley, Lawrence was not 'one for the ladies', although other people who knew him well had other ideas. Winifred Fontana remembered that 'Lawrence spared himself no pains for this woman's comfort and happiness – nor for that of other women who stayed there.'[32]

Lawrence said he never had a sexual relationship and most people who knew him found that credible. In 1927, he wrote to his friend the (homosexual) novelist E. M. Forster, 'I'm so funnily made up, sexually,'[33] and later that same year went further. Having read Forster's ghost story, 'Dr Woolacott', in which a man dies after a gay sexual encounter, Lawrence wrote that 'The Turks, as you probably know (or have guessed, through the reticences of the *Seven Pillars*) did it to me, by force . . . I couldn't ever do it, I believe: the impulse strong enough to make me touch another creature has not yet been born in me.'[34] The following year, with Robert Graves, the poet and at that point his biographer, he had a discussion 'about fucking': 'As I wrote (with some courage, I think: few people admit the damaging ignorance) I haven't ever: and don't much want to.'[35] The most important testimony, at this young, Carchemish stage of his life, comes from Lawrence's Oxford friend and fellow print-enthusiast Vyvyan Richards, who would have been stunned to know that there was anything sexual in Lawrence's relationship with Dahoum, as he had hoped for such intimacy himself. 'He had neither flesh nor carnality of any kind,' Richards wrote, after confessing his love for his friend.

'He received my affection, my sacrifice, in fact, eventually my total subservience, as though it was his due. He neither gave the slightest sign that he understood my motives or fathomed my desire. In return for all I offered him – with admittedly ulterior motives – he gave me the purest affection, love and respect that I have ever received from anyone . . . a love and respect that was spiritual in quality. I realise now that he was sexless – at least that he was unaware of sex.'[36] Even Woolley eventually mitigated his salacious remarks, insisting that Lawrence 'was in no sense a pervert; in fact, he had a remarkably clean mind. He was tolerant, thanks to his classical reading, and Greek homosexuality interested him, but in a detached way, and the interest was not morbid but perfectly serious.'[37]

Jeremy Wilson in *Lawrence of Arabia: The Authorised Biography* points out that Woolley was 'factually misleading' and 'libellously inaccurate'[38] even for suggesting that Lawrence and Dahoum were alone in the house, that Lawrence carved the naked figure when they were alone and, by inference from village disapproval, that they were lovers. There were many guests at the Carchemish that month and, even when the last of them had gone, Haj Wahid still lived in the house with his wife and children. More significant, Hubert Young was there when he made the carving, and was creating his own sculpture when Lawrence carved the gargoyle. Wilson points to jealousy on the part of Woolley. By the time he wrote the sugges- tion, Woolley was *Sir* Leonard Woolley, his name connected to Ur, the great Sumerian city he excavated so successfully between 1922 and 1934. At the time of Lawrence's death, however, he had not acquired a reputation or a following that could compare to his junior assistant, and he will have known that during the Carchemish exca- vations Lawrence, Hogarth and Kenyon found him 'a source of mirth and [that he] lent himself to delightful descriptions [by Lawrence]. These caused great enjoyment to the Ashmolean.'[39] In other words, Lawrence had mocked his boss behind his back and the others had found it funny. Woolley, when he read some of these comments soon after the end of the Great War, had other views.

All that lay in the not so distant future. They were very different characters, but they kept hidden any objections they might have had about each other and had developed an easy and successful working partnership. One thing Woolley expressed later but which struck him at this time was Lawrence's apparent lack of concern for others' opinion of him. 'He knew quite well what the Arabs said about himself and Dahoum,' but 'so far from resenting it was amused, and I think he courted misunderstanding rather than tried to avoid it'.[40] Lawrence had long nurtured an ability to sow confusion; it was one of the ways he had learned to protect himself from his mother's prying. After the war, it became an essential tool in his fight to preserve something of himself from journalists and others wanting to get at the man behind the legend.

Woolley returned to Carchemish – and Lawrence's new carving – at the beginning of October, having picked up potatoes, carpets and a light railway in Aleppo. The digging team had survived the latest Turkish recruitment drive, the days were warm and the nights comfortable: things were looking good. The expedition house, Lawrence's 'creation', was complete, extensions done, the roof repaired. 'Our sitting room is really rather delightful now,' he wrote to his mother with obvious satisfaction and reinforcing his independence in the process. 'We have a little good pottery (Turkish, Arab, Roman, and Hittite), some glass trifles, very good woodwork, and a few fine pieces of bronze; on the floor we have some exceedingly fine carpets and on the walls a Morris tapestry, and a large piece of Arab wool embroidery: I mustn't forget Dodd's drawing of Dahoum [the one Dodd gave to Dahoum that day at the Ashmolean], a really beautiful piece of work which gets more pleasant with familiarity: he has never summoned up, himself, enough courage to show it to his people.'[41]

Jerablus remained calm. Hostilities had ended in the Balkans and the Peace of Bucharest was agreed on 10 August, although the problems were far from being resolved. Three days after the treaty had been signed, political tensions, and ethnic and religious divisions, led the Austro-Hungarians to threaten 'defensive' action against Serb expansion. But while the Balkans hovered on the brink of a major war, none of this stirred Jerablus in the way the First Balkan War had done and Woolley felt sufficiently confident of the situation to write to Hogarth, in unusually forceful terms, insisting on 'a continuation of the dig beyond next summer; it would be ludicrous &

shameful to stop with our present prospects, & the thing couldn't anyhow be wound up decently by the end of next season'.[42] Hogarth assured him that there was money for the winter work and at least £2,000 already put aside for 1914.

The secure funding brought with it the pressure of greater expectations. Hogarth, Woolley and Lawrence had all made great claims for the Carchemish discoveries the previous season – the greatest British Museum dig since Nineveh, the most important Hittite discoveries and so on. The autumn dig continued in that vein, with both Woolley and Lawrence using superlatives to describe their progress. Woolley reported to the Trustees of the British Museum that seventeen reliefs, important inscriptions and other significant pieces of sculpture they had just uncovered made this 'the most successful month's work that has yet been done upon this site'.[43] Lawrence meanwhile wrote to his brother Will in excitement at having found near the King's Gate a carving of 'a seated goddess . . . followed by 15 servants, carrying either a mirror or sistrum & fillet [rattle and ribbon]. After this seven men carrying on their shoulders gazelles: these slabs alternate basalt and white limestone. Then came a break which turned out to be a door, flanked with huge inscriptions in Hittite. By some strange fortune the door had been rebuilt, and new inscriptions, in basalt put up by some acquisitive monarch. So we got not only the new inscriptions, in their places, but the old slabs turned face downwards and used to walk upon. A great find, the greatest we have made.'[44] A month later and, as Lawrence put it, 'we have been kept at it from morning to night',[45] although by then the discoveries had stopped and they were busy recording what they had found.

It was a short season. By December, a cold north wind turned everything in the village and on the *tell* to ice. Fragments of carving now filled several storerooms and large areas of the excavation site and, while it was too cold to dig, it was still possible to work on these pieces. A week before Christmas Lawrence reported that:

we are working over our many thousand fragments of carvings [Woolley reported two thousand], trying to make out which is which, and to group them again into sculptures fit to photograph. It is a most awful job . . . You will appreciate the difficulty of picking out of this pile (which takes half a day to turn over) the particular claw or ear or scrap of jaw required to complete a broken lion in the excavations. And it would require a genius to tell which is lion hair, and which human hair, in the tangle of tiny fragments, many of them no bigger than a penny: some of them weighing three or four tons.[46]

Woolley was no such genius, but noticed that his young assistant 'would look at a small fragment of a Hittite inscription and remark that it fitted on to an equally small piece found twelve months before, and although there were many hundreds of such in our store-room he was always right'.[47]

Woolley ascribed this ability to Lawrence's remarkable memory and his ability to focus exclusively on the work in hand. It helped that he was also enjoying the work and the life he was living. He could have been doing research at Oxford – he might have enjoyed that as well – but the life would have been different, and there would have been no leopard tied up outside, as there now was at the mission house, a gift from a government official, to remind him that he was somewhere beyond his usual range of experiences. 'It will only eat meat,' the mostly vegetarian archaeologist reported, 'but is otherwise good-looking and serves us as watch-dog: nearly everybody keeps clear of it.' A week later, he admitted that his pet 'is not very sweet-tempered, but not yet half-grown', adding that 'he will make a most splendid carpet some day, if the Zoo don't want him'.[48] Another week and there was the news that 'our leopard is loose! He broke away about 7 p.m. one evening:– men walk about by day revolver on hips in strong parties . . . by night they bar doors and shutter windows. Five women have miscarried in the upper village: the lower village is cut off from the world: the Baghdad construction-bridge is guarded night and day: railway work has ceased, though one train a day still runs . . . armoured . . . Hush, I hear scratching at the door! Only a cat!'[49]

Seduced by life in Carchemish, and by the prospects it offered – of being independent of his mother, of not having to consider his illegitimacy, of travel, perhaps with the Slayb Arabs, of writing *Seven Pillars of Wisdom* which he was doing in his spare time, of buying and selling *antikas* and carpets, of being with Dahoum and the others he had grown close to – he was finally forced to accept that he would not be returning to live in England. So he wrote to Vyvyan Richards to say that he was giving up the dream of setting up a printing press.

> The fault was in ever coming out to this place, I think, because really ever since knowing it I have felt that (at least for the near future) to talk of settling down to live in a small way anywhere else was beating the air: and so gradually I slipped down, until a few months ago when I found myself an ordinary archaeologist . . . I have got to like this place very much: and the people here – five or six of them – and the whole manner of living pleases me. We have 200 men to play with, anyhow we like so long as the excavations go on, and they are splendid fellows many of them (I had two of them:– headmen – in England with me this summer) and it is great fun with them. Then there are the digs, with dozens of wonderful things to find – it is like a great sport with tangible results at the end of things – Do you know I am keen now on an inscription or a new type of pottery? and hosts of beautiful things in the villages and towns to fill one's house with. Not to mention seal-hunting in the country round about, and the Euphrates to rest in when one is over-hot. It is a place where one eats lotos nearly every day . . .[50]

Work at Carchemish would continue for another four or five years, he wrote in farewell to Richards, and as 1914 approached, and 'I'm afraid that after that I'll probably go after another and another nice thing.'[51]

PART III

The Young Spy

Let us alone. Time driveth onward fast,
And in a little while our lips are dumb.
Let us alone. What is it that will last?
All things are taken from us, and become
Portions and parcels of the dreadful past.
Let us alone. What pleasure can we have
To war with evil?

Alfred, Lord Tennyson, 'The Lotos-Eaters',
The Poetical Works of Alfred, Lord Tennyson, p. 55

16

A Splendid Trip

Do you know that in January and February Woolley & I
explored the desert of the exodus, looking for the foot-prints
of the children of Israel?

T. E. Lawrence to James Elroy Flecker, June 1914[1]

January–February 1914

T
HE TURKISH POST was slow and irregular, but at the same time
as Lawrence wrote to tell Richards that he would be at
Carchemish for another four or five years, a letter arrived with a
different proposition. Kenyon was inviting Lawrence and Woolley
to take part in a Palestine Exploration Fund (PEF) mission to survey
Arabia Petraea, the borderland between Egypt and Ottoman Palestine.
The archaeologists cabled a reply. 'I hope they will still want us,'
Woolley wrote. 'It would be a splendid trip.'[2] But he was concerned
about the speed with which they would need to start for Jaffa and
the desert. There was still much to do at Carchemish and the PEF
survey could not compromise their Hittite work. Why, he might
wonder, was there such urgency to look for antiquities that had
remained in place for thousands of years?

The trip would indeed be splendid. It would be useful too, both
for the Palestine Exploration Fund and for the British Museum: if
the archaeologists were working for the PEF, the BM would be
spared covering their half-pay through the winter. But there was a
higher issue because the War Office was behind the PEF survey.

As much has been written about Lawrence's early work for British
intelligence as it has about his sexual preferences, most of which is

no more than speculation, occasionally deduction, but always impossible to verify. So it comes as a relief to pinpoint a moment when he does work for the War Office, however indirectly, and with evidence to support the claim.

The British government and its many agencies had been making preparations for a war that might involve some, perhaps all, of Britain's European rivals since at least the beginning of 1913. As part of those preparations, the Foreign Office in London had canvassed opinion of its diplomats in the Middle East as early as February 1913 as to the likelihood of Turkey attacking Egypt. Kitchener, the British Agent in Cairo with responsibility for running the Egyptian government, warned that Turkey might very well create trouble on its southern frontier after suffering such heavy losses in its northerly European territories. Sir Edward Grey, the British Foreign Secretary, broadly agreed: 'not a very probable event . . . [but] Turkish ambition, driven out of Europe, may well gravitate in other directions . . .'[3] Kitchener also knew that if there was a war, and if Britain were pitched against Turkey – increasingly likely as Turkey responded to German diplomatic overtures – then the Sinai and Negev deserts would need to be secured, if only to guarantee that Britain continued to control the Suez Canal, so vital to its interests in India and the East. Kitchener had worked with the Royal Engineers on a survey of those deserts in the 1870s and he knew that the maps were incomplete and that the work he had done on them was flawed. He also remembered that sensitivity over mapping this borderland had led, eight years earlier, to a standoff between Britain and Turkey.

Britain had invaded Egypt in 1882 and, although it had not officially annexed the country, its officials effectively ran the government and armed forces. This led to a need for clarity on frontiers between Egypt and Turkish-controlled Palestine. In 1892, the Egyptian, Turkish and British governments agreed that the border would follow a line from El Arish on the Mediterranean coast to the head of the Gulf of Aqaba. At the beginning of January 1906, W. E. Jennings Bramly, a British officer serving with the Frontier Administration of the (Egyptian) Sinai Peninsula, received orders to proceed to Umm Rashrash (now known as Eilat) to build an Egyptian border post. Bramly did as instructed and placed four Egyptian policemen at the frontier, but Turkish officials from Aqaba then questioned whether Umm Rashrash was on Egyptian or Turkish territory. The two sides were heading for conflict.

Before the Egyptian coastguard could support Bramly, Turkish troops from the modest Aqaba garrison, reinforced by thousands sent down from Maan, had marched into Sinai and occupied Taba. 'Undoubtedly it [Taba] was Egyptian territory,' Bramly wrote, 'and I knew of nothing which . . . could have altered this and made what was Egyptian then, Turkish now. Rushdi Pasha's [Turkish commandant at Aqaba] answer was that Turkey claimed Taba.'[4] Rushdi Pasha had received orders direct from the Grand Vizier in Constantinople to remove the Egyptians from Taba, by force if necessary. What started as confusion between low-ranking officers was quickly escalating. Bramly put fifty men on Gezirat el Faraon, just offshore from Taba and Umm Rashrash: the ruins of a Crusader-era castle were proof that the little island had long been of strategic importance. A British gunboat then appeared in the Gulf of Aqaba, the Turks increased the Aqaba garrison to 3,000 men and by the spring – for this standoff continued for several months – Britain prepared to land troops in Rafah, Turkish Palestine, and, to prove that gunboat diplomacy was not dead, the British Mediterranean fleet moved east to anchor off the Greek coast.

Behind this dispute lay a significant geo-political issue. The Turks were unhappy about the 1892 border because they were planning to extend the Hejaz Railway from Maan to Aqaba. More troubling for Britain, they then wanted to continue their railway across Sinai to Suez, claiming that a Suez branch line was essential for Egyptian pilgrims making the haj to Mecca. Both Britain and the British-administered Egyptian government thought the proposed branch line posed a security threat because it would give Turkish troops easy access to the Suez Canal.

The Turks suggested various compromises, including abandoning access to Suez in return for Sinai's eastern shore: Britain rejected this because the Turks would then have complete control of the Gulf of Aqaba. Things came to a head on 3 May 1906 when the British Ambassador in Constantinople gave Sultan Abdul Hamid II ten days to agree to the 1892 boundary, or face the consequences.

The Times supported this 'grave step', insisting that the Turks were not good neighbours and that their railway must never be allowed to run to Suez. 'Turkish railways in this region may be primarily intended for pilgrims,' an editorial on 5 May argued, 'but they have important strategic aspects as well. They have been constructed, we cannot forget, under the counsels and by the help of competent German advisers . . . to permit these railways to come within striking distance of Egypt, whose main defence has always lain in her isolation, and within striking distance of the great waterway to our Eastern possessions and markets . . . would be a folly too gross and palpable for the weakest and shallowest of politicians to make.'[5]

Ottoman diplomats sought German, Russian and French support for their claim to Sinai, but the three Powers colluded, the Ottoman Sultan was forced to concede and the frontier was fixed on a line between Rafah on the Mediterranean and Aqaba at the head of the Red Sea, something *The Times* and many in Britain considered a triumph. Then the German Kaiser made approaches to the isolated Sultan. Wilfred Scawen Blunt, the poet and political activist, recognised that forcing the Ottoman Sultan into this humiliating withdrawal was the first of the British Foreign Secretary's many blunders. 'The triumph', he wrote later and with the benefit of hindsight, 'proved an unfortunate one for our Foreign Office, as it was the beginning of the long quarrel between Sir Edward Grey and Constantinople.' This was the same moment that the Turks granted the Germans permits to excavate at several important archaeological sites, including Boghaz Köy. This 'long quarrel', Blunt continued, 'resulted eight years later in the Turkish alliance with the Central European Powers in the Great War, a combination which gave Germany its victory over Russia. Not a soul in England understood its importance or cared to understand.'[6]

In the summer and autumn of 1913, five officers from the Royal Engineers were already surveying Egypt-held Sinai Peninsula, under the eye of the British War Office's Geographical Section, MO4. This Geographical Section was soon merged into the fledgling British Military Intelligence and divided into various sections (MI6 being the most famous). MO4 was responsible for gathering information and intelligence in case of war, and that included the preparation of maps. On 19 September 1913, and following the correspondence with Kitchener in Cairo, the Director of MO4, Colonel W. Coote Hedley, Boer War veteran and keen county cricketer, wrote to the Foreign Office to suggest that the Royal Engineers' survey be continued across the Egyptian border into Turkish-held territory. 'The proposed survey is very desirable from a military point of view, and is essential for the proper study of the problem presented by the defence of the north-eastern frontier of Egypt.'[7] Knowing that the Turkish government would be unhappy at having British military personnel on its territory, it was decided to give the survey an archaeological cover.

Sir Louis Mallet, Britain's newly appointed Ambassador in Constantinople, approached the Turkish government for permission to allow the Palestine Exploration Fund (PEF) to look for evidence of the movement of Moses and the Israelites from Egypt to Palestine. On 29 October, he cabled London with the news that permission had been granted. By something other than coincidence, Colonel Hedley of MO4 had just been elected on to the Committee of the PEF. Also on the PEF Committee were David Hogarth of the Ashmolean and Walter Morrison, generous benefactor of the Carchemish dig.* On 30 October, the War Office wrote to the PEF to say that they would 'supply two officers and pay all the expenses',[8] although the Royal Geographical Society, another organisation with unofficial links to the British intelligence community and to which Hogarth belonged,† provided emergency funding.

The PEF Committee discussed the plan on 4 November. Sir Charles Watson, chairman, wrote to Hedley agreeing that 'It is a part of Palestine which has not been properly examined hitherto, and a careful investigation will probably lead to interesting results.'[9] There is a striking lack of conviction in Watson's words, but his conclusion was right: this part of Arabia Petraea, which now divides Israel from Egypt, had not been worked over by archaeologists, surprising given the long-standing enthusiasm for biblical archaeology. The Committee's first-choice archaeologist was an Oxford-educated Egypt scholar, Thomas Peet. But Peet was lecturing in Egyptology

---

* Morrison was the PEF Treasurer and had recently bought their central London headquarters building.
† Hogarth was President of the RGS from 1925 to 1927.

at Manchester University and sent his regrets. At this point, Hogarth, who knew of Woolley's plan to stay out in Syria that winter, encouraged the Fund to take on his two Carchemish archaeologists. The British Museum had no objections, so long as they were in Carchemish by the beginning of March to reopen the digs when the weather improved. 'Their names', Kenyon told Watson, 'are C. L. Woolley and T. E. Lawrence. The former is the senior man, with rather wider experience; the latter is the best at colloquial Arabic and gets on very well with the natives. He has, I think, more of the instincts of an explorer, but is very shy.'[10] Kenyon had already written to Woolley to put forward the offer, which included a daily wage of £1 for each of them, less than the £1 10 shillings Woolley was receiving from the British Museum, but more that the 15 shillings they paid Lawrence. It is interesting that Lawrence's value had risen because he could speak Arabic and got on with 'the natives'. Woolley, with his 'wider experience', must have been annoyed. Watson then sent instructions for the survey.

Watson's long letter sketched out the area they were to work, a block from Gaza to Rafah, across to Aqaba and up to the Dead Sea. 'This country, notwithstanding its proximity to Palestine and Egypt, is but little known, and, though it has been crossed by travellers in certain parts, is to a great extent unexplored.'[11] The mission had six specific goals. Most relevant to archaeologists were the making of plans of sites, taking photographs, making squeezes and collecting ancient stone and flint implements. But the mission was being run by a captain from the Royal Engineers and the military side had taken precedence, for they were also to produce an accurate map on a scale of half an inch to the mile, make plans of 'localities', photograph 'points of interest' and 'record carefully all names now in use'. The Committee, Watson wrote to Woolley and Lawrence, 'feel sure that you will understand the spirit of what is required, and will do all you can to collect useful and accurate information'.[12]

Watson suggested that they use as an assistant someone who had worked with previous Fund expeditions. It is interesting, in light of Woolley's salacious comments about Dahoum and Lawrence, that he replied to say that he preferred using 'one of our Jerablus men, who is a good photographer and excellent at squeeze-work . . . a very useful fellow'. Woolley went so far as to insist on Dahoum. 'Should you not approve of this step I should be prepared to pay his wages myself; but I must point out that for a short piece of work, a man who knows one's ways and objects is more use than a stranger, however good that stranger may be.'[13] So the three of them would travel from Jerablus.

Christmas passed quietly. When Woolley insisted on singing, Lawrence sent him to the outer courtyard where he performed two short carols and 'Auld Lang Syne'. The day after Christmas, Lawrence wrote a jaunty letter to Emily Rieder to say that they were off to help survey Arabia Petraea and that there were 'dark suggestions of horrible political complots'.[14] On 29 December they left for Gaza, where they consulted the British Consul. After that, they continued to Beersheba, the last major Ottoman outpost in the Negev desert, a town of single-storey houses (only the police station had an upper floor) and a central square whose orderly municipal plantings failed to cover the scrappiness of the place. Beyond Beersheva, there was nothing but desert, and the mountains in which they had been instructed to look for Captain Stewart Newcombe and his Royal Engineers and, beyond them, traces of Moses and his people. 'We are obviously only meant as red herrings, to give an archaeological colour to a political job,' Lawrence had written to his mother while sailing down the Palestine coast. 'We have Dahoum with us, and are warned that we may have to ride camels some of the time . . .'[15] Given Lawrence's later exploits, and the way he has been forever associated with camels, it is ironic to see how reluctant he was to ride: he would still have preferred walking.

Newcombe, a Welsh bachelor ten years older than Lawrence, had already served fifteen years with the engineers. He had fought in the Second Boer War and been with the Egyptian Army since 1901. He was known as 'skinface' to his colleagues, as his skin was prone to burn and peel, but the rest of him was as hard as the landscape they travelled through. He had had a slow start to the mission, spending five days haggling over the price of camels in Gaza and admitting to being 'bored with myself for having taken so long getting a start on this show'.[16] He had, however, planned out how they would map the area, and which of the engineers would work out the triangulations for which sectors. Now he was on his way to Beersheva to meet the archaeologists. They, however, had had a similarly chaotic start. Newcombe was expecting them to arrive fully equipped for the expedition, while Woolley had been told that everything from tents, kitchen equipment, food and water to cameras and measuring tapes would be supplied. The archaeologists had brought some clothes and basic equipment, but no more than a donkey-load of kit and certainly not enough to go into the desert to research for a month or two. Woolley's terse letter to Watson at the PEF reminds him 'that we were asked to join an expedition already fitted out for the work in hand; we were not asked to furnish ourselves any kind of equipment and supposed therefore that, as is usually the case, all such equipment had been provided for us'. He added that 'necessarily our work will be to some degree hampered by the want of various things'.[17] Lawrence had packed his camera, and they had brought some notebooks and squeeze paper with them. Alexander Knesevitch, the British consular agent in Gaza (whom Lawrence called Creswick), found them second-hand tents, a cook and some other necessities, and then arranged for whatever else they needed to be sent from Cairo.

Newcombe had imagined that two British Museum archaeologists coming down from the Hittite heartland would be older, more conservative, more eminent – more boring. Instead, he was met by 'two young and very bright young people . . . [who] looked about twenty-four and eighteen respectively'[18] and were, he thought, 'quite nice fellows'.[19] They were also, at the same time, both irritated and curious. Newcombe realised he had shown much too much respect in his letters and now set about asserting his authority: he was, after all, the officer in overall charge of the survey, even if they had very different missions and very little time to complete either to their satisfaction.

Lawrence had been wrong to suggest that their expedition was only a cover for Newcombe's mapping team. Although the PEF would not have sent them if the War Office had not wanted the area to be mapped, there was a serious archaeological aspect to the mission. Biblical associations had long been the driving force behind archaeology in the Holy Land, hoping to satisfy the desire for evidence to substantiate the Bible. The story of the forty years that Moses and the Israelites spent in the Sinai between pharaonic Egypt and the promised land is one of the most potent. Yet considering the implications of a significant discovery, relatively little work had been done in the area they were travelling towards. This might be an opportunity to make a name for themselves. But among the many obstacles they needed to overcome was the intention of the Turkish authorities 'to throw all possible difficulties in our way'.[20] This included denying that they had any antiquities in their possession, but Lawrence discovered a pile of Greek tombstones stored under a sofa in the Beersheva police station.

Logistics were a greater problem and the expedition to what was known as the Wilderness of Zin continued as chaotically as it had started: the PEF had wired money to Thomas Cook in Jerusalem, fifty miles away, but with no time to travel back north, Woolley had to draw on his own funds to cover their expenses. When they had gathered money and stores, they left on camelback and, with a caravan of donkeys, headed for Khalasa. Khalasa had stood on the incense route across the desert to the Mediterranean Sea and it proved an encouraging place to start for they found Nabataean inscriptions, and were the first people to draw a plan of the site. From there they moved deeper into the desert to Shivta, another Nabataean site. No more than a few inches of rain fell there each year, but the people of Shivta had learned to catch and store moisture and from the fourth to the ninth centuries it grew into a thriving city. Most traces of this city had long since disappeared, but a recent report on Lawrence and Woolley's work concluded that 'their overall success in recording low-status archaeological features (and not just standing architecture) was a major advancement, methodologically well in advance of their day and even much subsequent fieldwork until the 1970s.'[21]

The work was demanding. 'The Palestine fund wants to find sites illustrating the Exodus, which is supposed to have passed this way,' Lawrence wrote home after ten days on the move with camels, 'but of course a people 40 years out of Egypt could hardly leave much trace of themselves in their later camping grounds.'[22] The comment shows up the impossibility of their task, but also the depth of Lawrence's analysis of the problem. The longer they looked, the more acute the problem. On 17 January 1914 he admitted that 'it isn't much good identifying a Bible site with a town no older than Christian Greek'.[23] A week later there was still 'not a sign or smell of Israelites wandering about here: only on the old road from Gaza to Akaba did we find two little scraps of early pottery'.[24] Their break came early in February, after they had crossed the border into Egyptian territory, and reached Kadesh Barnea, 'a filthy dirty little water-hole, and we more than sympathise with the disgust of the Children of Israel when they got there'.[25] Woolley went further and thought that 'it speaks wonders for the Children of Israel that they left Moses alive after he brought them to a place like that'.[26]

A few miles beyond Kadesh Barnea they reached Ain el Guderat, a very different prospect, a valley oasis created by a spring of the cleanest water and with a stream deep enough to bathe in, and constant enough to support trees and corn. The Israelites, Lawrence suggested, had stayed there forty years and the Zin party would spend an enjoyable week, waiting for photographic and other supplies to come from Egypt. The sense of relief was as much for the living as for the archaeology, although they had found remains of a fort, which Woolley described as 'of early date'[27] and Lawrence thought optimistically came from the period of the Exodus. But Woolley had to admit his 'fear that the results of the Survey as a whole can hardly but be a disappointment to the Society at least so far as biblical research is concerned'.[28] They had found much that was Byzantine, but very little that they could confidently call ancient.

Lawrence was as reluctant a rider as on his previous journeys, writing to Leeds that 'Over the consequences of much riding of camels I draw thick veils: but take it as a summing up that we are very unhappy.'[29] Then there was the problem of food: the cook whom Consul Knesevitch had found was inept and supplies were limited. 'Our menu is a broad one: we eat bread and eggs: and Turkish delight. Only yesterday we finished the eggs, and the nearest hens are three days journey to the N.'[30] The bedding was no more satisfying than Turkish delight sandwiches and all this was clearly taking its toll. 'Woolley is the more uncomfortable,' Lawrence confessed to Leeds, 'since he is a flesh-potter: I can travel on a thistle, and sleep in a cloak on the ground. Woolley can't, or at least, is only learning to, quite slowly.' Life improved with the arrival of more supplies – lentils, rice, potatoes, figs and marmalade – but the cook did not. When Woolley finally cracked, Lawrence concluded that 'our cook can't grasp a word of English, which explains his continued presence with us: after Woolley in a clear tone last Thursday had expressed his desire (in front of the whole camp) to bugger him with a rough stick'.[31]

More important, for the war that was coming and for Lawrence's role in it, were the things he learned about desert travel. On 27 January, they were late leaving El Auja because, although it was a sad place that had been recently plundered to provide material for new government buildings, it was still, as ever, of great strategic value. 'The fort is well placed to block the great Wady Hafir, which leads up from the central plateau of Tih,' Lawrence wrote in *The Wilderness of Zin*, showing off his knowledge of Middle Eastern military structures and strategy, and echoing some of his later writing, 'and its garrison would command not inadequately the old Shur road that runs past Bir Birein. The wide valley would supply the soldiers with food, and water was to be found at no great depth. Actually fortresses are of little avail against a mobile enemy in a desert country where roads run everywhither; and the event proved worthless here; but on paper El Auja, Ahda and Kurnub may well have looked an admirable chain of defence.'[32]

The morning they were leaving El Auja, they sent their baggage camels ahead, keeping Dahoum with them, expecting to catch the others before they reached that night's camping place. Woolley picked up the narrative:

> We struck eastwards, and hitting the Darb el Shur, where we had crossed it two days before, followed it southwards to Bir Birein, where we found an early building on the hill-top, and thence on to Ras Seram, a stony pass looking over the plain across which runs the Kossaima road. Going straight on, we missed our baggage animals (which had taken the Kossaima road) and had to spend the night in the open; on the next day we secured a guide and went straight for Ain Kadeis. The fact that our two camels had bolted in the night proved to be rather an advantage, for the tracks which we followed were almost impossible for camels. We climbed up and down steep

scree-covered hills rising about a thousand feet above narrow wadies; nowhere was there any cultivation, nor the possibility of any; it was the most impressive mountain landscape, and the most barren that we had seen since leaving Gaza.[33]

Lawrence told his parents that they had been stalking a gazelle. 'Our baggage men . . . were alarmed at our non appearance: they warned the Egyptian police here, who sent out to look for us (Woolley, self, and Dahoum) and found two wandering camels: result was wild telephoning all over the frontier: 20 of the 25 camel police here at Kuseime [sic] were wandering over the hills all day and a night: the Turks were wandering over their hills: about 40 Arabs were arrested and brought in as hostages for our reappearance: and meanwhile we were sitting quietly in Ain Kedes [sic], wondering where in the world our tents had got to.'[34] At midday, the three men decided to walk up to the police post at Kossaima and 'were received with enormous relief. Some of the searchers are not back yet. They were just going to report our strange disappearance to Cairo.'[35]

Other people might have learned the importance of giving precise instructions to the camel train, or having a back-up plan in case things went wrong, or of not splitting up in the desert. But Lawrence extracted something more useful and, in the light of the way he shaped the Arab revolt, more significant: 'It shows how easy it is in an absolutely deserted country to defy a government.' From this realisation that one could hide from even the most determined of seekers came his game-changing ideas on how to fight the Turks – not by facing them on the battlefield, but by using a superior knowledge of the terrain to attack them when they least expected it, to be, as he put it in *Seven Pillars*, 'an idea, a thing intangible . . . a vapour, blowing where we listed'.[36] A regular soldier, he now knew, was helpless without a target. The idea of not being a target, of evasion, of disappearing into and striking out of the desert, an idea he had considered when staying in the Assassins' castle during his first visit to Syria, now blossomed in his mind like desert flowers after brief rain, suddenly and fully.

The Zin survey was the first journey of any length that Lawrence had made in the region with another European. Until then, around the Crusader castles and across the Euphrates, he had travelled on his own or with people from the area. Being with Woolley had clearly brought out his competitive streak, although he should not have worried. Gertrude Bell, at first sight of Lawrence, had said she thought he would make a traveller. Kenyon, when recommending the two men for the Zin survey, had described Lawrence as having the instincts of an explorer. Woolley might be the more experienced and more skilful archaeologist, but he found the going hard.

Competitiveness was not the reason why they went their separate ways after Kadesh Barnea. There was still much ground to cover if they were to be back in Carchemish by early March, as they had promised the British Museum, so Woolley headed north, working his way through the ancient *tells* and Byzantine towns towards Beersheva and from there to Gaza and Aleppo. Lawrence and Dahoum, meanwhile, headed east to join Newcombe and some of the survey party.

From the engineers, Lawrence learned how to read a landscape by its geological make-up, to see strata and to understand how landmass had been formed by the movement of the earth and subsequently shaped by wind, by rain and, even in the remote desert, by humans. Lawrence had an extraordinary facility both to observe and to recall, and his descriptions of the journey are as vivid and memorable as the landscape he passed through. At first, the land was 'only an exaggeration of the northern country. There are the same great stretches of flaky limestone . . . overlaid with brown flints, sand-polished.'[37] After several days, they reached the end of this limestone plateau and the pass that would lead to Aqaba.

> The way down is very splendid. In the hill-sides, all sorts of rocks are mingled in confusion; grey-green limestone cliffs run down sheer for hundreds of feet, in tremendous ravines whose faces are a medley of colours wherever crags of black porphyry and diorite jut out, or where soft sandstone, washed down, has left long pink and red smudges on the lighter colours . . . The road finally reaches sea level on the extreme north-west beach of the Gulf of Akaba, and runs over the sand of the shore and through the old site of Aila between the palm-gardens into the modern village.[38]

Lawrence's name is forever linked to Aqaba: in the war, he and a force of Arab fighters from various tribes, under the joint command of Auda abu Tayi and Sherif Nasir, surprised the Turkish garrison by attacking from the desert. As with his realisation, when he was lost in the desert, that a small raiding force could defeat a larger army, so this visit, 'on foot, since my idiot camels went astray',[39] coming from the west and leaving to the north, provided knowledge of the terrain that was critical to the 1917 attack. Only by under-standing the terrain, recognising how Aqaba was squeezed between the sea and the desert mountains, seeing that the main defences were all facing out to sea, was he able to achieve victory over the Turks.

When Lawrence reached the coast in February 1914, he found Newcombe and a problem: the Kaimmakam had received no word of their arrival. Given the diplomatic and military confrontation that had followed the 1906 boundary dispute, it is easy to understand Newcombe's reluctance to confront the official, even though he had permission from the highest authority in Constantinople. 'At present,' Newcombe wrote to the PEF on 15 February, 'I am being held up, quite courteously, by the Kaimmakam at Akaba who says he has no information about us being allowed to survey in his province.'[40]

This was less of a problem for the Royal Engineer than for the archaeologist. Newcombe now received a message from no less a figure than Kitchener instructing him not to exceed the limits of his permit: the field marshal was keen not to antagonise the Turks. But Lawrence had work to do and was not to be stopped. 'Kaimmakam of Akaba was a bad man,' he wrote to Leeds. 'He had (or said he had) no news of us and our little games: and so he forbade Newcombe to map, and me to photograph or archaeologise. I photographed what I could, I archaeologised everywhere.'[41] In particular, there was the little island of Gezirat el Faraon, Pharaoh's Island, not far offshore, where Bramly had landed troops during the 1906 standoff. Lawrence and Dahoum were hoping to find a boat to take them over to the island to see the Crusader ruins, but were forbidden to go. Swimming was not recommended because the bay was known for sharks and poisonous fish. 'I sent word to the Kaimmakam that upon his head was the forbidding me to go, and he said yes . . . and while his police were carrying out mutual recriminations I puffed a zinc tank full of air, tied to its tail another for Dahoum, and one for a camera and tape and things . . . and splashed off for the island with a couple of planks as paddles. The police returning a little later found my fleet sailing slowly seawards, and they had no boat, and no zinc tanks, and so could only weep while we worked.'[42] It was a typical Lawrence prank – in keeping with the ones at Carchemish and Oxford. And it worked, for they inspected the island, although as Lawrence's reference in his report to 'the extreme poverty of the remains'[43] suggests, it was not really worth the effort, nor the risk of antagonising the Kaimmakam, who retaliated by detailing a lieutenant and half a company of soldiers to follow Lawrence. 'The Turkish government', he concluded, 'now repents itself that it gave permission for the survey to be done.'[44]

He left Newcombe with an invitation to visit Carchemish, and travelled north with Dahoum and their Turkish 'minders'. They were intending to visit Petra, the ancient Nabataean city carved into the rocky walls around a deep gorge on the edge of the desert. The Turks were determined to hinder them in every way. Lawrence wrote several accounts of his visit to Petra, but in all of them the soldiers were 'a horrible nuisance'.[45] He sent the camels with their baggage direct to Wadi Musa, the village above Petra, while he and Dahoum headed for the hills beside the ancient city. The soldiers followed them, obeying orders 'not to let me out of their sight, and I took them two days afoot over such hills and wadies as did for them all. I have been camped here for two days, and they are still struggling in from all over the compass: the first was ten hours after me: and the last is still missing. It is a country of awful crags and valleys, impassable for camels, and very difficult on foot. The lieutenant has gone home.'[46]

Lawrence and Dahoum were walking towards Mount Hor, above Petra, which legend identified as the burial place of Moses' brother, Aaron. They reached the mountain with a sense of achievement, but without any supplies and with the weather turning: it can freeze up there in winter. 'Perfect peace without,' Lawrence wrote to Leeds, but 'a rather strained situation within, mitigated partly by a sweet rain-pool, partly by the finding of my tents next afternoon after a two-day absence. I shot a partridge on the hill at dawn, and we cooked it over brushwood, and ate half each. A very good partridge but a small one. The night just under the hill-top was bitterly cold, with a huge wind and blinding squalls of rain.' He and Dahoum found warmth together. 'We curled up in a knot under a not-sufficiently-overhanging-rock and packed our sheepskin cloaks under and over and round us, and still were as cold and cross as bears.'[47]

The next morning they walked down into Petra, 'the most wonderful place in the world',[48] he announced, and not just because they had found their tents and some food. Petra is notoriously difficult to evoke, and he knew it, having read the accounts of earlier travellers. His attempt, written while there on 25 February, captures some of the beauty of the place. 'It is', he told his parents,

> a running together of narrow stony gorges, between great cliffs of red sandstone. And up and down the cliffs, all over are great rock-cut tombs. Of the town ruins there is very little remaining: it has all been washed down and buried by torrent-bursts. But the tombs all stand undamaged, though the soft sandstone has rubbed in very curious patterns. The rock is dark red, with veins of grey and black, very narrow and regular running through it. So you get strange effects of colour, like surface ornament, everywhere. Some of the tombs are enormous:– that is their fronts are big, spreading over half a cliff, with only a couple of tiny rooms behind cut out of the rock, for perhaps twenty bodies at most. Some are Greek in style, some more Egyptian. There is almost no fine work: the beauty of the place lies in the contrast between the green oleander and the red of the sandstone, and in the queer way in which without plan the tombs are dotted over the cliffs of the valleys.[49]

Later, when he had left Petra (having come in from what today would be regarded as the back end), he finally saw the finest and most iconic of all Nabataean structures, the Treasury.

Reunion with their baggage did not solve all their problems because they were short of money. Fortunately, two Englishwomen walked up while Lawrence was having his first lunch at Petra and they camped near by for a couple of days. In his first letter home, Lawrence branded them as 'nothing over much'. But later, from Damascus, he decided they were 'curious'. 'One of them, Lady

Evelyn Cobbold, improved vastly. Would F[rank] look her up at the Union, and let me know *what* she is? I expect she's in *Who's Who*.'⁵⁰ Lady Evelyn Cobbold turned out to be extremely 'curious'. The daughter of an aristocrat who had bankrupted himself extending his Scottish castle to impress the woman he wished to marry (it worked), she and her parents spent winters in Algeria when she was young, as an economy. As a result, she acquired some Arabic and a taste for Arab customs. At the age of twenty-four, Lady Evelyn married the heir to a brewing company, John Cobbold, with whom she had three children, the last in 1900. But she retained her passion for Arab life throughout motherhood and, once the children were a little older, started to travel in North Africa again. When Lawrence met her, she was forty-seven years old and would have impressed him as much for speaking good Arabic as for being an excellent shot.* She also provided a solution to his most pressing problem by lending enough money for him and Dahoum to take the Hejaz Railway north from Maan. They travelled third class on the Damascus-bound service from Medina. Far from being an express, it took twenty-eight hours to cover 230 miles, which would have given an observant young man with a keen memory ample opportunity to observe the lie of the land, the significant stations, the facilities and the vulnerabilities of the line, observations he would make use of and vulnerabilities he would exploit three years later. From Damascus, they continued by train to Aleppo and Jerablus. They went home.

---

* Lawrence and Lady Evelyn Cobbold met again in Cairo during the war. She later divorced her husband, converted to Islam and, in 1933, with Emir Feisal's permission, became the first British-born Muslim woman to perform the pilgrimage to Mecca.

17

Another Step, a Long Way

> I wonder why Arabia is the best-looking land, however you
> see it. I suppose it is the name that does it.
>
> T. E. Lawrence, 1916[1]

Spring 1914

HE HAD ARRIVED as an Oxford undergraduate looking for
evidence that would challenge the accepted view of medieval
castle-building and had spent more of the intervening four and a
half years in the Middle East than in England. That first summer
he had boasted that he had become Orientalised, and there was
more truth than he knew in his insistence that he would 'have
such difficulty in becoming English again'. The part of him that
continued to wear shorts and a Magdalen College blazer on the
excavations and that needed to mortify the flesh was completely
and always English. But he recognised another side to his character,
the one that talked of travelling in the desert with the Bani Slayb
and their saluki hunting dogs, living far from the cold touch of
an increasingly homogenised West with all the trappings of progress.
Far also from the stigma of his illegitimacy. But he was many years
away from understanding that there was a price to pay for what
he called this 'Yahoo life', for being caught between two cultures.
For now, he relished this new aspect of himself and, as he warmed
himself by the copper-shaded fireplace in the house he had built
in Carchemish, as he sat on one of the Kurdish rugs over the Roman
mosaic floor he had laid in the sitting room, with the mound outside
to be excavated, with Dahoum and the others around every day, he

was as happy as he had been in his adult life, as he was ever to be.

Little had changed at Carchemish in his absence. He returned to a pile of post and the pleasing confirmation that he had earned £66 in Zin, a significant boost to his finances.* Elsewhere, as he knew from Sinai, there were the rumblings of war,† but in Jerablus the grass was green, a sudden pleasure after Sinai's unrelenting browns and yellows. If he had a concern, it was that their permission to dig had expired and because there was again, as so often, a shortage of funds. Permission to dig came through on 21 March 1914. The money took longer.

Hogarth had been putting pressure on Woolley to deliver something eye-catching to spell out the significance of the Carchemish work, particularly in relation to recent discoveries elsewhere in the region. There was a practical reason behind this: with Walter Morrison's £5,000 donation almost spent, he needed to attract further funding. On 24 January, two articles appeared in the British press reporting progress at Carchemish. Woolley wrote a story for *The Times* about 'discoveries of such great importance'. In a paragraph headed 'The Principal New Finds' he explained that the main excavation at the foot of the *tell* had revealed several important structures. One was the great ceremonial staircase, lined with decorated slabs. Another was the east wing of the palace, where a series of chambers ran around two sides of a cobbled courtyard.

> The main chamber, apparently a small shrine, had walls of blue glazed bricks decorated with flowers in relief, and resting upon polished blocks of limestone. A single wooden column rising from a plain dolerite drum supported the roof; the door-jambs are of dolerite, covered with inscriptions in the Hittite hieroglyphic script. In front of the door stood the altar of burnt sacrifice. On a stone base between this and the doorway we have been able to restore a colossal dolerite group of two bulls flanking a deep basin.

* Equivalent to £5,300 in comparative income today.
† Improved German–Ottoman relations were a concern for both Russia and Britain, especially when General Liman von Sanders arrived in Turkey with forty German officers to restructure the defeated Ottoman army. When Liman took command of the Constantinople garrison, pressure from Britain and France led, in January 1914, to him being given the less contentious post of Inspector General of the Ottoman armed forces.

It was, he suggested, very similar to one that stood at Solomon's temple in Jerusalem. Future excavations would be as rich and rewarding as the past few seasons' 'should funds be forthcoming'.[2]

On the same day Woolley's article appeared, Hogarth wrote about 'Revealing the Civilisation of the Hittites of Syria' in the *Illustrated London News*. He called the Carchemish dig 'the largest, and in many respects the most important and fruitful, excavation which they [the British Museum] have ever promoted', in spite of difficulties 'and even their dangers, for Jerablus lies in a lawless region, among Kurdish tribes excited by recent events in Turkey'. He was more forceful than Woolley had been in his plea for funds. 'By the end of next spring season the Trustees, who have been splendidly supported by private munificence, will have expended some £10,000 on the site; but the work, which is opening up Hittite history for us, and the nature of the civilisation occupying the geographical space between the Semites and the Hellenes, will not be much more than half done.' In case that was not sufficient reason, there was the scare factor: 'if we do not finish it, the German scholars who follow up the Baghdad Railway, now running to Jerablus, will surely do so . . .' And after a lengthy description of the site and the various ruins excavated, Hogarth claimed that through the Carchemish discoveries they could now trace 'the development of Hittite plastic art . . . from its cradle to its grave'. All this, and at any moment the possibility of finding a bilingual inscription that would allow the translation of Hittite hieroglyphs. 'When so much can be said for three years' work on a part only of this great site, it will be agreed that it is well worth digging completely.'[3]

Walter Morrison had already agreed. A week before the articles appeared, he wrote to tell Hogarth of his plan to put another £10,000 for 'excavation at Carchemish, possibly removal of sculptures to London, and publication of results . . . I get the responsibility off what I am pleased to call my mind, the work can be carried on systematically and the money is assured.'[4]

'We are preparing ourselves and our house for a long stay,' Lawrence wrote home when news of the gift reached him, and in doing so prepared his parents for a 'long stay' as well, 'waterproofing the roofs with asphalt, cementing floors, getting a couple of tables and chairs and table-cloths and things'.⁵ When work did restart, there was more than ever to do: two hundred workmen to run, the cleaning and cataloguing of finds, and a crowd of guests to entertain including Dr Altounyan, 'the best carpet authority in Aleppo'. The doctor had looked over his collection of carpets in the expedition house, after which Lawrence, always hoping for appreciation, was pleased to tell his parents that 'you will next year have as good a floor as Mr. Hogarth . . . which means the best in Oxford'.⁶ He was living to the full, with the added tasks of completing *Seven Pillars of Wisdom* and writing a report on archaeology in the Wilderness of Zin for the Palestine Exploration Fund. But results at Carchemish remained hard to come by: 'we haven't found anything as yet'.⁷

One thing they didn't have to worry about were relations with their workers, mainly thanks to the villagers' admiration for Lawrence. He motivated them by being playful, to which Woolley had added small bonuses if antiquities were found. The German railway engineers paid higher wages, but had no such rapport and treated their people harshly, setting armed Circassian guards to watch over them. At times this seemed to pay off and they made good progress, with the German press reporting that 125 miles of track would be open and services running east across the Euphrates from Jerablus by the end of the year. Then things went wrong.

'The paymaster', Lawrence wrote in a detailed description to Flecker in Switzerland,* 'was a German clerk, an awful rotter who used to treat his men as beasts, & to swindle them in wages right & left; he used to charge for water and for bread, even though the men never ate the Company's bread. Of course they had to drink the water – but that was Euphrates, & the only cost of it was the wage of a water-boy to carry it.'⁸ This particular conflict erupted when the German clerk underpaid a Kurd worker. When the worker protested, the clerk ordered the Circassians to beat him. The ensuing fight saw more than a hundred Kurds and Arabs throwing stones at Germans and Circassians. When windows were broken in the company shed, the Germans inside came out with rifles and revolvers. 'After that of course everyone, Kurd or Arab, took cover behind

---

* Flecker died in Davos, Switzerland, in January 1915.

the upper bank, & those who had revolvers let them off at the office. The Germans telephoned over the bridge & to their camp, & soldiers & Circassians rushed down with other engineers & foremen & mechanics, till they had about 30 wildly excited men with rifles about the bridge-head, shooting up & down stream, & across the bridge & at the embankment & in the air like lunatics.'[9]

The workers – some three hundred of them now – looked for cover in the Carchemish ruins, using the ancient city wall for protection. Those who owned guns had brought them. Others had crowbars or axes and all were ready to charge down and force the foreigners into the river. The archaeologists held back, watching the Germans firing at a man with a rifle on the island in the river. It turned out to be 'an unfortunate German . . . He had been working there, & was about 100 yards from the bank: but the bullets were fairly whizzing round him. He was dancing about & shaking his fist at them & talking in German, not softly, until finally some Kurds in a boat landed on the island & took him ashore.'[10] At that point, 'for lack of other targets the German idiots began shooting again at us. They shot very badly, only hitting one boy next to me, but it made the Kurds by us very wild.'[11] They also shot at Woolley. By what Consul Fontana called superhuman efforts and good humour, Lawrence and Woolley persuaded the workers to back away, leading them up towards Jerablus village.

The threat of an uprising was taken so seriously that when news of fighting Kurds and Arabs reached Aleppo, the 'amateur fire-brigade' was sent to restore order. Even *The Times* in London reported 'a serious riot on the Baghdad Railway',[12] mentioning three dead, five possibly drowned and many wounded, as well as Woolley's and Lawrence's efforts to stop the fighting. The following morning, with German officials pointing to the fight as proof that Arabs and Kurds hated Christians, 250 soldiers arrived to help keep order. Other visitors that day included 'all the Consuls & Valis & Kaims. & Mutasarrifs & Commandants'. Nor was that the end of it. The young Kurd who had been killed belonged to Busrawi's clan and the Agha was calling for blood, vowing that the railway would never cross the Euphrates. The following night the German Consul in Aleppo, Walter Rössler, appeared at the mission house to ask the Englishmen to negotiate a settlement. 'We of course were inwardly chortling,' Lawrence remembered, 'but quite polite, I hope. We pointed out how serious the matter was.'[13] They suggested that blood money be paid for the young Kurd who was killed and to others who were wounded, and also that the German clerk and one of the engineers be removed, along with all Circassian guards. When this was agreed, Busrawi went to Aleppo to sign the agreement with Fontana and the German diplomat, and to receive the money. 'The improvement in German manners is incredible,' Lawrence noted when calm had been restored, 'only they don't seem to love us more than before.'

Fontana in his report on the attack to Ambassador Mallet in Constantinople proposed suggesting to the Vali of Aleppo 'that distinguished Ottoman Decorations conferred upon both Mr. Woolley and Mr. Lawrence, who saved the situation at Jerablus and who have, besides, rendered such signal services to the Ottoman Museum, would serve to materially demonstrate the well-earned gratitude of the Ottoman Government. Distinguished German Decorations might also be conferred upon them with equal reason.'[14] The suggestion seems to have met with some enthusiasm in Constantinople but Lawrence mentioned that he and Woolley refused them. 'Stupid nonsense,' he wrote home. 'They are such expensive things!'[15]

It was hard to imagine that Jerablus could remain peaceful when so much of the region was not – and when it had been so disturbed by the German–Kurd shootout – but that is how Hogarth found it when he arrived towards the end of March. Several trains a day from Aleppo brought a different sort of life to the place. While Hogarth was there, the Fontanas visited, Professor Cowley from Oxford came with his wife, the Altounyans, Professor Porter from Beirut, Dr Mackinnon from Damascus and a crowd of others, many of whom stayed. So many, in fact, that over two months there were only four evenings the archaeologists did not have guests for dinner. Lawrence became so used to this social life that he found it strangely quiet when no one else was staying in the house. The digs, which had been less successful during Hogarth's stay, became more promising after his departure. Among the objects they uncovered, it was a Hittite greave, a bronze leg armour, that caught Lawrence's eye. This was an unusual item because most of what they had found so far was carved stone. With his love of knights, it is perhaps not surprising that he thought this 'one of the most interesting things of all found in Carchemish'.[16]

One of the last visitors of the season was Stewart Newcombe, the Royal Engineer officer who had led the survey of Zin. In the desert, Newcombe had been enthralled by the stories that Woolley and Lawrence told late into the night. 'To discuss on the spot with two very alert people, weigh the different theories of the forty years' Wanderings and to learn a good deal of ancient history with the correct local colour, gave a mental balance to the ultra physical life of a surveyor.'[17] More mental balance was now on offer at Carchemish. Newcombe had asked Kitchener for permission to travel to Constantinople via Jerablus on the assumption that there was military intelligence to be gleaned from the progress of the railway over the Euphrates, something he already knew about as he had compiled a report on the possible effects of the railway on British interests for the Foreign Office in 1909.[18]

He arrived at Jerablus in mid-May with Lieutenant Greig, also with them in Sinai, and for several days they were offered what had become the traditional pleasures of the house – a walk through the ruins, a swim in the river, a paddle to the island and a feast cooked by Haj Wahid. Newcombe, who became one of Lawrence's lifelong friends,* enjoyed the archaeologist's 'vivid and amusing' stories about the German railway builders, learning more from him about local customs than about the Hittites.

The two officers left Jerablus to travel north over the Taurus Mountains into Anatolia, following the route of the Baghdad Railway. The journey had its difficulties, which they were to recreate for the Royal Geographical Society later in the year. The mountains were perhaps the greatest obstacle, but angry German and Turkish officials working on laying the railway had no desire to allow British military personnel into the area. The horses they had hired posed other challenges: 'horse', Newcombe observed wryly, 'is rather a misnomer

* Newcombe, who named his first son Stewart Lawrence Newcombe, was one of six pall-bearers at Lawrence's funeral.

for the animals obtained'. In the middle of the mountains they were stopped at a sentry post. 'Unless the traveller has a pass here,' they were to tell the RGS audience, 'the sentry is liable to stop him, since the road is private and belongs to the railway company. A few well-chosen words in French to an Austrian, who could only understand Italian, and the acceptance of a cigar, were sufficient to get us through.'[19]

Lawrence, who had planned a longer summer break in England this year, expected to leave Jerablus on 22 June, but at the beginning of the month he wrote that he would be delayed because he had an opportunity of travelling to Baghdad and from there down the Tigris River to the Persian Gulf. The next post brought news that this Eastern trip had been shelved. Then Newcombe wrote from Constantinople asking if Lawrence and Woolley could do what he and Greig had failed to do and follow the construction road through the Taurus Mountains. The Royal Engineers might have told the fellows at the RGS that they got through with a cigar and a joke, but they needed the two archaeologists to bring back details for their report and map.

Lawrence left Jerablus in mid-June with no more thought about it than when he and Woolley had gone to Sinai in January, or when he had taken Dahoum and Hamoudi to London the previous summer. They had catalogued as much as they could, recorded more than two thousand inscribed stone fragments and made long lists of their pottery finds, all now locked away in the storerooms with the portable antiquities. Whatever was left outside and could be covered up was buried.

Lawrence wrote a last, proud description of his recent improvements about the house he had built. He had brightened the thirty-five-foot sitting room by whitening the walls with powdered chalk, hung curtains of red leather, put carpets on the wall and a dado-rail of hemp stalks. He had even built a second sitting room in case the rumour was true that architects and another archaeologist would be joining them in the autumn.

The things he did not need for the journey had been put away, including the heavy camel-hair robe with which he could have melted the North Pole, and he had shown Dahoum where he had left his revolver: it was too much trouble to pass it through customs and he was hoping they would not need it on their way through the mountains. Some of his little *antikas* were packed and ready to go, as was an Aleppo-weave quilt he had bought for his parents, 'silver and coloured silks: old, and now becoming rare, for they burn them all to get out the metal, when they tarnish'.[20] For himself, he had Dodd's portrait of Dahoum sketched that happy day at the Ashmolean, the previous summer, and which Dahoum seems to have given to Lawrence. His camera was in its leather case. Passports, money, maps and notebooks . . . and he had packed the manuscript of *Seven Pillars of Wisdom*. His shorts, the buttonless shirt and the gaudy Kurdish sash with its multi-coloured tassels that held the ensemble together, had been put away and with them went some of the easy manner he had found at Carchemish. What Winifred Fontana called an absorbed, discomfiting aloofness settled around him as he dressed in his travelling clothes and boots, although there was no mistaking that he was, as she had seen him, 'a young man of rare power and considerable physical beauty'.[21]

Gregori had already left for Cyprus and Busrawi was across the Euphrates in his forty-pole tent. Lawrence and Woolley said their farewells to Haj Wahid, Hamoudi, the workers, the women of the village and Dahoum. It would be the first time Lawrence had been away from his young friend and protégé for more than a year and a half.

They went first to Aleppo, to the head office of the Baghdad Railway Company to ask for permission to travel along the construction road, saying they had heard it offered spectacular views. The German chief engineer in Aleppo laughed when he interviewed them and forbade them to go anywhere near it. So they went anyway, heading north by train. When Lawrence checked out of Baron's Hotel on 8 June, his bill (which was still hanging in the hotel's reception a few years ago) included a bottle of Cordon Rouge champagne, unexpected for a man who claimed that water had more taste and character than wine.

Heading towards the mountains, they had one of those happy coincidences that can transform a journey, for they found themselves sharing a compartment with a man who worked for the Kaiser Friedrich Museum in Berlin.* The German was taking photographs of antiquities, but had been unable to see Carchemish, something Woolley assured him could easily be arranged: he was invited to visit the following season. When Woolley then explained their own difficulty, the German wrote letters of introduction to some of his engineer friends working on the line. Realising that the chief engineer might have sent a message down the line about them, Woolley asked him to give them assumed names: he chose Jones and Robinson.

At the railhead, they hired mules to carry their baggage and continued on foot into the mountain passes. By a second stroke of luck, at one of the first construction camps they met an Italian engineer who had just been sacked and who seemed not to care that two British travellers should ask for a full set of plans of the mountain-section of the politically sensitive railway, the crucial gap that needed to be tunnelled in some sections. Woolley's fluency in Italian might have helped. The man's anger at being dismissed certainly did, for he gave them blueprints of the whole line and even pointed out areas where the engineers were having construction problems. On the other side of the mountains, they took the train to Constantinople. Woolley later wrote that it was 'the only piece of spying I ever did before the war'.[22] Lawrence never mentioned the journey. He was in Oxford by the end of June.

* Now called the Bode Museum.

18

Shooting and Burning

I don't think I will ever travel in the West again: one cannot tell, of course, but this part out here is worth a million of the rest. The Arabs are so different from ourselves.

Lawrence writing home from Carchemish, 23 April 1914[1]

Summer 1914

H E SAID HE would be in England for six weeks, but as soon as he arrived there he wrote to Flecker that he would stay only another two or three, 'thereafter Eastward'.[2] His parents were in Oxford, older – his father now in his late sixties – and a little frail, struggling to recover from niggling infections, but the Polstead Road house seemed unchanged, quietly rich and solid, and now overlaid with Baluch, Kurd and Persian carpets, an exotic note, a different palette of colours, and giving off a whiff of the Orient. News in Oxford was of a Suffragette 'disturbance' at the Union. When he heard about it, Will Lawrence wrote from Delhi, where he was teaching, to say that he wished 'they were agitating for something worth while talking about'.[3] Bob, the eldest brother, was studying medicine at Bart's Hospital in London, Frank, the fourth of them, was following Ned's example, reading history at Jesus College where he had just sat his first-year exams. Arnold was still at the City High School. Life in Oxford seemed as normal and dependable as ever, as did the news from elsewhere. On Saturday 27 June 1914, for instance, *The Times* reported that a Suffragette had been found guilty of possessing 'explosive substances', stones and hammers, while Lord Curzon (who had applied for Lawrence's original *iradés* in

246

Constantinople) was speaking in London at the National League for Opposing Woman Suffrage about the dangers of giving women freedom. King George V and Queen Mary were back at Buckingham Palace after a tour around the north of England. A collection of Old Masters had sold particularly well at Christie's saleroom. Three people had died in a motorbike accident on Holland Park, London. The weather continued fine and warm. Under 'Imperial and Foreign Intelligence', it was reported that the Greek and Turkish governments had agreed to an exchange of population in the areas that had recently changed hands; also that the Ottoman Sultan would hold a dinner in honour of Sir Berkeley Milne, Admiral of the British Mediterranean Squadron, at which, no doubt, the delivery of the two British-built battleships that Turkey had paid for would be quietly discussed.* Of most relevance to Lawrence was the news that a sixty-mile stretch of the Baghdad Railway, running east from Jerablus into Mesopotamia, would open on 1 July.

In what the family still called Ned's house, the bronze head of Hypnos stared unseeing at the books, the files of papers, the final typescript of his Crusader castles thesis, the journal from his walk along the Euphrates three summers before. The sight and smell of the place belonged to another life. (Were the brass rubbings still there, or put away?) Dahoum and Hamoudi had slept in there the previous summer, but Lawrence made it his own again as he unpacked things brought from Carchemish, his camera, the manuscript of *Seven Pillars of Wisdom* and Dodd's sketch of Dahoum in his striped robe. On the table were notes and drawings for his report on their findings in the Wilderness of Zin. In spite of what he called 'our non-success',[4] the Palestine Exploration Fund wanted to publish something significant with maps, floorplans, sketches and photographs. The drive behind this came from Kitchener, in Cairo. In a note to Basil Liddell Hart, who began work on his biography in 1929, Lawrence explained that 'Turkey was not in the war, but was sore about the Sinai survey, which it felt had been a military game.'[5] It was hoped that the publication would convince them that the Zin survey had

---

* Winston Churchill, as First Lord of the Admiralty, was determined not to deliver them.

been academically rigorous and important in its discoveries. He had noted while still in Carchemish that they were halfway through writing the report for publication, but it was obviously going to take him more than a couple of weeks to finish. As well as going to the Bodleian Library for research, and writing in the bungalow, he needed time at both the British Museum and the Ashmolean to unpack and catalogue the crates of seals, bronzes and other antiquities that the Royal Navy had brought back from Syria over the past year. Returning to Syria in a couple of weeks seemed overly optimistic.

But neither the PEF nor the museums dictated his movements that summer because on 28 June the Archduke Franz Ferdinand, nephew of the octogenarian Emperor Franz Joseph and heir to the Austro-Hungarian throne, was assassinated in Sarajevo. Because the murder took place in Bosnia, which Austria had annexed in 1908, and because the assassin, Gavrilo Princip, was a Yugoslav nationalist and a declared member of the Young Bosnians, a movement dedicated to ridding the country of Austrians, the tragedy had political meaning. In hindsight, the consequences seem impossible to ignore: unless one of the Powers intervened, war would break out between Austria and Serbia. The British government's attitude was less far seeing, typified by the Chancellor David Lloyd George, who thought that 'such official reports as came to hand did not seem to justify the alarmist view'.[6] Who, one wonders, was writing 'such' reports? But then no one was taking seriously the alarmist view of what was happening in Syria where, inspired by the audacity of the assassination in Sarajevo, Arab nationalists were becoming bolder, as pamphlets distributed in Damascus suggest: 'O you, the heirs of the Orient Glory who cannot endure wrong done to them, this is the voice of your dead fathers calling to you from their coffins . . . Enough suffering! Arise and form societies and bands to punish the aggressors and free yourself from the oppressors and you have God and the high mountains to protect you . . .'[7] The writer ended by reminding the glorious heirs that freedom could be bought only by soaking the land with their blood.

Yet July passed calmly, a flat still sea of a month before war broke over them. As it passed, with Lawrence hard at work, the situation in Europe deteriorated and a sense of foreboding grew. Lawrence was a dreamer, so might be forgiven for thinking that all this was just a bad dream, uniquely so for him for it stood in the way of his return to Carchemish, to Dahoum, to his own life. He would need to stay longer at home, with all the problems which that presented to someone who five years earlier had admitted to having difficulties becoming English again and who needed to keep some distance from his mother. Perhaps it was at this moment that he began to work out the steps of an Arab uprising and to think through what it would take to hustle into being the new Asia that he had first imagined many years before in Oxford.

The previous year, Consul-General Cumberbatch had wondered whether Arab reformers were showing themselves too early, and so it proved when the Young Turk government reversed its earlier liberal policy, scattering the Arab deputies and outlawing their societies. Forced underground, they changed, in Lawrence's words, 'from liberal clubs into conspiracies'.[8] Arab officers serving in the Turkish army formed themselves into secret groups – he reckoned as many as 70 per cent of Mesopotamian-born officers belonged to it. Secret societies in Egypt, those known to al-Qalam al-Siyari, the government's Secret Service Bureau, and a clutch of others that had not been infiltrated, had expanded, while in Syria, one organisation, al-Fatah, had attracted significant support from lawyers, landowners, doctors and other public figures. These and many others were waiting for the moment to rise against the Turks.

It is impossible to know how aware of all this Lawrence was in July 1914 as Europe staggered from the shots fired by Gavrilo Princip to a war of words, to open warfare. Probably he knew few of the details. But he understood perfectly the political, social and religious make-up of the place where he had been living, he knew of the aspirations of its intellectuals and the urges of his workers, and he would have already thought through what might happen next. Planning was a quality his brother Will had recognised in him: after hearing of his defiance of the authorities at Aqaba, he had written that Ned had 'the gift of seeing the whole campaign as well as the detailed manoeuvres, so never fear for him'.[9]

He was not in Arabia, but he found relief at Hogarth's house, particularly during the July days when Gertrude Bell came to stay. She was gratified that her prediction of his becoming a traveller had come true and they exchanged stories and information: Bell had just returned from Arabia and talked of the tribes along the Hejaz Railway, including the Howeitat, who were to become so important to Lawrence during the Arab revolt. But instead of travelling in Arabia, he was working on *The Wilderness of Zin*, as the PEF publi-cation was to be called. This had now become urgent. With Turkey standing back, Kitchener did not want the Sinai survey to be a cause of friction between London and Constantinople. In Lawrence's words, the man about to become War Minister 'insisted on the Palestine Exploration Fund's bringing out its record of our archaeological researching p-d-q as whitewash. Woolley and I had instructions to get it done instanter.'[10]

On 28 July, Austria-Hungary declared war on Serbia. Russia mobilised its army in defence of its Slav ally. On 2 August, Germany signed a secret treaty with Turkey and declared war on Russia. France, bound by treaty to defend Russia, declared against Germany on 3 August. This provoked a German advance into Belgium. On 4 August, Britain entered the war to stand beside Belgium. At this point, all of the initial players in this tragedy were now in place, except one. In spite of the new treaty with Germany, the Turkish government continued to stand back from the conflict and, for as long as it did, Lawrence might have clung to the vain hope that he might be able to ignore the whole mess and return to Carchemish, to his life and work and friends.

The British government called for 100,000 troops to fight what it anticipated would be a short war, but almost 300,000 men volun-teered. After the first British defeat, at the Battle of Mons at the end of August, there was a further spike in recruiting: almost half a million volunteered in September, one of them being Ned's brother Frank.

It made as much sense for Frank to sign up as it did for Bob to complete his medical training. The phrase 'sign up' is a literal one: he filled in a form offering to join the Special Reserve. He had taken this decision 'not lightly nor without thought'.[11] As he was already in summer camp in Yorkshire, his mother delivered the form to the Oxford recruitment office. Will's response was eloquent and revealing. He was glad that Frank had volunteered: 'if Frank is sent to the front there'll be one of the five of us doing something, which is as it should be'.[12] And he asked his mother whether Ned would 'stop at home or go East again and steer his country into safe waters?'[13]

Ned stopped at home. It has been suggested that he wanted to fight but was too short for the army, but his brother Frank was only two inches taller. By Ned's own account he did not even try to enlist. Not that he did not want to be involved: most people he knew wanted to help the war effort and anyone with his sort of expertise would be much needed, on both sides of the trenches: Baron von Oppenheim was already at work drawing up plans for the Kaiser on how to destabilise the British in India and elsewhere. But Lawrence already had a job to do and one that Kitchener, in England and appointed Secretary of State for War on 6 August, wanted finished. Turkey was still not in the war and the Sinai book needed to be published.

To begin with he stayed in Oxford, keeping in close touch with Hogarth and enlisting the help of several Oxford scholars to translate ancient inscriptions, while the RGS in London worked on the survey map. Towards the end of August, after his twenty-sixth birthday, he moved to London to share digs with Woolley and work intensively on the book. After London, he would find a way to follow his brother's example and go to war, to what, it was becoming increasingly obvious, might be his death.

Before he left, he tidied up the bungalow. He rearranged the books and made sure the photograph files were in order. He had always been scrupulous in that way. Then there was the manuscript, *Seven Pillars of Wisdom*, that queer book that he had found so hard to write but that he had written, which recounted his adventures in 'seven type cities of the East'.[14] The book that was 'a moral symphony', that no one else had read.

If he had been working in intelligence and had written about his adventures in the manuscript, he might not have wanted that to outlive him. But he would have trusted his parents' judgment on that and would have known that, if he died and they had found something compromising, they would have destroyed it, or placed it in safe keeping. But if he had written about himself and his relationships in the East, if he had exposed himself in a way that revealed the person he had become, if he had expressed even indirectly his rejection of so many of his parents' values, and his happiness at being free, or even his love of Dahoum, then he would not have wanted the manuscript to outlive him. He provided one convincing reason for this, after the war: 'I have a terror of her [his mother] knowing anything about my feelings, or convictions, or way of life. If she knew they would be damaged, violated, no longer mine.'[15] This echoed two things he had written while on his long French bike ride. One was that he did not want to tell his parents about himself. The other was that if you wrote a book and then died, it was 'almost terrible' that your ideas, yourself, would be picked over by people after your death. Because he found this sort of exposure impossible, he crouched by the fireplace, as he had done as a student on so many winter nights, piled the papers in the grate and struck a match – not to his Crusader castles thesis, his 1911 diary nor any of his other immature writings that have survived, only to *Seven Pillars of Wisdom*.

He had been quite clear about why his mother behaved in this way towards him: she could not bear to see him grow as a person, 'because she has not grown since we began'.[16]

He no longer needed the words written on the pages that now curled and caught in the grate, because he had them in mind. If he could not return in all innocence to dig again at Carchemish with Dahoum, then he would go to war and fight his way back there. He was about to grow again.

19

Of Arabia

. . . the rocky North,
From storm and silence drove me forth
Down to the blue and tideless sea.
I do not fear the tinkling sword
For I am a great battle-lord,
And love the horns of chivalry.
   James Elroy Flecker, 'The Masque of the Magi'[1]

IT TOOK MORE than a few weeks to finish writing about their findings in Sinai. They were still working on it in late September 1914 when, in Lawrence's words, 'Woolley lost heart, waiting, and wangled a Commission in the Artillery'.[2] Around the same time, Mrs Lawrence wrote to Will in India to say that Ned was still hoping to return to Carchemish, to which Will replied, astonished: 'Turkey has mobilized through Syria and digging will be absurd. Perhaps there's a political motive.'[3] But Turkey had not yet joined the war and there was no political motive, just a very personal one.

Lawrence continued working on *The Wilderness of Zin* for some weeks, but by the end of September it was mostly done, and he was restless in a city gripped by enthusiasm for war and stories of 'our boys' signing up. He complained about being bored and having to put up with 'all the rumours and theories and anxieties of everybody all round you'.[4] His own anxieties were different from anyone else's. While some of the people around him worried about finding a suitable commission and others feared being killed, Lawrence was anxious about the possibility of the Turks not entering the war. He needed them to fight so that he could fulfil his plan to reduce or remove them from Asia Minor and to help Arabs – Dahoum – be free.

There was a great need for manpower, but it was not easy to find a job to suit his very specific skills and talents, so – as he had done many times in the past – he went to consult Hogarth. At this point, presumably at Hogarth's suggestion, Kenyon offered him a job arranging the British Museum's Hittite collection. It is interesting to consider what might, and might not, have happened had he accepted the £4 a week and become a museum curator. We will never know because another of Hogarth's promptings resulted in an interview with Colonel Coote Hedley. Hedley was a Committee member of the PEF and was working on the Sinai survey map, so he knew all about Lawrence. He was also Director of MO4, which concerned itself with both military operations and intelligence, and had lost all but one of his assistants. By the second half of October Lawrence was working in what was known as the GSGS (General Staff Geographical Section) and, without so much as a medical, had been commissioned as a temporary second lieutenant-interpreter.

With Lawrence it was never going to be just about maps. That much was clear soon after he joined Hedley when he wrote to Winifred Fontana (back in England) to express his frustration at Turkey not fighting, 'because I wanted to root them out of Syria',[5] and to ask if she had any news from Carchemish. He was not alone in agitating against the Turks. On 5 October, Lord Cromer, the great proconsul who had run Egypt as Britain's 'veiled protectorate' for thirty years, called for Arabic-speaking British officers to be sent to the Middle East to stir an uprising against Turkish occupation. Ten days later, he added the suggestion that the Kurds and Armenians would also rise.[6] Two weeks later, Turkey went to war and Lawrence's pieces were falling into place.

'The war brought the archaeologist out in a new light,' Woolley remembered, 'and his habit of prying about in countries little known, his knowledge of peoples, and his gift of tongues, were turned to uses far other than his wont.'[7] Turkey's entry into the war gave purpose to many people who knew the region from peacetime. At the beginning of December, Woolley, Newcombe and Lawrence were all on their way to Cairo and the headquarters of British action against the Turks. Hogarth, who was in Athens on intelligence work, would soon be there, as would Gertrude Bell, Harry Pirie-Gordon whose map Lawrence had used on his Crusader castle walk, Hubert Young with whom he had made limestone carvings during that happiest of all summers a year and a half earlier, and many others who had enjoyed sharp conversation and warm hospitality at the Carchemish house. All of them had inside information on the people of the Near East. But only Lawrence was driven by an urgent and specific desire. Before he left for Calais (he and Newcombe were going overland to Marseille and from there to Egypt by boat), Lawrence wrote again to Mrs Fontana for news of Carchemish. He had pushed Raphael Fontana to ask the Vali of Aleppo to allow the Jerablus people, Dahoum among them, to perform their military service as guards at Carchemish. He was also hoping that Dahoum and Haj Wahid would empty the house of anything of value, including his revolver, before the Turks sacked it. 'It would grieve me if any Turk shot me with my own revolver.'[8]

Lawrence and Newcombe reached Cairo on 14 December and discovered there was no intelligence department. 'They thought all was well without it,' Lawrence explained to Hogarth, 'till it dawned on them that nobody in Egypt knew about Syria.'[9] Although he had an extremely lowly rank, he had already been mentioned to the Commander in Chief in Egypt as someone 'who has wandered about in the Sinai peninsula'.[10] They were soon to discover that he had done more than wander: in the past five years, he had travelled through Syria, Palestine, Turkey and Egypt, much of it on foot, had visited Aqaba, Cairo and the Suez Canal, knew his way through the Taurus Mountains and was familiar with the hotels of Constantinople. Lawrence could speak several dialects of Arabic – not perfectly, but well enough for most purposes – and he was comfortable wearing the clothes of Arabs and Kurds, with whose manners and customs he was familiar. In an intelligence department, he ought to have been an asset and yet within weeks he was complaining to Hogarth – hoping the Turks were making better use of the expertise they had to hand, and lamenting that while Newcombe was running 'a gang of most offensive spies' and Woolley was writing 'windy concealers of truth for the press . . . I am map officer, & write geographical reports, trying to persuade 'em that Syria is not peopled entirely by Turks . . .'[11]

Shelves have been filled with descriptions and analyses of the Arab revolt and Lawrence's part in it, the extent and effectiveness of which are still a matter for hot debate and the popularity of which have risen and fallen with the passing decades. Books have also been written about the activities and more clear-cut duplicities of Western diplomats and generals in their dealings with Sherif Hussein, the Emir of Mecca, and his sons, particularly Sherif Feisal, the future King of Iraq. For my story, however, what Lawrence did and the effect it had on the region is less important than *why* he did it and *how* he managed.

The latter part is easily answered: the years of training himself as a young man in England and of living in Carchemish made Lawrence uniquely suited to overcome the demands of war in general and of this desert conflict in particular. He understood the people of that region, he knew what pleased them and how they were angered, how to make them fight. He also knew the history of thousands of years of conflict in the region, why Pharaoh Necho had struggled beneath the walls of Carchemish, which route Alexander the Great had taken along the Mediterranean coast, how Saladin had conquered the Crusaders and who, in turn, had terrified Saladin and how they had done it. He had been dreaming of this moment for years, even before there was Dahoum and Carchemish. And his military judgments were usually inspired. The Sykes-Picot agreement, the secret deal to divide Turkey's Asian empire between Britain and France, had not yet been negotiated, but he was already suspicious of France's political aspirations and deeply disapproving of its behaviour in its North African colonies of Morocco, Algeria and Tunisia. This in part explains how and why, when he had been in Cairo for just three months and was still a very junior officer in the geographical section, he wrote a war plan for Hogarth that revolved around a landing at Alexandretta, 'a wonderful harbour'[12] as he knew from personal experience. 'A landing in Alexandretta in Feb. 1915', he wrote after the war, 'would have handed over Syria and Mespot. [sic] to their native (Arab) troops, then all in their home stations, and complete, and automatically established local governments there.'¹³* Four days after urging Hogarth to talk to 'Winston', Lawrence went further and wrote one of the most remarkable sentences of the war: 'I want to pull them [Arab leaders] all together, & to roll up Syria by way of the Hedjaz in the name of the Sherif . . . we hope we can rush right up to Damascus, & biff the French out of all hope of Syria.'¹⁴ He wrote those visionary words in March 1915. The Sykes–Picot agreement was secretly concluded more than a year later, on 16 May 1916. Sherif Hussein called for an Arab uprising against the Turks the following month.

There were other people – even in Cairo now – who had great knowledge of the region and its patchwork of people, but very few combined that knowledge with physical toughness in the way that Lawrence did. The physical element was important because the campaigning would be demanding. He knew he could survive whatever was required of him: long bike rides as a youth and long walks as a young man, including the summer walks through Syria, had taught him to ignore pain and discomfort. As he had shown on many occasions, most recently during the Zin survey, he was used to living rough, to not washing or changing his clothes, to sleeping on the ground with a cloak thrown over him. But to physical and mental strength, Lawrence also brought a great knowledge of previous campaigns, a fluency in Arabic and an ease with people; his comment to Sir John Rhys on his return from the Crusader castle walk five years earlier, that 'I have perhaps, living as an Arab with the Arabs, got a better insight into the daily life of the people'¹⁵ finally rang true. His apprenticeship was done and there were few people in Britain better equipped to liaise with the inhabitants of Syria and Arabia, whether sherifs in the Hejaz or sheikhs in Mesopotamia, just as there were few who knew the place as well as he. Hubert Young, who worked with him in Arabia, recognised this and echoed the reason Dahoum had put forward for loving him. 'What the Arabs admired most in him was his utter disregard of danger and his readiness to endure not merely discomfort but the

* The French in particular refused to allow this, realising they would never regain control of their future colony if there was a local Arab government. A landing was made at Gallipoli instead, with the loss of over 100,000 lives.

worst kinds of hardship. Not only did he beat them all at their own game, shoot straighter, ride harder, and eat and drink less, but he shone out among them all in the qualities which they would like to have possessed.'[16]

As for why he did what he did . . . He claimed in 1919 that he had four motives in what he called 'the Arab affair'. These were a desire to win the war, 'to feel what it was like to be the mainspring of a national movement', and to see a Commonwealth of free peoples created in the Near East, 'an Arab Dominion' initially under British sovereignty but ultimately independent. The fourth motive, which he listed first and which by his own reckoning was the most important, was personal: 'I liked a particular Arab very much, and I thought that freedom for the race would be an acceptable present.'[17]

He had hidden this personal motive throughout the fighting, which was easy as he was used to hiding such things – he had done it for years from his mother – and because they were in such constant physical and mental activity there was little time to wonder why. Most people around him in Arabia and Cairo had no idea that everything he achieved was driven by a need to recover a life and a person he had left behind at Carchemish, and to help those people and people like them towards what he thought would be a better life. A long list of notable names praised his efforts, yet none of them understood the personal desire that drove him just as none of them knew he had burned the only copy of the book he had written before the war. None, perhaps, except Hogarth.

It was finally revealed in a postscript to the second *Seven Pillars of Wisdom*, a page that does not appear in the first, subscription edition, the only one to be published during his lifetime. The first public edition, which appeared immediately after his death in 1935, ends with the confession that 'the strongest motive throughout had been a personal one, not mentioned here, but present to me, I think, every hour of these two years. Active pains and joys might fling up, like towers, among my days: but, refluent as air, this hidden urge re-formed, to be the persisting element of life.'[18]

When he reached Damascus, on 1 October 1918, he was just three hundred miles from Carchemish. If the roads were open, he could have driven there in six hours. The train took much longer.

Turkish troops and Allied prisoners had often passed through on the Hejaz and then the Baghdad Railways. There had been no fighting around Jerablus and Lawrence knew that Dahoum had been working as a guard on the site – perhaps his request had reached Fontana and perhaps Dahoum had been relieved of military service elsewhere. He had certainly stayed safe at least until October 1916. But a shortage of food and medicine, and a hard winter, led to famine, which was followed by a typhus epidemic. A third of the village died this way, among them as many as a half of the Carchemish labour force.

Some time, some weeks perhaps, before he followed the Arab army into Damascus, Lawrence heard from Hogarth – probably – that Dahoum was dead. His most pressing motive for fighting had been taken from him. Dahoum had probably died in the winter of 1916, before Lawrence had even started fighting with Feisal and the Arab army, before the taking of Aqaba, before the long march north to Syria, to Damascus, towards Jerablus.

Lawrence was still in Damascus the night after its the liberation, so he was there when the muezzin called the faithful to prayer – *Allahu akbar, ashhadu an-la ilaha illa allah* – and when they added one extra line, chanting that Allah had been good to the people and had delivered Damascus to the Arabs that day. As this call went out, into the streets, around mosques and into houses across the city, the faithful bowed down in happiness and relief to give thanks for the freedom that Lawrence thought would be an acceptable present for the man he had loved. 'Only for me,' he wrote, having heard the call, 'of all the hearers, was the event sorrowful and the phrase meaningless.'[19]

Epilogue

An Unpeaceful Peace

> When Feisal had gone, I made to Allenby the last (and also I
> think the first) request I ever made him for myself – leave to
> go away. For a while he would not have it . . . In the end he
> agreed; and then at once I knew how much I was sorry.
>
> T. E. Lawrence, *Seven Pillars of Wisdom*[1]

> The East has been rather impressed by our having taken the
> most unlikely material in the world, and pushed it to undreamed
> of success.
>
> T. E. Lawrence to Geoffrey Dawson, 17 November 1918[2]

A T THE END of the fighting, Colonel T. E. Lawrence could have
enjoyed fame and fortune. 'I had meant to be a general and
knighted, when thirty,' the thirty-year-old acknowledged just before
the war ended in 1918. 'Such temporal dignities (if I survived the next
four weeks) were now in my grasp – only that my sense of the falsity
of the Arab position had cured me of crude ambition.'[3] Dahoum's
death robbed him of whatever was left. This was no strange quirk on
his part. The loss of his 'personal motive' and the failure of his plan
to secure independent Arab states of the Middle East weighed heavily
on him. In his war-shattered mind, the dream had become a nightmare
and everything seemed irrelevant, ridiculous or wrong.

But there was already celebrity: the capture of Aqaba on 6 July
1917 was the beginning and soon afterwards he was recommended
for many decorations. Colonel Wilson, an old Arabia hand, urged
'that Lawrence be granted a DSO immediately',[4] while General
Wingate, who the previous year had accused him of amateur
soldiering, recommended to the Chief of the Imperial General Staff,

the highest-ranking officer in the British army, that he be awarded a Victoria Cross, the army's highest award for valour, for the skill, endurance and pluck he had shown. Lawrence did not qualify for the VC on a technicality – his pluck needed to be witnessed by a British officer – but he was made a Companion of the Order of the Bath (Military Division). Later Allenby proposed him for a knighthood, but Lawrence wanted neither rewards nor decorations. His reasoning was sound. He believed that the British government had been duplicitous when it appeared to promise Feisal, Sherif Hussein's son, Arab independence in return for help fighting Turkey, a promise it could not keep because of a prior agreement with France. Lawrence felt that he had been implicated in this deceit. His inspiration and knowledge had helped in the fight against the Turks and he had offered it believing he was helping the Arabs achieve independence. 'One of the sorest things in life', he knew at the end, 'is to come to realise that one is just not good enough.'[5] He felt he had not been good enough to bring about the thing he most desired; instead, he had been used by others to deceive his Arab friends. For that reason he felt he did not deserve awards and later would express unease about benefitting in any way from the significant sums that *Seven Pillars of Wisdom* generated.*

In his usual flippant way, he had written to his parents after Aqaba to say that all the decorations and honours he had been offered 'are so many nuisances afterwards, & I'll never wear or use any of them'.[6] He made an exception for the French Croix de Guerre, but that was intended to be ironic, given his opposition to a French presence in Arabia or Syria. He assumed that his views on awards and medals were widely known when he attended a private audience with King George V on 30 October 1918, just days before the end of the war. The event had been announced in the press, but Lawrence did not read that sort of report, so he appears not to have known that he was attending a private investiture of the Order of the Bath. It became clear as he entered the room and saw the King, Queen,

---

* Initial royalties covered the high cost of producing the book – the illustrations were extravagant – after which royalties from book sales went to help some people he knew and to the RAF Benevolent Fund. After his death, the Seven Pillars of Wisdom Trust was created to distribute royalties.

their attendants and the decorations. According to the King's private secretary, Lawrence apologised for any embarrassment and hoped he was causing no offence, but could not accept. He then called the British Cabinet a 'set of crooks'.

By the winter of 1918, Lawrence's thoughts were not on glory. Allenby, Feisal and their staff had arrived in Damascus on 3 October that year and Lawrence had left the following day, going first to Cairo and then back to England. And then where? The dream was dead, the strongest motive gone, the monument shattered. Even his plan for the new Arab states was compromised by the machinations of British and French diplomats and by the mistrust that existed between the various Arab tribes. Lawrence was still wanted, of course − needed even − and for a while he gave himself as fully as before, arguing for the right to Arab self-determination, self-administration, at the post-war peace conference. 'My objects', he explained, 'were to save England, & France too, from the follies of the imperialists, who would have us . . . repeat the exploits of Clive or Rhodes. The world has passed that point.'[7] In that he was wrong. He had suggested that the former Ottoman provinces be refashioned as a confederation of independent or autonomous Arab states, with Britain overseeing the transition. It was a good idea and the world would be a very different place today had he got his way. But he did not: the follies of the imperialists were repeated.

He was back in London in December 1918, staying at the Carlton Hotel on Pall Mall from where he wrote to old man Doughty, on Christmas Day, to say that he 'had been over much of your country, (more securely and comfortably, but in somewhat the same fashion) meeting many of the people, and sons of the people who knew you out there. It has been a wonderful experience.'[8] There must have been a feeling of circularity in writing that letter, a reaching out to the old life. Perhaps he still thought there was a way for him to live it − a pale shadow of it − for him to follow Hogarth's example and become 'a travelled, archaeological sort of man, with geography and a pen as his two standbys'.[9] For a while that winter he thought so because he contacted Kenyon at the British Museum to ask about the possibility of going to dig at Carchemish.

Many of his old friends returned to their old lives. Gertrude Bell was involved in creating the state of Iraq, but Hogarth went back to the Ashmolean, Sir Frederic Kenyon continued to run the British Museum and Reginald Campbell Thompson, who had worked in intelligence in Basra through the war, went digging in Iraq using Turkish prisoners as labourers.

In 1915 Woolley had left Lawrence and the rest of the Arab Bureau team in Cairo to work at the Port Said intelligence office, where he had control of British and French spy ships in the Eastern Mediterranean. In the summer of August 1916, he was sailing off the Turkish coast on Lord Rosebery's yacht when it hit a mine. He was taken captive and spent the rest of the war in a Turkish prison camp. A few months after the armistice, he was sent back to Syria as a political officer, and by June 1919 he was at Carchemish, preparing to dig for the British Museum. The area was officially under French control but there were Turkish soldiers, Kurdish militia and others disputing the French claim and the French were nervous about the site because of its proximity to the Baghdad Railway crossing over the Euphrates.

Woolley was delighted to find that some of the old team had survived the war and the typhoid epidemic and were still at Jerablus, most notably Haj Wahid, and Hamoudi, who was to work with him for the next couple of decades. Woolley reported to Hogarth and Kenyon in England, as before, which is how he heard that Lawrence had asked to return to Carchemish. Lawrence said that he owed Hogarth everything that had come to him since the age of seventeen, 'which is the age at which I suddenly found myself',[10] but this was one thing not even Hogarth could fix for him.

Woolley had mixed feelings about working with his assistant again and for several reasons. Lawrence was increasingly covered in glory while Woolley had sat out much of the war in a Turkish prison, writing his archaeological memoirs. The younger man had often pushed, challenged and mocked Woolley and his ways and would be even more insufferable now. Perhaps Woolley did seriously consider renewing their partnership, for in September 1919 he wrote to Kenyon to say, 'I hope that he still has the intention, expressed last winter, of continuing work as my assistant.' But somehow Colonel

Lawrence was never likely to answer to acting Major Woolley and most obviously because of politics.

The region was unsettled in a way that was depressingly familiar from before the war: the Turks and French were confronting each other, while Arabs, Kurds and Armenians threatened to rise against yet another foreign occupation. In those circumstances, the name and fame of 'el Urens', cheered through the many-poled goat-hair tents during the war years, would be too potent a rallying cry in a divided country hoping for peace. 'In the present state of affairs in Syria,' Woolley wrote, '& until there is a formal settlement of that country with a permanent form of government constituted & functioning, it will not do for him to come out.'[11] It took Kenyon three months to reply and by then 'it is pretty plain that it will be inexpedient for Lawrence to go out at present; but I hope the atmosphere for political suspicion will blow over in time, and that he will be able to return to archaeology, as he desires'.[12] His desires were not to be, and things became more complicated, more bloody. Feisal came away from the Paris peace talks believing that Britain and France had not kept their promises about Arab self-rule. Without the blessing of the European powers, he was crowned King of Greater Syria by the Syrian National Congress on 7 March 1920. In April, France took control of Syria. On the 11th of that month, a 400-strong French garrison at Urfa, besieged for two months by a Turkish unit, accepted a ceasefire only to be massacred. A week later, with the whole region threatening to rise, Woolley abandoned the site. The imperialists, whom Lawrence had tried to outmanoeuvre, had won and most of the Middle East was divided into British and French spheres of interest. Lawrence never returned and Carchemish never revealed the multilingual inscription, the 'Hittite Rosetta Stone' that Hogarth had hoped for.*

Before Woolley wrote to reject the idea of working again with his assistant, another part of Lawrence's life changed when his father died of pneumonia. Two years later, his mother, mourning the loss

---

* Hittite cuneiform was deciphered by the Czech scholar, Dr Friedrich Hrozný during World War I. Excavations at Carchemish were finally resumed in 2011.

of two sons in the war and now her partner, sold the house in Polstead Road and with it 'Ned's bungalow'.

He had discovered there was a price to pay for daring to dream in the day. He still loved all waste and solitary places, but he could no longer taste the pleasure or believe them to be boundless. Later, hoping not for boundlessness but for a quiet corner, he changed his name – twice. He knew by then that Lawrence was not his real name anyway – his father had been a Chapman, his mother a Junner. So when he needed to escape the attention of the press, the name Ross and then Shaw would do just as well, or even 338, the abbreviation of his service number, which is how Noël Coward referred to him. Churchill offered him responsibility and power, took him to the 1921 Cairo Conference and there were rumours of various posts he might be offered, including that of British High Commissioner in Egypt. But he wanted none of it and in July 1922, shattered emotionally and distrustful of politicians and those in power, he relinquished his commission, changed his name to John Hume Ross and enlisted as a lowly aircraftman in the Royal Air Force, where he hoped to hide himself.

Among the things Lawrence carried with him wherever he went was a copy of Homer's *Odyssey*, a book he said he 'loved'. In 1928, serving under the name of Shaw in the Engine Repair Section of an RAF base in Karachi, he agreed to create a new translation of the *Odyssey* from the Greek. Perhaps it appealed because he recognised the connection between his story and that of the ancient hero Odysseus, returning from war, whom the gods stop from reaching home, because Lawrence had just written these words in a letter to a friend: 'Woe's me, I suppose I'll never dig again.'[13]

Hogarth had died in Oxford the previous year and there were now no gods to look down on his plight, no Athene to argue his case or smooth his way back to the only place he had been happy, to the person who had helped make him so. 'This lamentable tale give over,' he wrote, translating the words of the ancient bard, 'the sorrow of it slowly melts my heart within my bosom; for you tell of the event which has brought down upon me . . . this unappeasable pain. So continually does my memory yearn after that dear head.'[14]

These words were published in 1932. Three years later the man who translated them was dead.

After his death, the poem he had written about Dahoum as a dedication to *Seven Pillars of Wisdom*, was finally published:

To S.A.

I loved you, so I drew these tides of men into my hands
    and wrote my will across the sky in stars
To earn you Freedom, the seven pillared worthy house,
    that your eyes might be shining for me
        When we came.

Death seemed my servant on the road, till we were near
    and saw you waiting:
When you smiled, and in sorrowful envy he outran me
    and took you apart:
        Into his quietness.

Love, the way-weary, groped to your body, our brief wage
    ours for the moment
Before earth's soft hand explored your shape, and the blind
    worms grew fat upon
        Your substance.

Men prayed me that I set our work, the inviolate house,
    as a memory of you.
But for fit monument I shattered it, unfinished: and now
The little things creep out to patch themselves hovels
    in the marred shadow
        Of your gift.[15]

Acknowledgements

I have been collecting stories about Lawrence and the places in this book for more than two decades, and have had more conversations, recommendations, advice and warnings about him and the impact he had on the region than I can list here. But the decision to write about this early part of his life is a more recent one and came out of conversations with several people, particularly Sylvie Franquet, Gillon Aitken, Peter Lydon, Richard Sattin, Rose Baring, Barnaby Rogerson and Peter Straus. I must also thank Jan Morris: when I saw her in Wales and told her what I wanted to write, she drove me round to Tremadog to stand outside the house where Lawrence was born.

People who write or have written about the same area or even the same character can be less than generous in offering advice, but Jeremy Wilson, the authorised Lawrence biographer who has devoted much of his working life to Lawrence, has been unstinting in providing help, advice, opinion and introductions from the moment I contacted him to the time he finished reading the proofs. I am extremely grateful for his input. So much of the research for this book was made easier by his own *Lawrence of Arabia*. James Barr, author of the excellent *Setting the Desert on Fire*, and Dr Eugene Rogan, Director of the Middle East Centre at St Antony's College, Oxford, were also extremely helpful and generous with time and thoughts. Also in Oxford, Deb Manley, Felicity Wood, Jean Fleming, Clara Semple and Dr Jaromir Malek provided guidance and welcome suggestions. At the Ashmolean Museum, Cath Casley, Dr Paul Collins, Alison Roberts and Ilaria Perzia all helped provide access to information about Lawrence and Hogarth. At the Bodleian Library, Colin Harris, Superintendent of the Special Collections Reading

Rooms, showed great patience with yet another person wanting to see Lawrence material. By my deduction, all roads lead back to him when it comes to looking for anything about Lawrence in the Bodleian Library. Thanks also to Dr Alice Stevenson, Curator at the Petrie Museum, London, for access to Professor Petrie's papers.

I owe a big debt to the Rt Hon. Rory Stewart, MP, whose documentary on Lawrence is among the more perceptive views of the man to be created in recent years, and who took time to talk through my ideas about young Lawrence. Cathy Giangrande, UK Director of the Global Heritage Fund, provided information and help with Carchemish. I also owe thanks to Ted Gorton for advice about writers on Lebanon, Kerry Webber who is working on a biography about 'skinface' Newcombe, Professor David Gill for sharing thoughts and information on intelligence work in the Middle East in the years leading up to World War I. Julian Wilson went out of his way to provide access to his grandfather the late Philip Kerrigan's notes and draft for *Two Oxonian Scholars*, an unfinished biography of Lawrence and Hogarth. The people at wordworth.org put me in touch with Aurelia Perry and her excellent thesis on Hogarth. Hugh Bett at the rare book dealer Maggs Bros allowed me to touch books I would not otherwise have seen, and to hear about others I can only dream of, although he has yet to find me a copy of the manuscript Lawrence burned in Oxford in August 1914.

At the British Museum, Nigel Tallis, Curator of the Museum's Assyrian and Babylonian collections, gave generous access to the Lawrence papers and to his extensive knowledge about the Carchemish dig. Felicity Cobbing, Curator and Executive Secretary at the Palestine Exploration Fund, London, was generous in her time and thoughts concerning the Wilderness of Zin project. Staff at the London Library, always my first port of call, and at the British Library Humanities and Rare Books reading rooms, made life easier with their efficiency.

I was lucky to be helped by a number of wonderful people when I went travelling in Lawrence's footsteps. In Cairo, HE James Watt, British Ambassador to Egypt, Max Rodenbeck and Karima Khalil, Ahdaf Soueif, Mona Anis, Cecilia Udden and Otto

Mannheimer, Salima Ikram, Olivier Sednaoui, Youssef Rakha and many others provided assistance, advice, opinion and inspiration, listened to my stories and added their own. In Beirut, HE Tom Fletcher, British Ambassador to Lebanon, George Asseily, Chairman, and Alexandra Asseily, Governor of the Centre for Lebanese Studies, St Antony's College, Oxford, Professor Samir Khalaf of the American University in Beirut, Kamal Mouzawak, Alice Eddé in Jebail and Rita Saad of Le Gray all helped me locate places that Lawrence knew. In Turkey, Caroline Finkel, Köyüm Önal of TURSAB, Mety Arici at Mama Shelter Istanbul, Songula, Sabahattin Alkan of Alkans Tours provided rooms, meals and plenty of encouragement. Professor Nicolò Marchetti, head of the University of Bologna team who have picked up at Carchemish where Woolley and Lawrence left off, has been generous both with his time and experience. I must also thank Bashir and Bashar al-Ash of Syriana Travel in Damascus who looked after me and made arrangements for my travels in Syria over so many years. I look forward to the moment we can start planning together again.

I have written much of this book in splendid isolation, so must thank David and Sonja Sims for the loan of their apartment in Cairo (I thought curfews would help me to concentrate) and Amanda and Nicholas Mellor for letting me write in Thorpeness – the Peter Pan connection seemed appropriate. Christine Walker, then of the *Sunday Times*, Tom Robbins at the *Financial Times* and Sarah Spankie at *Condé Nast Traveller* all commissioned stories that helped me visit Lawrence locations.

Sylvie Franquet, Jeremy Wilson, Alan Spademan, Christine Walker, Max Mulhern and Johnny-Paris Sattin all read through earlier versions of the book and gave crucial feedback on what they liked and what they did not. Many thanks to all at John Murray, including Peter James for combing through the text, Juliet Brightmore for picture research, Nick de Somogyi for proofreading, Douglas Matthews for the index, Rodney Paull for drawing maps, Lyndsey Ng for publicity and Caroline Westmore for overseeing the whole project.

I owe a huge debt to Peter Straus, my agent at Rogers, Coleridge & White, and to Melanie Jackson of the Melanie Jackson Agency

ACKNOWLEDGEMENTS

in New York and to my editors, Roland Philipps at John Murray and Starling Lawrence at Norton. All had the vision to see the Lawrence story I wanted to tell and have made it possible for me to tell it. Living with a writer is not the easiest thing to do, but my wife Sylvie and sons Johnny and Felix have all (more or less willingly) become Lawrence experts, having had so many conversations, meals and other moments interrupted by thoughts of the man. To them I owe the biggest thanks for love, encouragement and patience.

Copyright Acknowledgements

Text

The author would like to thank the following for granting permission to quote material in this book: the Seven Pillars of Wisdom Trust for permission to quote from the writing of T. E. Lawrence and from *T. E. Lawrence by his Friends*; the Keeper of Special Collections, Dr Chris Fletcher and the Bodleian Libraries, University of Oxford, for permission to quote from the T. E. Lawrence material; the Trustees of the British Museum for permission to publish from their Carchemish correspondence; the National Archives at Kew, London, for permission to quote Foreign Office correspondence; the Palestine Exploration Fund for permission to quote from correspondence relating to the Wilderness of Zin survey; the Griffith Institute, University of Oxford, for permission to quote from the Petrie diaries; Oxford University Press for permission to quote from *Dead Towns and Living Men: Being Pages from an Antiquary's Notebook* by C. Leonard Woolley.

Illustrations

The Gertrude Bell Archive, Newcastle University: 8 below (Q225). © The British Library Board: 7 above left and right (MS 50584 f115-116). © The Trustees of the British Museum: 4 below left (bronze head of Hypnos, 1st–2nd century AD/GR 1868.6-6.9 (bronze 267). © The Trustees of the British Museum (Carchemish photo Vols 1 and 2): 9/neg. 033799, 10 below/neg. 033819, 11 above/ neg. 033816, 11 below/neg. 033828, 12 above/neg. 083705, 12 below/

neg. 043180, 13 above/neg. 033804, 13 below/neg. 033809, 14 below/ neg. 033827. The Bodleian Library, University of Oxford: 1 (MS. Photogr.c.126, fol.2v). *Carchemish Report on the Excavations at Djerabis*, Part I, 1914, by D. G. Hogarth: 10 above. Getty Images: 3, 16/ Gamma-Keystone. Mary Evans Picture Library: 4 above/Tal/Epic, 5 below/Epic/Collection Gregoire, 15 below/Imperial War Museum/ Robert Hunt Library. Library of Congress, Washington DC, Prints and Photographs Division: 14 above. Courtesy of the Palestine Exploration Fund, London: 15 above (PEF-DA-ZIN-101). Private collections: 4 below right, 5 above left, 6 below. © The Seven Pillars of Wisdom Trust: 2, 6 above. *Some Letters from Abroad of James Elroy Flecker*, 1930: 8 above left and right. Topham Picturepoint: 5 above right. © War Archive/Alamy: 7 below.

Every reasonable effort has been made to trace copyright holders, but if there are any errors or omissions, John Murray will be pleased to insert the appropriate acknowledgement in any subsequent printings or editions.

Notes

Abbreviations

BHF:	*T. E. Lawrence by his Friends*, ed. A. W. Lawrence
BM/A:	British Museum Archive
CC:	T. E. Lawrence, *Crusader Castles*
DG:	*The Letters of T. E. Lawrence*, ed. David Garnett
DTLM:	Leonard Woolley, *Dead Towns and Living Men*
FO:	Foreign Office Archive, Kew
HL:	*The Home Letters of T. E. Lawrence and his Brothers*
JW:	Jeremy Wilson, *Lawrence of Arabia: The Authorised Biography of T. E. Lawrence*
KB:	Karl Baedeker, *Palestine and Syria: Handbook for Travellers*
LTEL:	*Letters to T. E. Lawrence*
MB:	*Lawrence of Arabia, the Selected Letters*, ed. Malcolm Brown
OA:	T. E. Lawrence, *Oriental Assembly*
PEF:	Palestine Exploration Fund archive
PS:	R. Campbell Thompson, *A Pilgrim's Scrip*
SPW:	T. E. Lawrence, *Seven Pillars of Wisdom*
TEL to ETL:	*Letters to Leeds*
TELLH:	Basil Liddell Hart, *T. E. Lawrence to his Biographer*
TELSJ:	*Journal of the T. E. Lawrence Society*
WZ:	T. E. Lawrence and C. Leonard Woolley, *The Wilderness of Zin*

PROLOGUE: THE FIRST SPARK

1. BHF p. 76
2. DG p. 431
3. Ibid.
4. HL, p. 304
5. HL p. 232
6. *Listener*, 25 December 1947
7. SPW, p. 8
8. *The Times*, 20 May 1935, p. 15

CHAPTER 1: LANDING

1. *The Oxford Book of English Mystical Verse* (Oxford University Press, 1917), p. 415
2. HL p. 86
3. BHF p. 81
4. BHF p. 37
5. HL p. 86
6. HL p. 87
7. HL p. 86
8. Ibid.
9. *Levant Herald & Eastern Express*, 13 May 1909
10. Ibid., 19 May 1909
11. Bell, *Amurath to Amurath*, p. 320
12. Ibid., p. 321

CHAPTER 2: ORIGINS

1. Homer, *Odyssey*, Book I, p. 7
2. Jean-Jacques Rousseau, *Confessions* (Penguin, 1953), p. 26
3. BHF p. 53
4. BHF p. 41
5. BHF p. 65
6. BHF p. 53
7. BHF p. 56
8. Ibid.
9. BHF p. 29

10. Report of the Keeper of the Ashmolean Museum to the Visitors, in *Oxford University Gazette* (Oxford, vol. xxxvii, no. 1203, 30 April 1907, pp. 552–6). Quoted in *Wilson, Lawrence of Arabia,* p. 28.
11. DG p. 553
12. Bodleian MS. Res. C13
13. HL p. 23
14. HL p. 43
15. Bodleian MS. Res. c.569
16. MB p. 345
17. MB p. 344
18. DG p. 491
19. TELLH, p. 51
20. L. R. Jane to R. R. Graves, 27 July 1927, in Bodleian R
21. BHF p. 62
22. HL pp. 80–1
23. HL p. 61
24. HL p. 64
25. HL p. 65
26. Percy Bysshe Shelley, *Julian and Maddalo: A Conversation*, ll. 14–17
27. HL p. 66

Chapter 3: Father Confessor

1. Fedden, *Syria*, p. 146
2. Bell's, BL Add. MS 63549
3. Hogarth, *Arabia*, p. i
4. SPW p. 58
5. Hogarth, *Antiquary*, p. 1
6. BHF p. 26
7. BHF p. 34
8. BM Add. MS 45903, quoted in Wilson, *Lawrence*, p. 25
9. Amendment to typescript of R. R. Graves, *Lawrence and the Arabs* (1927), quoted in Graves, *T. E. Lawrence to his Biographer*, p. 61
10. Graves, *Lawrence and the Arabs*, p. 25
11. Ibid.
12. Ibid.
13. DG p. 553
14. LTEL p. 37

15. TEL to Doughty, 8 February 1909, Gonville and Caius College, Cambridge, quoted in Wilson, *Lawrence*, p. 54

CHAPTER 4: ON FOOT AND ALONE

1. Flecker, *Collected Poems*, p. 146
2. CC p. 118
3. KB, p. 276
4. HL p. 93
5. Ibid.
6. HL p. 94
7. Ibid.
8. HL pp. 87–8
9. Ibid.
10. HL p. 94
11. HL p. 92
12. LTEL p.37
13. BHF p. 29
14. HL p. 94
15. CC p. 73
16. HL p. 95
17. Ibid.
18. HL p. 96
19. KB p. 265
20. BHF p. 64
21. CC p. 93
22. Ibid.
23. HL pp. 96–7
24. HL p. 97
25. HL pp. 98–9
26. HL p. 99
27. Ibid.
28. HL p. 87
29. HL p. 88
30. HL p. 90
31. HL p. 91
32. HL p. 100
33. DG p. 74

Chapter 5: A Glorious Country for Wandering In

1. Quoted in Lawrence, *Minorities*, p. 198
2. DG p. 74
3. HL p. 100
4. KB p. 339
5. BHF p. 67
6. HL p. 102
7. Ibid.
8. Ibid.
9. Ibid.
10. Ibid.
11. Ibid.
12. KB p. 337
13. HL p. 103
14. Ibid.
15. Ibid.
16. HL p. 104
17. Ibid.
18. Ibid.
19. KB p. 371
20. Bell, *Letters*, vol. 1, p. 197
21. HL p. 104
22. CC p. 93
23. CC pp. 93–4
24. CC p. 94
25. HL p. 104
26. Ibid.
27. HL p. 105
28. SPW p. 192
29. HL p. 106
30. HL p. 105
31. Ibid.
32. HL p. 107
33. BHF p. 67
34. HL p. 107
35. Ibid.
36. KB p. xxvi

37. HL p. 106
38. Ibid.
39. Ibid.
40. Ibid.
41. CC p. 58
42. CC p. 63
43. Ibid.
44. *Los Angeles Herald*, 5 June 1909, p. 5
45. KB p. 379
46. Hogarth, *Antiquary*, p. 161
47. Ibid., pp. 161–2
48. HL p. 164
49. CC p. 57
50. HL p. 108
51. HL p. 81
52. TEL to ETL pp. 5–7
53. BHF p. 65
54. HL p. 107
55. Ibid.
56. HL p. 108

Chapter 6: Pushing the Boundaries

1. HL p. 207
2. DG p. 81
3. SPW pp. 30–1
4. BHF pp. 59–60
5. BHF p. 31
6. DG p. 82
7. LTEL p. 38
8. BHF p. 68
9. BHF p. 62
10. CC p. 25
11. CC p. 26
12. Ibid.
13. CC p. 93
14. CC p. 118
15. W. H. Hutton to Robert Graves, 21 November 1927, Bodleian R (quoted in Wilson, *Lawrence*, p. 67)

16. BHF p. 60
17. Ibid.
18. HL p. 603
19. HL p. 602
20. HL pp. 110–11
21. DG p. 87
22. Hogarth, *Carchemish*, p. 12
23. TEL to ETL p. 11
24. TEL to ETL p. 12
25. Ibid.

Chapter 7: Forgotten Far Off Things

1. HL p. 132
2. HL p. 113
3. Ibid.
4. HL p. 114
5. HL p. 115
6. HL p. 114
7. HL pp. 115–16
8. HL p. 117
9. Ibid.
10. Ibid.
11. HL p. 118
12. HL p. 119
13. Ibid.
14. HL pp. 119–20
15. HL p. 122
16. BM/A, Kenyon, Dec 1910
17. DG p. 93
18. BHF p. 70
19. HL p. 132
20. HL p. 124
21. BHF p. 70
22. HL p. 124
23. Ibid.
24. BHF p. 383
25. HL p. 129
26. HL p. 132

27. Ibid.
28. BHF p. 383
29. Quoted in Knightley, p. 29
30. DG p. 94
31. DG p. 96
32. Ibid.
33. Bell, *Letters*, vol. 2, p. 264
34. PS p. 295
35. HL p. 133
36. Hogarth, *Antiquary*, p. 152
37. PS p. 296
38. HL p. 135
39. HL p. 137
40. Ibid.
41. PS p. 298
42. FO 861/60, Kenyon to Fontana, 13 January 1911
43. PS p. 298
44. Hogarth, *Antiquary*, p. 1
45. PS p. 10

Chapter 8: The Apprentice

1. HL p. 174
2. HL p. 141
3. HL p. 140
4. MB p. 31
5. HL p. 144
6. Meyer's *Neues Konversationslexicon*, quoted in Ceram, *Narrow Pass*, p. 4
7. Hogarth, *Carchemish*, p. 6
8. *The Times*, 12 July 1880, p. 4
9. PS p. 294
10. HL p. 143
11. *The Times*, 1 July 1911, p. 5
12. HL p. 148
13. HL p. 151
14. Lock, 'D. G. Hogarth (1862–1927)', pp. 175–200
15. HL p. 148
16. HL p. 146
17. Hogarth, *The Penetration of Arabia* (1904)

18. HL p. 207
19. HL p. 206
20. Doughty, p. 280
21. HL p. 207
22. FO 861/60, Fontana to Lowther, 20 March 1911
23. BM/A, Hogarth to Kenyon, 24 April 1911
24. BM/A, Hogarth, Report to the British Museum, 20 May 1911, pp. 39–40
25. MB p. 38
26. BM/A, Thompson to Kenyon, 14 June 1911
27. HL p. 164
28. HL p. 167
29. HL p. 168
30. HL p. 149
31. Bodleian MS Eng. d.3335
32. Bell, *Letters*, vol. 2, p. 300
33. Bodleian MS Eng. d.3335, p. 19
34. HL pp. 161–2
35. Bell, *Letters*, vol.2, p. 293
36. HL p. 162
37. Ibid.
38. PS p. 7
39. PS pp. 5–6
40. HL p. 151
41. Ibid.
42. PS p. 26
43. HL p. 144
44. HL p. 170
45. HL p. 163
46. Mores Romanorum, Bodleian MS Res. C13, quoted in TELSJ, Vol. 3, No. 1, pp. 10–11
47. HL p. 163
48. DG p. 114
49. Ibid.
50. DG p. 115
51. HL p. 173
52. DG p. 115
53. Ibid.
54. HL pp. 173–4

CHAPTER 9: THE WANDERER AFTER SENSATIONS

1. Homer, *Odyssey*, Book VII, p. 95
2. HL p. 160
3. Ibid.
4. HL p. 168
5. DG pp. 111–12
6. Ibid
7. DG pp. 112–13
8. HL p. 169
9. BM/A, Thompson to Kenyon, 24 June 1911
10. HL p. 172
11. BM/A, Thompson to Kenyon, 24 June 1911
12. *The Times*, 1 July 1911, p. 5
13. BM/A, Minutes of the Standing Committee, British Museum, 8 July 1911
14. PS p. 319
15. HL p. 173
16. HL p. 175
17. HL p. 173
18. HL p. 174
19. Ibid.
20. BHF p. 115
21. Ibid.
22. DG p. 81
23. HL p. 149
24. HL p. 148
25. OA, p. 5
26. OA p. 2
27. OA p. 3
28. OA p. 9
29. OA p. 10
30. OA p. 12
31. OA p. 15
32. OA pp. 13–14
33. OA p. 18
34. OA p. 19
35. OA p. 32
36. OA p. 43
37. OA p. 26

38. HL p. 176
39. OA, p. 43
40. OA p. 45
41. OA p. 46
42. HL p. 47
43. HL p. 48
44. BHF pp. 98–9
45. OA p. 51
46. OA p. 55
47. DG p. 118
48. DG p. 119
49. OA p. 58
50. Flecker, *Letters*, p. 51
51. Ibid., p. 64
52. DG p. 120
53. Bodleian MS, TEL to Mrs Rieder, 11 August 1911
54. Ibid.

CHAPTER 10: IF THE ITALIANS PERMIT . . .

1. HL p. 541
2. DG p. 125
3. DG p. 120
4. *The Times*, 8 August 1911, p. 10
5. *The Times*, 9 August 1911, p. 2
6. BM/A, Hogarth to Kenyon, 1 February 1912
7. *The Times*, 27 December 1921, p. 4
8. DG p. 123
9. Hogarth to Petrie 11 July 1911, Ashmolean Archives
10. 1910 postcard (private collection)
11. Quoted at www.grandhotelsegypt.com
12. HL p. 183
13. Petrie Journal ii.1.1, Petrie Museum Archive U.C.LCXIX/WFPI/16/1/4 (14)
14. Ibid.
15. HL pp. 184–5
16. HL p. 190
17. Drower, *Flinders Petrie*, p. 320
18. TELLH p. 54

19. HL p. 186
20. DG pp. 132–3
21. DG p. 143
22. DG p. 134
23. Quoted in Tauber, p. 8
24. HL p. 191
25. MB p. 44
26. DG p. 135
27. HL p. 192
28. Ibid.
29. HL p. 194
30. Lawrence, 'An Essay on Flecker', in TELSJ, Vol. 3, No. 1, p. 16
31. Flecker, *Collected Prose*, pp. 70–1
32. Flecker, *Letters*, p. 55
33. HL p. 194
34. DG p. 132
35. FO Fontana to Kenyon, 2 January 1912 (camera)
36. Quoted in Winstone, *Woolley*, p. 16
37. DTLM p. 150
38. DTLM p. 153
39. DTLM p. 155
40. HL p. 197
41. DTLM p. 156
42. HL pp. 196–7
43. DTLM pp. 173–4
44. DTLM p. 177
45. HL p. 109
46. DTLM p. 77
47. DTLM pp. 94–5
48. HL p. 197
49. HL p. 203
50. Bodleian MS3340
51. HL p. 203
52. Ibid.
53. HL p. 208
54. HL p. 213
55. Bodleian MS Eng. d.3340
56. BM/A, Hogarth to Kenyon, 10 May 1912
57. BM/A, Hogarth to Kenyon, 19 May 1912
58. HL p. 208

59. BM/A, Hogarth to Kenyon, 10 May 1912
60. HL p. 215

Chapter 11: Because He Loves Us

1. Flecker, *Collected Poems*, p. 222
2. HL p. 218
3. HL p. 217
4. FO 195/2371, p. 287, Cumberbatch to Lowther, 6 November 1911
5. HL p. 217
6. Ibid.
7. BHF p. 83
8. DG p. 140
9. DG p. 141
10. HL p. 225
11. Storrs, *Orientations*, p. 134
12. FO 195/2370, p. 234, 10 April 1911
13. FO 195/2371, Fontana to Lowther, 24 October 1911
14. HL p. 225
15. HL pp. 223–4
16. HL p. 248
17. *Jesus College Magazine*, Vol. 1, No. 2, January 1913
18. HL p. 227
19. HL p. 228
20. Flecker, *Letters*, pp. 57–9
21. Ibid., p. 68
22. Flecker, *The Story of Hassan*, Act V, Scene 2
23. HL p. 229
24. BHF p. 80
25. DG p. 149
26. HL p. 233
27. DG p. 149

Chapter 12: An Old Story

1. HL p. 239
2. HL p. 229
3. *The Times*, 9 October 1912, p. 6

4. HL p. 237
5. SPW p. 56
6. HL p. 239
7. *The Times*, 9 September 1912, p. 5
8. HL p. 232
9. HL p. 236
10. All from *The Times*
11. HL p. 238
12. HL p. 217
13. HL p. 237
14. BM/A, Woolley to Kenyon, 1 December 1912
15. Ibid.
16. HL p. 241
17. Ibid.
18. HL p. 239
19. HL p. 242
20. BM/A Woolley to Kenyon 9 November 1912
21. BM/A, C. L. Woolley, Report to the Trustees of the British Museum, November 1912
22. HL p. 243
23. HL p. 239
24. This and subsequent passages from Bodleian R: Report by F. Willoughby Smith, 9 December 1912. Quoted in JW pp. 945–8

Chapter 13: The Happiest Time, the Richest Dig

1. DG p. 153
2. BM/A, Lawrence to Hogarth, 17 January 1913
3. BM/A, Kenyon to Hogarth, 29 January 1912
4. BM/A, Hogarth to Kenyon, 20 December 1912
5. FO 195/2457, p. 70
6. BM/A, Lawrence to Woolley, 25 January 1913
7. FO 195/2457, Fontana to Cumberbatch, 24 February 1913
8. BM/A, Woolley to Hogarth, 8 February 1913
9. BM/A, Lawrence to Woolley, 25 January 1913
10. FO 195/2451, pp. 484–5
11. DTLM p. 189
12. FO 195/2451, Fontana to Lowther, 15 June 1913
13. Ibid.

14. HL p. 246
15. HL pp. 246–7
16. BM/A, Lawrence to Hogarth, 8 February 1913
17. MB p. 48
18. Ibid.
19. DG p. 151
20. Ibid
21. HL p. 247
22. MB pp. 49–50; also BM/A
23. Ibid.
24. Ibid.
25. HL p. 250
26. BM/A, Woolley to Hogarth, 18 March 1913
27. BM/A, Woolley to Hogarth, 20 April 1913
28. BM/A, Lawrence to Hogarth, 28 April 1913
29. *The Times*, 18 April 1913, p. 6
30. HL p. 251
31. Ibid.
32. Flecker, *Letters*, p. 64
33. BM/A, Fontana to Hogarth, 23 April 1913
34. BHF p. 84
35. DTLM p. 129
36. BHF p. 84
37. IIL p. 250
38. DG p. 154
39. BM/A, Lawrence to Hogarth, 14 May 1913
40. BM/A, C. L. Woolley, Report to the Trustees of the British Museum, April 1913

CHAPTER 14: GATHERING STORM

1. BM/A Kenyon to Hogarth, 28 March 1913
2. FO 195/2452 – 124, pp. 217–18
3. DG p. 152
4. SPW p. 661
5. DTLM p. 193
6. DTLM p. 194
7. DTLM p. 195
8. HL p. 254

9. HL p. 257
10. TEL to ETL p. 74
11. FO 195/2451 484/20, May 1913, p. 63
12. *The Times*, 12 June 1913, p. 9
13. Article in *Haaretz*, Weekend Section, 12 November 2012
14. Ibid.
15. SP p. 33
16. Suleiman, *Arabic Language*, p. 93

Chapter 15: Eating Lotos

1. *The Poetical Works of Alfred, Lord Tennyson*, p. 58
2. HL p. 254
3. HL p. 257
4. HL p. 259
5. *Jesus College Magazine*, Vol. 1, No. 2, January 1913, pp. 37–9
6. Wilson, *Lawrence of Arabia*, p. 96
7. MB p. 51
8. MB pp. 51–2
9. BHF p. 98
10. TEL to ETL, p. 76
11. HL p. 262
12. HL p. 265
13. HL p. 260
14. HL p. 264
15. HL p. 260
16. TEL to ETL, p. 77
17. HL p. 396
18. HL p. 437
19. HL p. 442
20. HL pp. 443–4
21. Young, *Independent Arab*, p. 14
22. HL p. 446
23. HL p. 447
24. HL p. 467
25. BHF p. 104
26. Young, *Independent Arab*, p. 41
27. TELLH p. 53
28. HL p. 269

29. HL p. 271
30. BHF p. 89
31. BHF p. 90
32. BHF p. 83
33. MB p. 368
34. MB p. 383
35. MB p. 414
36. Quoted in Knightley p. 29
37. BHF p. 83
38. JW pp. 128–9
39. TEL to ETL p. 79
40. BHF p. 89
41. HL p. 268
42. BM/A, Woolley to Hogarth, 3 November 1913
43. BM/A, C. L. Woolley, Report to the Trustees of the British Museum, October 1913
44. HL p. 270
45. HL p. 273
46. HL p. 277
47. BHF p. 87
48. HL p. 275
49. TEL to ETL, 17 December 1913, p. 88
50. DG p. 161
51. Ibid.

CHAPTER 16: A SPLENDID TRIP

1. DG p. 176
2. BM/A, Woolley to Kenyon, 17 December 1913
3. FO 195/2452, 1124, p. 217
4. Jennings Bramly papers in the Royal Geographical Society, London, quoted in Warburg, 'The Sinai Peninsula Borders'
5. *The Times*, 5 May 1906, p. 11
6. Blunt, *My Diaries*, vol. 2, p. 144
7. FO 371/1812, ff. 279–80
8. PEF ZIN5, War Office to Sir Charles M. Watson, 30 October 1913
9. PEF, Watson to Hedley, 5 November 1913
10. PEF ZIN12, Watson to Kenyon, 21 November 1913
11. PEF ZIN23, Watson to Woolley, 16 December 1913

12. Ibid.
13. PEF ZIN32, Woolley to Watson, 28 December 1913
14. DG p. 163
15. HL p. 280
16. PEF ZIN37, Newcombe to War Office, 7 January 1914
17. PEF ZIN38, Woolley to Watson, 10 January 1914
18. Newcombe, 'T. E. Lawrence', p. 162
19. PEF ZIN37
20. HL p. 281
21. WZ p. xxiv
22. HL p. 282
23. Ibid.
24. MB p. 59
25. HL p. 285
26. PEF ZIN48/49
27. Ibid.
28. Ibid.
29. TEL to ETL p. 89
30. MB p. 58
31. Ibid.
32. WZ p. 156
33. WZ p. 6
34. HL p. 284
35. Ibid.
36. SPW p. 193
37. WZ p. 10
38. WZ p. 11
39. DG p. 165
40. PEF ZIN47
41. DG p. 165
42. DG p. 166
43. WZ p. 173
44. HL p. 287
45. DG p. 168
46. HL p. 287
47. DG p. 166
48. DG p. 167
49. HL p. 286
50. HL p. 287

CHAPTER 17: ANOTHER STEP, A LONG WAY

1. HL p. 316
2. *The Times*, 24 January 1914
3. *Illustrated London News*, 24 January 1914, p. 132
4. BM/A, Morrison to Hogarth, 19 January 1914
5. HL p. 291
6. HL p. 293
7. HL p. 292
8. DG p. 172
9. DG p. 173
10. DG p. 174
11. Ibid.
12. *The Times*, 25 March 1914, p. 7
13. DG p. 175
14. FO 371/2132, no. 16157, Fontana to Mallet, 26 March 1914, enclosed in Mallet to Foreign Office, 8 April 1914, no. 240
15. HL p. 297
16. HL p. 296
17. BHF p. 106
18. FO 195/2327
19. *Geographical Journal*, December 1914, p. 578
20. HL p. 298
21. BHF p. 84
22. Woolley, *As I Seem to Remember*, p. 93

CHAPTER 18: SHOOTING AND BURNING

1. HL p. 295
2. DG p. 176
3. HL p. 537
4. DG p. 176
5. DG p. 181
6. Lloyd George, *War Memoirs*, Vol. 1, p. 33
7. FO 195/2453, p. 350, Consul Devey, 29 June 1914
8. SPW p. 46
9. HL p. 541
10. DG p. 181
11. HL p. 615

12. HL p. 573
13. HL p. 565
14. DG p. 431
15. MB p. 344
16. Ibid.

CHAPTER 19: OF ARABIA

1. Flecker, *Collected Poems*, p. 71
2. DG p. 181
3. HL pp. 572–3
4. DG p. 186
5. DG p. 187
6. Quoted in Owen, *Lord Cromer*, p. 386
7. DTLM p. 6
8. DG p. 198
9. DG p. 190
10. Callwell to Maxwell, 19 November 1914, quoted in Wilson, *Lawrence in Arabia*, p. 154
11. DG p. 192
12. DG p. 193
13. DG p. 195
14. DG p. 196
15. DG p. 81
16. Young, *Independent Arab*, p. 157
17. MB p. 178
18. SPW p. 661
19. SPW p. 652

EPILOGUE: AN UNPEACEFUL PEACE

1. SPW p. 660
2. MB p. 170
3. SPW p. 562
4. FO 882/7, Wilson to Wingate, p. 28
5. DG p. 813
6. HL p. 340
7. DG p. 578

8. DG p. 271
9. DG p. 553
10. Ibid.
11. BM/A, September 1919
12. BM/A, 6 December 1919, Kenyon to Woolley
13. DG p. 565
14. Homer, *Odyssey*, trans. T. E. Shaw, Book I, p. 10
15. SPW p. 114

Bibliography

Andrew, Sir William, *Euphrates Valley Route to India* (W. H. Allen, 1882)

Antonius, George, *The Arab Awakening* (Hamish Hamilton, 1938)

Baedeker, Karl, *Palestine and Syria: Handbook for Travellers* (Baedeker, 1912)

Barr, James, *Setting the Desert on Fire* (Bloomsbury, 2006)

Bell, Gertrude, *Syria: The Desert and the Sown* (William Heinemann, 1919)

——, *Amurath to Amurath* (Macmillan, 1924)

——, *The Letters of Gertrude Bell*, 2 vols (Penguin, 1939)

Blunt, Wilfred Scawen, *My Diaries*, 2 vols (Alfred A. Knopf, 1921)

Boulanger, Robert, *Lebanon* (Hachette, 1955)

Brett, Peter, *Far Arabia: Explorers of the Myth* (Weidenfeld & Nicolson, 1977)

Brown, Malcolm, *Lawrence of Arabia: The Life, The Legend* (Thames & Hudson, 2005)

Bullard, Sir Reader, 'James Elroy Flecker in Constantinople', *Listener*, No. 1146, 15 February 1952, p. 268

Burney, Charles, *Historical Dictionary of the Hittites* (Scarecrow Press, 2004)

Burns, Ross, *The Monuments of Syria* (I. B. Tauris, 1992)

Ceram, C. W., *Narrow Pass, Black Mountain: The Discovery of the Hittite Empire* (Readers Union, 1957)

——, *Gods, Graves and Scholars* (Penguin, 1984)

Chapman III, Rupert L. and Shimon Gibson, 'A Note on T. E. Lawrence as Photographer in the Wilderness of Zin', *Palestine Exploration Quarterly*, No. 128, 1996, pp. 94–102

Clark, Christopher, *The Sleepwalkers* (Allen Lane, 2012)

Darke, Diana, *Syria* (Bradt, 2010)

——, *Eastern Turkey* (Bradt, 2011)

Darvill, Timothy, *The Concise Oxford Dictionary of Archaeology* (Oxford University Press, 2002)

Dawn, C. Ernest, 'The Rise of Arabism in Syria', *Middle East Journal*, Vol. 16, No. 2, Spring 1962, pp. 145–68

——, *From Ottomanism to Arabism: Essays on the Origins of Arab Nationalism* (University of Illinois Press, 1973)

Doughty, Charles M., *Travels in Arabia Deserta*, with a new introduction by T. E. Lawrence (Jonathan Cape, 1921)

Doyle, Paul, *Lebanon* (Bradt, 2012)

Drower, Margaret S., *Flinders Petrie: A Life in Archaeology* (University of Wisconsin Press, 1995)

Dunand, Maurice, *Byblos* (Imprimerie Catholique, Beirut, 1973)

Emmerson, Charles, *1913: The World before the Great War* (Bodley Head, 2013)

Encyclopaedia Britannica (1932)

Fedden, Robin, *Syria* (Robert Hale, 1955)

Fieldhouse, David, 'The Decline of the Ottoman Empire in the Middle East and the "Arab Awakening" before 1914', in *Western Imperialism in the Middle East 1914–1958* (Oxford Scholarship Online, 2010)

Finkel, Caroline, *Osman's Dream: The Story of the Ottoman Empire 1300–1923* (John Murray, 2005)

Flecker, James Elroy, *Collected Poems* (Martin Secker, 1916)

——, *Collected Prose of James Elroy Flecker* (William Heinemann, 1922)

——, *Hassan: The Story of Hassan of Bagdad and How He Came to Make the Golden Journey to Samarkand. A Play in 5 Acts* (Heinemann, 1922)

——, *Some Letters from Abroad* (William Heinemann, 1930)

Florence, Ronald, *Lawrence and Aaronsohn* (Viking, 2007)

Gilibert, Alessandra, *Syro-Hittite Monumental Art and the Archaeology of Performance* (De Gruyter, 2011)

Gill, David W. J., 'Harry Pirie-Gordon: Historical Research, Journalism and Intelligence Gathering in the Eastern Mediterranean (1908–18)', *Intelligence and National Security*, Vol. 21, No. 6, 2006, pp. 1045–59

Gingeras, Ryan, *Sorrowful Shores: Violence, Ethnicity and the End of the Ottoman Empire 1912–1923* (Oxford University Press, 2009)

Goodwin, Jason, *Lords of the Horizons* (Chatto & Windus, 1998)

Gorton, T. J. and A. Féghali, ed., *Lebanon through Writers' Eyes* (Eland, 2009)

Gossman, Lionel, *The Passion of Max von Oppenheim* (Open Book Publishers, 2013)

Graves, Robert, *Whipperginny* (Alfred A. Knopf, 1923)

——, *Lawrence and the Arabs* (Jonathan Cape, 1936)

——, *T. E. Lawrence to his Biographer* (Faber & Faber, 1938)

Hall, Richard C., *The Balkan Wars 1912–1913* (Routledge, 2000)

Hamm, Geoffrey, 'British Intelligence and Turkish Arabia: Strategy, Diplomacy, and Empire, 1898–1918' (D.Phil. thesis, Department of History, University of Toronto, 2012)

Hanioglu, M. Sukru, *A Brief History of the Late Ottoman Empire* (Princeton University Press, 2008)

Hanssen, Jens, *Fin de Siècle Beirut: The Making of an Ottoman Provincial Capital* (Oxford University Press, 2005)

Heffernan, Michael, 'Geography, Cartography and Military Intelligence: The Royal Geographical Society and the First World War', *Transactions of the Institute of British Geographers*, New Series, Vol. 21, No. 3, 1996, pp. 504–33

Hitti, Philip K., *Lebanon in History* (Macmillan, 1962)

Hodgson, Geraldine, *The Life of James Elroy Flecker* (Basil Blackwell, 1925)

Hogarth, D. G., *The Penetration of Arabia* (Lawrence & Bullen, 1904)

——, 'Problems in Exploration: Western Asia', *Geographical Journal*, Vol. 32, No. 6, December 1908, pp. 549–70

——, *Accidents of an Antiquary's Life* (Macmillan, 1910)

——, *Carchemish: Report on the Explorations at Djerabis on Behalf of the British Museum, Part I* (British Museum, 1914)

——, *The Life of Charles M. Doughty* (Oxford University Press, 1928)

——, 'Hierapolis Syriae', in *Annual of the British School at Athens*, No. XIV (Kraus, 1971)

Homer, *The Odyssey*, trans. T. E. Shaw (pseud. T. E. Lawrence) (Oxford University Press, 1932)

Hourani, Albert, *A History of the Arab Peoples* (Faber, 1991)

Journal of the T. E. Lawrence Society

Karsh, Efraim and Inari Karsh, *Empires of the Sand: The Struggle for Mastery in the Middle East 1789–1923* (Harvard University Press, 1999)

Kassir, Samir, *Beirut* (University of California Press, 2010)

Kayali, Hasan, *Arabs and Young Turks: Ottomanism, Arabism, and Islamism in the Ottoman Empire, 1908–1918* (University of California Press, 1997)

Khairallah, Shereen, *Railways in the Middle East 1856–1948* (Librairie du Liban, 1991)

Khalidi, Rashid et al. (eds), *The Origins of Arab Nationalism* (Columbia University Press, 1991)

Kliot, Nurit, *The Evolution of the Egypt–Israel Boundary: From Colonial Foundation to Peaceful Borders* (International Boundaries Research Unit, 1995)

Knightley, Philip and Colin Simpson, *The Secret Lives of Lawrence of Arabia* (Nelson, 1969)

Kociejowski, Marius, *Syria through Writers' Eyes* (Eland, 2006)

Korda, Michael, *Hero: The Life and Legend of Lawrence of Arabia* (Aurum, 2012)

Lane-Poole, Stanley, *Saladin and the Fall of the Kingdom of Jerusalem* (G. P. Putnam's Sons, 1906)

Lawrence, A. W., ed., *T. E. Lawrence by his Friends* (Jonathan Cape, 1937)

Lawrence, T. E., 'The Kasr of Ibn Wardani', *Jesus College Magazine*, Vol. 1, No. 2, January 1913

——, *Seven Pillars of Wisdom: A Triumph* (Jonathan Cape, 1935)

——, *The Letters of T. E. Lawrence*, ed. David Garnett (Jonathan Cape, 1938)

——, *Oriental Assembly* (Williams & Northgate, 1939)

——, *The Home Letters of T. E. Lawrence and his Brothers* (Blackwell, 1954)

——, *Minorities*, ed. J. M. Wilson (Jonathan Cape, 1971)

——, *Crusader Castles* (Immel, 1992)

——, and C. Leonard Woolley, *The Wilderness of Zin* (Stacey International, 2003)

——, *Lawrence of Arabia: The Selected Letters*, ed. Malcolm Brown (Little Books, 2005)

Le Strange, Guy, *Palestine under the Moslems* (Alexander Wyatt, Palestine Exploration Fund, 1890)

Lewis, Bernard, *The Emergence of Modern Turkey* (Oxford University Press, 1968)

——, *The Assassins* (Phoenix, 2003)

Liddell Hart, Basil, *T. E. Lawrence to his Biographer* (Faber & Faber, 1938)

Lloyd George, David, *War Memoirs of David Lloyd George* (Odhams, 1938)

Lock, P., 'D. G. Hogarth (1862–1927): ". . . A Specialist in the Science of Archaeology"', *Annual of the British School at Athens*, No. 85, 1990, pp. 175–200

Maalouf, Amin, *The Crusades Through Arab Eyes* (Saqi, 2006)

MacMillan, Margaret, *The War that Ended Peace* (Profile, 2013)

McMeekin, Sean, *The Berlin–Baghdad Express* (Allen Lane, 2010)

Maloney, Arthur P., *The Berlin–Baghdad Railway as a Cause of World War I*, Center for Naval Analyses, Virginia, Professional Paper 401, January 1984

Mansel, Philip, *Constantinople: City of the World's Desire, 1453–1924* (John Murray, 1991)

——, *Levant: Splendour and Catastrophe on the Mediterranean* (John Murray, 2010)

Marchetti, Nicolò, 'Leonard Woolley et l'archéologie proche-orientale', in *Pionniers et protagonistes de l'archéologie syrienne 1860–1960* (Documents d'Archéologie Syrienne XIV, Ministry of Culture, Damascus, 2008)

——, 'Karkemish on the Euphrates: Excavating a City's History', *Near Eastern Archaeology*, Vol. 75, No. 3, 2012, pp. 132–47

Meeker, Michael E., *Literature and Violence in North Arabia* (Cambridge University Press, 1979)

Meyers, Jeffrey, *Homosexuality and Literature 1890–1930* (Athlone Press, 1977)

Milam, Major Curtis S., 'The Art of the Possible: T. E. Lawrence and Coalition Liaison' (MMAS thesis, Fort Leavenworth, Kansas, 2001)

Mohs, Polly A., *Military Intelligence and the Arab Revolt* (Routledge, 2008)

Moorey, P. R. S., *Cemeteries of the First Millennium B.C. at Deve Hüyük, near Carchemish, Salvaged by T. E. Lawrence and C. L. Woolley in 1913* (BAR, 1980)

Morrison, Walter et al., *The Recovery of Jerusalem* (Appleton, 1871)

Murphy-O'Connor, Jerome, *The Holy Land* (Oxford University Press, 1998)

Newcombe, S. F., 'T. E. Lawrence: A Personal Reminiscence', *Palestine Exploration Fund Quarterly Statement*, July 1935, p. 110

—— and J. P. S. Greig, 'The Baghdad Railway', *Geographical Journal*, Vol. 44, No. 6, December 1914, pp. 577–80

Ocampo, Victoria, *338171 T.E.* (Victor Gollancz, 1963)

Orlans, Harold, *T. E. Lawrence* (McFarland, 2002)

Owen, Roger, *Lord Cromer* (Oxford University Press, 2005)

P&O, *Pocket Book* (A & C Black, 1908)

Petrie, W. M., *Flinders, Tarkhan I and Memphis V* (School of Archaeology in Egypt, 1913)

Reynolds-Ball, Eustace, *Cairo of Today* (A. & C. Black, 1916)

Richards, Vyvyan, *Portrait of T. E. Lawrence* (Scholastic, 1967)

Rogan, Eugene, *The Arabs: A History* (Allen Lane, 2009)

Rogerson, Barnaby and Alexander Munro, eds, *Desert Air: A Collection of the Poetry of Place of Arabia, Deserts and the Orient of the Imagination* (Baring & Rogerson, 2001)

Runciman, Steven, *A History of the Crusades* (Cambridge University Press, 1951–4)

Satia, Priya, *Spies in Arabia: The Great War and the Cultural Foundations of Britain's Covert Empire in the Middle East* (Oxford University Press, 2008)

Sconzo, Paola, 'Leonard Woolley, Lawrence d'Arabie et les fouilles de Karkémish', in *Pionniers et protagonistes de l'archéologie syrienne 1860–1960* (Documents d'Archéologie Syrienne XIV, Ministry of Culture, Damascus, 2008)

Searight, Sarah, *The British in the Middle East* (East–West Publications, 1979)

Sheffy, Yigal, 'British Intelligence and the Middle East, 1900–1918: How Much Do We Know?', *Intelligence and National Security*, Vol. 17, No. 1, 2002, pp. 33–52

Sherwood, John, *No Golden Journey: A Biography of James Elroy Flecker* (William Heinemann, 1973)

Steadman, Sharon R. et al., eds, *The Oxford Handbook of Ancient Anatolia (10,000–323 BCE)* (Oxford University Press, 2011)

Stéphane, Roger, *Portrait de l'aventurier* (Sagittaire, 1950)

Storrs, Sir Ronald, *Orientations* (Ivor Nicholson & Watson, 1937)

Suleiman, Yasir, *The Arabic Language and National Identity: A Study in Ideology* (Edinburgh University Press, 2003)

Sykes, Mark, 'Journeys in North Mesopotamia', *Geographical Journal*, Vol. 30, No. 3, September 1907, pp. 237–54, and No. 4, October 1907, pp. 384–98

——, 'The Kurdish Tribes of the Ottoman Empire', *Journal of the Royal Anthropological Institute of Great Britain and Ireland*, Vol. 38, July–December 1908, pp. 451–86

Tabachnick, Stephen E., *Explorations in Doughty's Arabia Deserta* (University of Georgia Press, 2012)

Al Tahtawi, Rafi', *The Book of Distillation of Pure Gold, Even the Distillation of Paris* (Cairo, 1905)

Tauber, Eliezer, 'Egyptian Secret Societies, 1911', in *Middle East Studies*, Vol. 42, No. 4, pp. 603–23 (Frank Cass, 2006)

Tennyson, Alfred, *The Poetical Works of Alfred, Lord Tennyson* (Macmillan, 1926)

Thompson, R. Campbell, *A Pilgrim's Scrip* (Bodley Head, 1926)

Tuscon, Penelope, *Playing the Game: Western Women in Arabia* (I. B. Tauris, 2003)

Warburg, Gabriel R., 'The Sinai Peninsula Borders, 1906–47', in *Journal of Contemporary History*, Vol. 14, No. 4, A Century of Conservatism, Part 2 (October 1979)

Wilson, Jeremy, *T. E. Lawrence: Catalogue* (National Portrait Gallery Publications, 1988)

——, *Lawrence of Arabia: The Authorised Biography of T. E. Lawrence* (William Heinemann, 1989)

Winstone, H. V. F., *The Illicit Adventure* (Jonathan Cape, 1982)

——, *Woolley of Ur* (Secker & Warburg, 1990)

——, *Gertrude Bell* (Barzan, 2004)

Woolley, C. Leonard, 'Hittite Burial Customs', in *Annals of Archaeology and Anthropology*, Vol. VI (University of Liverpool, 1914)

——, *Dead Towns and Living Men* (Humphrey Milford, 1920)

——, *Carchemish: Report on the Excavations at Jerablus on Behalf of the British Museum, Part II* (British Museum, 1921)

——, *Carchemish: Report on the Excavations at Jerablus on Behalf of the British Museum, Part III* (British Museum, 1952)

——, *As I Seem to Remember* (George Allen & Unwin, 1962)

Young, Hubert, *The Independent Arab* (John Murray, 1933)

Index

Ranks and titles are generally the highest mentioned in the text.
Works by Lawrence (TEL) appear directly under title; works by others
under author's name